DEEP PURPLE

WAIT FOR THE RICOCHET

The Story of Deep Purple In Rock

SIMON ROBINSON

STEPHEN CLARE

PUBLISHED BY **easy on the eye** BOOKS

a **darker than blue** PRODUCTION

contents

	Introduction	3
1	From Deeves Hall to Deep Purple	4
2	Hanwell Community Centre	12
3	Writing the album	15
4	On the road - July to December 1969	29
5	The equipment	47
6	The studios	58
7	Recording the album	64
8	Black Night	75
9	On the road - January to June 1970	82
10	Album release and artwork	97
11	Reviewing the album	101
12	Touring the album - June 1970 to early 1971	117
13	Concert listing	155
14	Deep Purple In Rock discography	160
15	Credits / easy on the eye / ST33 books	166

easy on the eye books
Nethergate
Sheffield

www.easyontheeyebooks.wordpress.com

easy on the eyebooks

Second edition 2017

Text copyright © Simon Robinson / Stephen Clare / Easy On The Eye Books 2017
Designed by easy on the eye copyright © Easy On The Eye Books 2017

British Library Cataloguing in Publication Data. A catalogue record for this book is available from the British Library.

ISBN 978-0-9561439-6-9

All rights reserved. No part of this publication may be reproduced, stored in a retrieval system, or transmitted, in any form or by any means, electronic, mechanical, photocopying, recording or otherwise, without the prior permission of the publishers.

set in adobe caslon pro

DESIGNED SHEFFIELD ENGLAND

Introduction

"Although In Rock was done over quite a long period that was a most wonderful time for the band." Jon Lord

Deep Purple In Rock proved to be a milestone in the history and development of rock music, and an album which has influenced countless groups and musicians in the four decades after it first appeared. *In Rock* is also Deep Purple's most important album, which not only marked a defining change of direction in their music but firmly established the group's reputation amongst a generation of rock fans. A European hit single extended the band's reach and, coupled with the album, helped lay the groundwork for a period of creative and financial sucess over the next few years.

This book documents the story of the album's evolution during a period of upheaval within the group. Early - and impressive - American success proved to be short lived and had not been repeated back-home, leading to tough internal decisions. It was only through personnel changes coupled with a period of intense rehearsal, writing and touring that they managed to reverse their fortunes, doing so in spectacular style.

Deep Purple In Rock took almost twelve months to complete, with sessions taking second place to live work. Yet it remains both a perfect snapshot of the band at this crucial point in their career as well as a reflection of an extraordinarily prolific and progressive period in the story of British hard rock overall, just as the psychedelic sixties gave way to the more aggressive and focussed rock music of the seventies.

The album itself is only half the story. Deep Purple was (and remains) primarily a band which existed to perform. No matter how productive their time in a studio, it was on the stage that the group really came into their own. Ian Gillan perhaps summed this up in a line fundamental to understanding the way the group operated at this time: *"We don't plan things. People like Jon and Ritchie just play what they want to play. If Ritchie wants to play a 150-bar solo he'll play it - and no one will stop him."* • IG to Melody Maker, 11th September 1971.

And this applied equally to the rest of the musicians, the practice of improvisation flowing strongly through everyone in the band. It is this which as much as anything else set them apart from many of their contemporaries and indeed from their original incarnation.

For Deep Purple it meant that from one show to the next they were never completely sure how each 'song' (a somewhat inadequate word for pieces which might develop over half an hour) would express itself. Not only did this keep them alert but it also put a creative and personal pressure on everyone concerned. And Deep Purple appear to have thrived on it, revelling in an almost telepathic interaction on stage. It was this inate ability which made the band so special and which led directly to the material recorded for *Deep Purple In Rock*.

The band's approach to recording in the studio took much of its inspiration from these live skills. Rather than spend hours writing, they would instead improvise together around ideas suggested by one or more of the group, drawing on their live experience to structure and develop the finished song. In turn, rather than then slavishly copy the album tracks on stage, the group saw them often as yet further kicking off points for more improvisational work, which in turn fed back into future recordings. *Deep Purple In Rock* was the album where they finally captured the live spirit of the band within a studio.

Ian Paice attempted to explain it over a decade later: *"Purple should never have worked. Basically we had five egomaniacs. There was just a magical chemistry that allowed us to get some good stuff. I can't think of any other band that's been allowed that much freedom for all the members to do exactly what they wanted. We were just lucky that the chemistry was right and people felt it."* • IP to Robyn Flans, Modern Drummer, December 1984.

Various aspects of the *In Rock* story have been documented over the years in interviews, articles, books, liner notes, etc. The aim here has been to bring all this together for the first time and expand the story with new material and research to give a complete and detailed narrative of this important phase of Deep Purple's career. We have taken a prismatic approach to the story; there is both a chronological narrative, interespersed with expanded sections which look at the writing, recording and ananlysis of each track in detail. Inevitably in dealing with events which are over forty years old there are some discrepancies in individual accounts and recollections and in these cases we have attempted to present both opinions.

It is also a sad truth that not everyone from those early days is still around. Both the band's managers have passed on in recent years and more critically from an artistic point of view, Jon Lord died in 2012. He was interviewed specifically for this book by Stephen Clare and did his best to describe the time around *In Rock* as he remembered it. Talking with warmth and fondness about all his fellow musicians he obviously held that time as a unique and very special period in his life. *"Although In Rock was done over quite a long period that was a most wonderful time for the band."* • JL to SC.

Roger Glover has also provided new insights on the writing of the album and Ian Gillan offered a fresh look at *Child In Time*.

Stephen Clare first approached me with the idea of collecting together my sleeve notes from various Deep Purple reissues. In the end we decided to focus on one period in the band's long history. I am grateful to Stephen for his determination in making this happen. Inevitably putting this all together and expanding into areas not documented properly (if ever) before, who actually wrote what has to some extent been lost, so we're both going to plead guilty.

I'm not a musician (so any references to the science of chords and the like are clearly Stephen's) but *Deep Purple In Rock* came to my notice just as I was first discovering rock music in 1969/70, and had a lasting impact on my life one way and another. Every time I find myself writing about this period, I'm still filled with the urge to abandon the computer and disappear to the music room for a blast of *In Rock*. So I'll finish here.

Simon Robinson.

1 • Deeves Hall to Deep Purple

"For the first few years Purple had no direction whatsoever. We used to follow what Jon wanted to do, because nobody else had any ideas." Ritchie Blackmore

Deep Purple as a band came together over the winter of 1967. You don't need this book to further mythologise the decade but clearly it was a unique period in Britain's cultural history. Post-war austerity had been followed by investment in infrastructure, health, education and the arts, with the result that as living conditions improved and social attitudes changed many more people could make the most of their opportunities.

Tony Edwards was one such person, albeit for him there was less of a struggle. Working in his parent's established ready-to-wear fashion business (and without having to worry too much about the next pay-cheque) Tony became caught up in the heady whirl of late sixties London. Always with a theatrical bent (he trod the boards briefly) and looking to do something in the entertainment industry, he began managing singer Ayshea Brough. Meeting former Searcher Chris Curtis socially, Tony agreed to back his new band. Musicians came and went but Chris brought Ritchie Blackmore and Jon Lord on board. By early 1968 bassist Nick Simper had joined. Holed up in a modest country farm house Deeves Hall (left), just off the A1, auditions produced singer Rod Evans and through him drummer Ian Paice. Thanks largely to the music industry connections of producer Derek Lawrence, Deep Purple got an early leg up the ladder and in particular struck a huge chord in America, where their psych updating of an already popular club record *Hush* reached No. 4 in September 1968. Seizing the moment but with no real direction the band turned out two cover-led albums inside six months to capitalise on their American success and spent the last three months of 1968 touring there.

It was not until they started recording their third album in early 1969 that Deep Purple were able to find any breathing space. They put some real effort into burying the Vanilla Fudge influences they had hung their early records on and started to develop a more individual direction. That is not to say the first two albums hadn't demonstrated a Deep Purple sound, but they were clearly still finding their way. More promising individual tracks like *Wring That Neck* and *Mandrake Root* showed a harder edge, but this was often overlooked amidst the eclectic output, rubbing up against dramatic overblown covers of Beatles or Ike & Tina Turner numbers. By contrast, apart from just one track, their third album (titled *Deep Purple*) comprised entirely self-penned progressive material, as was their final single *Emmaretta*.

Nick Simper saw the way the band were moving: *"From the beginning Ritchie and I were always trying to make rock music, but Jon with his classic intentions and love of softer music tended to hold us in check during recording sessions. On stage it was another story, and we proved time and time again that we were true hard rock pioneers that could hold up against any opposition. That was why they chucked us off the tour with Cream. I believe the seed of hard rock had already begun to bloom on our third album."* • NS to Gabriel Gonzalez, Argentina, 2006.

If they allowed Jon more leeway, there was a good reason; few of the others had any real alternative idea of where the band ought to be going. Rather than a group of mates who had forged a band from shared backgrounds, Deep Purple had essentially been brought together by a couple of businessmen. So it was natural that it would take them a while to find out what made each other tick. As this was essentially done on the fly and having to cope with demands from their American label, having someone like Jon Lord contributing did at least give them something to hang the albums on. And what was the rush? Despite being a new band they had worldwide record deals, were scoring hits and touring heavily (albeit mostly in America). Time enough to develop new ideas once they were established. And while Nick confirms the band was capable of moving towards a more overtly heavy rock direction sooner, he does acknowledge that on balance it was a good idea to let Lord guide them over that first year or so. Ritchie was of a similar opinion: *"For the first few years Purple had no direction whatsoever. If anything, we used to follow what Jon wanted to do, which was OK because nobody else had any ideas."* • RB to Trouser Press, July 1978. *"At the time we thought we were pleased with the early things, but when you look back they are a really different style altogether, more of a ballad style. It is like it ws someone else playing, and I suppose in a way it was."* • RB to Zigzag, Aug 1970.

There wasn't much guidance or direction from their management either, who were themselves new to the world of rock and pop, certainly on this level. Many of the big bands of the day had hard-nosed operators with years of experience in the music business, capable of taking on labels and promoters.

Deep Purple's first line-up in 1968. L-R Blackmore, Evans, Paice, Lord, Simper

Ivy Lodge, which housed the Ivy Lodge Club in the 1960s. It was here that Jon and Ritchie came to check out Ian Gillan at an Episode Six concert.

Deep Purple's two main backers came from other industries, Tony as we've seen from the rag trade (!) and John Coletta, who joined the band's management team early on, from an advertising agency. There were also problems with the band's American label during 1969 as well, which had been spending lavishly without much other success. It came to a head towards the end of the year as Coletta recalled: *"We had some minor success over there, but we couldn't break Europe at all. We had Kentucky Woman which was the follow-up which did reasonably well. We had the Taliesyn album which was a follow-up which did fairly well and then we had Deep Purple which also did quite well. Then the record company went bankrupt, Tetragrammaton, and of course we had all these royalties which we weren't going to get and the market of course was dead."* • Voxpop, 1972.

If initially the musicians rubbed along, artistic differences began to surface during another lengthy tour of America through April and May 1969. Derek Lawrence recalls them discussing possible changes in the group as early as The Book Of Taliesyn sessions in 1968: *"Ritchie wanted to get the original Hollies bass player [Eric Haydock] in."* • DL to SR. Now, six months on, Ritchie and Jon decided they wanted to steer the band in a more overtly rock direction and, having discussed this with Ian Paice, felt vocalist Rod Evans wasn't capable of fronting the louder, more aggressive material they wanted to develop. They also came to the conclusion that Nick Simper's musical direction was a little old school. Rather than let the potential of their new band wither, Ritchie, Jon and Ian Paice felt they shared a common aim and made the decision to sack Nick and Rod in persuit of their ambitions. Or rather let their managers do it when they were ready. The band flew back to Britain at the end of May. The task uppermost for three of them was to find a new singer and bass player. Ian Paice explains their thinking: *"The three of us had a discussion in New York. We thought that Rod and Nick had gone about as far as they could. We decided that if it was going to be a break, it was going to be a substantial one to refocus the band to look forward, to break this feeling of stagnation."*
Jon was of the same mind: *"Ritchie, Ian and I had come to the conclusion that Rod couldn't take us to where we wanted to go. We wanted to become harder, to write our own material. Rod was a bit of a cabaret singer. We needed a lyricist. It was a very cold decision. Rod was a really nice guy and didn't deserve to be treated in such a cavalier fashion."* • JL and IP to Kieron Tyler. Mojo Magazine, Jan 2003.
"Although we were going down quite well there was something lacking. Quite honestly Jon, Ian and I were going down well, but the other two were really just passengers. So we looked at it from a cold point of view and decided they'd have to go." • RB to Zigzag, Aug 1970.

Having spent so long on the road in America Ritchie, Jon and Ian Paice found themselves a little out of touch with the changing scene back home and unsure of where to begin looking for new musicians. Ritchie wanted to contact singer Terry Reid, who only a year earlier had declined a similar opportunity to front a band which became Led Zeppelin. Though Reid (who coincidentally had opened for Cream on their 1968 farewell U.S. tour after Deep Purple had lost the gig for being 'too good') found the Deep Purple offer "flattering" he was still bound by an exclusive recording contract with his producer Mickie Most and wanted to follow his solo career instead.

With this avenue closed Ritchie rang up his old mate Mick Underwood (they'd played together in Joe Meek's houseband The Outlaws) to see if he had any ideas on who might be both available and suitable. Mick was then drumming in Episode Six and Ritchie was a little taken aback when Mick suggested he check out their singer Ian Gillan. Mick explained that Episode Six were doing a session on the radio the following day so Ritchie could have a listen. He must have been interested as they decided to go and see Ian Gillan at Episode Six's next gig. There was some irony in wanting to see the singer, as Nick Simper recalls he had raised Gillan's name when Deep Purple first got together, but an approach via a mutual friend had apparently been rebuffed.

On Wednesday June 4th 1969 Ritchie and Jon drove over to the Ivy Lodge Club, a small church youth club in Woodford, North East London, to see Episode Six play. Mick had given Ritchie Ian Gillan's number so he could have a chat and Ian told his friend and band-mate Roger Glover on the day of the gig that someone from Deep Purple had called with the possible offer of a job. It was no secret that Ian Gillan felt Episode Six were getting nowhere fast and he had already broached the idea of forming a new band with Mick Underwood and Roger Glover (Episode Six's drummer and bassist respectively) and Peter Robinson[1].

Fondly remembered by locals who saw many bands there in the late 1960s, the Ivy Lodge Club was in a large Victorian house[2] taken

Episode Six in 1968, clockwise from bottom left: Graham Carter, Tony Lander, Roger Glover, Mick Underwood, Ian Gillan, Sheila Carter.

KINGSTON COLLEGE OF TECHNOLOGY
PENRHYN ROAD, KINGSTON-UPON-THAMES, SURREY
ENTERTAINMENTS COMMITTEE PRESENTS
EPISODE 6
THE GIANT ★ ORANGE RAINBOW
MAIN HALL, Saturday, 26th April, 8-12.30, LICENSED BAR
TICKETS IN ADVANCE 6/-, AT DOOR 8/-. Tel: 546 4836

Episode Six with previous drummer John Kerrison back centre. Roger far left, Ian far right.

over by the church next door. Volunteers converted a couple of the big reception rooms into a youth club for discos and then live bands. During the gig, the rest of Episode Six, who were a close-knit band, realised something was going on when Ritchie got up for a jam (which the rest of the band felt in retrospect was a cheeky move). Roger recalled his first contact with Jon and Ritchie: *"I certainly hadn't heard of Deep Purple, the first I knew of them was when Ian Gillan told me they had a hit in the States. I didn't meet them that night, but I thought they were very nefarious characters. Ritchie got up and had a jam, a blues. I was quite impressed, but my overriding impression was they all wore black. They looked mysterious. They had dyed black hair, and lots of it."*

Ian Gillan almost blew it as he confessed later: *"It was only the fact that I had a stinking cold and no money that stopped me bursting out laughing when I first actually came face to face with Jon and Ritchie. It was the haircuts! These bouffants seemed dated to me, didn't bear any relevance to what was actually happening in London at the time."* • RG + IG to Kieron Tyler. Mojo Magazine, Jan 2003.

Jon's recollections of that first meeting with Ian also lasted: *"He was a handsome bugger you know, obviously there wasn't a woman in the audience who wasn't madly in love with him, that's a plus for a lead singer. Tall, good sense of humour and that amazing range. I never thought he was what you might say a great blues singer, which was probably a little bit more of what we were looking for after Rod who had almost been a pop singer. But he had this startling range, lovely sounding voice, powerful and this character. I think it was 50/50 on his voice and his character vying for each other. I just remember thinking 'my god he is going to look great in front of our band'. You do not want someone standing up there who has got no presence; Ian had presence by the ton. Ritchie was very much in love with Ian's voice and style and everything for a couple of years. It was only later that Ritchie started to fall out with him, I think over personality issues, I think Ritchie found him a bit full on. Ian was mad as a box of wasps; he would do anything for the crack, for the fun of it. They (singers) have got to have that get up and go, that madness to get up there in front with that spotlight without an instrument to protect them. The only instrument that they've got is a God given one, not something bought from a guitar shop. I have got a huge amount of respect for singers, I've always been slightly in awe of them rather than guitarists, just because of that chutzpah they require, that's what Ian had, that's what Ritchie liked."* • JL to SC.

Yet curiously Jon got the distinct impression that Episode Six were not making the best of Gillan. *"Ian was not, in a strange way, not the lead singer of Episode Six, it was Sheila (Carter) who was. Ian just did these occasional pieces which were his party pieces almost, he sang backup quite a lot of the time. Occasionally he would play a little keyboard. His party piece was an astonishing song by a singer called Lorraine Ellison called Stay With Me Baby; if it don't give you goose bumps there's something wrong with you. Ian used to do that, it's got this astounding climax, she goes way up above the stave and he managed that."* JL to SC

Jon was clearly sold, though to be fair to Shiela Carter it was her who handled the lead vocals on this track, with Ian doing harmonies, playing the keyboards and yes, matching Sheila on the high notes at the end of the verses. Still, there is no denying that Episode Six were musically a very schizophrenic lot and had an act which ran more along cabaret style lines at times.

Ritchie also remembers his first exposure to Gillan: *"Why we thought we had to change singers was because of Robert Plant. We were playing at Mother's in Birmingham and Robert Plant got up to sing with Terry Reid. We thought 'Christ almighty.' He was so dynamic. And the next two weeks we were looking for a singer, people who had Roger Plant's dynamic approach. So it was thanks to him. Ian was amazing, his voice, the way he looked and everything else. Stupendous. We took him right there."* • RB to Classic Rock. Feb 2009.

For 'took' read 'pretty much offered Gillan the job backstage' as Jon explained; *"We felt really bad about it cause it was Episode Six and one of their singers. I wanted him to join right then and there!"*

Ian Paice was happy to go along with Jon and Ritchie's verdict and recalls Ritchie telling him he'd been *"blown away with this shattering voice of Ian Gillan's."*

Ian Gillan was really up for it but there were some details to be worked through. The following day the members of Episode Six made their way to manager Gloria Bristow's place for a meeting to discuss what to do about Ian's job offer. Roger Glover knew that Ian taking the job was a real blow for them and that the band might fold. Nevertheless they accepted Ian's decision and decided to look for a permanent replacement. Ian promised to honour their confirmed bookings so the band wouldn't lose any work or income.

Even as they were reaching this decision, Roger became aware that Deep Purple were also looking for a bassist. He and Ian were close friends, and Ian told Roger that he should be putting himself forward. Roger wanted none of it though, feeling he was letting Episode Six down by even considering it. The pair reached a compromise. Roger and Ian had both been writing together, hoping to sell songs to other performers; Ian suggested that Roger submit one or two ideas to Purple. So on Saturday June 7th 1969 (we know as Roger kept a diary at the time), accompanied by Ian Gillan, Roger made his way round to Jon Lord's flat on Gunter's Grove to play him a few songs they'd written. This was the first time the pair had properly met and Roger took to him: *"In person (Jon) wasn't anything like I imagined. He was such a nice man. I was blown away with his geniality. We nervously played our songs, about monkeys and lions, monkeys always appeared in our lyrics those days. But there was nothing that interested him."* • Roger Glover., Mojo 2003.

Anyone who has heard early Episode Six material with the Gillan / Glover writing credit (they were sometimes allowed a b-side) would hardly be surprised at this polite lack of interest. As for the monkeys, much of what they'd written was whimsical pop, likeable but fairly lightweight. Which is not what Deep Purple wanted to be anymore. Instead, Jon countered with an acetate he had, getting Roger to take a listen: *"He played a demo of Hallelujah and said 'what do you think of that? Do you think it's a hit?'"*

There was a certain irony in the choice of this track; with the layered vocal harmonies it actually sounded more like a potential Episode Six track than a Deep Purple one. Jon explained to Roger that they had already decided to record it, and asked if he fancied playing on the recording on a session basis. Neither Ian nor Roger were overimpressed by the demo, later confiding to one another that the choice of Hallelujah was a bizarre one. Ian: *"I was appalled, I thought it was absolute..."* Roger: *"It was a bit limp."*

The track had already been earmarked as Deep Purple's next American single. It had been sent to their producer Derek Lawrence as a demo titled *I Am The Preacher* and the band had a studio booked that afternoon. Jon, Ritchie and Ian Paice were keen to try out Ian Gillan on the song to get a feel for how he would cope in a studio. *"Blackmore and I thought it would be perfect for auditioning Ian Gillan in the studio and Roger came along to play bass. We worked up an arrangement in an hour. All that Hallelujah bit, I added those chords and got Ian Gillan in three part harmony and we were all just sitting there with goose bumps thinking 'this is fantastic'."* • JL to SC.

The session was done at De Lane Lea's Kingsway Studio on June 7th and 8th 1969. It was engineered by 'BA' (we assumed this was Barry Ainsworth, who had worked on the Mk 1 albums, but he says not). They did ten takes, half of which were complete, and went for take nine (in the key of A) as the "possible master". Although the track didn't presage *In Rock*, it did show how determined the band were to strike out on their own. Manager John Coletta later said that even he didn't know the session was taking place. It was also the first time the band had produced themselves, an idea which they would continue for the new album. A second reel from the same date has three more complete backings out of a further five takes. On the next day they did takes 11 and 12, the latter in the key of G, and decided this would be the final master.

Derek thought it didn't really work and he told the group he felt it wasn't right for them (he would later record a soul / gospel version on his own label.)[3]

If Roger's own song ideas back at the flat had not won over Jon, then his playing and suggestions during the session certainly did. Roger recalls the moment clearly. *"I walked into the studio, early evening. The thing that impressed me most was their clothes. They all had new clothes. I didn't buy clothes, I used hand me downs. I used to make my own stage gear. I had no socks on, the bottoms of my jeans were frayed, and they were held up by string. There were a couple of Marshall stacks, a Precision bass, it all looked very new. I made a suggestion about the middle eight of the song, which worked, and they seemed to like me. At the end of the session Jon came up and said 'we've had a chat, me and the boys, would you like to join our band?' I was floored."* • RG to Kieron Tyler, Mojo.

In fact Jon had already discussed the idea with Ian Paice and Ritchie, based on what they had heard from Roger when they had gone to check out Episode Six: *"When we were watching Ian in the Ivy Lodge Club I'd been aware of Roger's bass playing. He's a great bass player, very rhythmic, he's a rock solid terrific player. I became aware that he was a song writing partner of Ian Gillan and that they were really, really close, so I said to the other guys in the band 'there's a bass player sitting right there', they said 'You can't take two out of their band'."* • JL to SC.

"We had no thoughts of including Roger Glover in our plans but our drummer heard him and realised that he would blend in perfectly with his percussion." • JL to Record Mirror, Oct 1970.

The band fully expected Roger to jump at the opportunity, and Jon felt the offer was a good one. *"We were offering £20.00 a week (the band were all on that amount) which was £1000 a year. I remember my dad coming home in the mid sixties saying 'I have just had a raise and I am a £1000 a year man'."* • JL to SC.

BELOW : I Am The Preacher tape box from De Lane Lea Kingsway session

FRUSTRATED THATS DEEP PURPLE
By Keith Altham

Instead Roger asked to think about the offer and wrote in his diary that evening: *"A very important day. Did the session at De Lane Lea. They were impressed and offered me a job!! I said I would think about it."* Roger was in fact thrown by the offer and recalled the emotional turmoil the decision left him in: *"I couldn't leave the band 'cos if Ian's leaving my group, and if I leave, we've been through so much together and everyone's out of a job, and I can't handle the responsibility. (Jon) was quite taken aback by that."*

If this now seems a bit sentimental, Roger had helped form Episode Six with friends from school and had been with them from day one (Ian Gillan had been recruited later on). Even so the offer was tempting. Roger and Ian left the studio and made their way back to Gillan's flat where Roger slept over, or tried to sleep. *"The challenge was eating away at me; I wanted to join Deep Purple, it was too good an opportunity to miss. I didn't even know why, cos I hadn't heard the music, it was just the feeling. I wanted a change, and I called up 9 o'clock the next morning, and woke up Jon."*

Jon told him he'd have to speak to the others first. Roger made his way back home to find a message from Ian Gillan; he was in. Roger: *"I was put on three months trial, though I didn't know it at the time."* His diary entry for the 8th of June 1969 summed it up: *"I've decided to accept Deep Purple's offer after a sleepless night. Phoned Jon and he said he'd ring me back with the answer...... feeling ten miles high."*

Roger now had to break the news to Episode Six's manager. Having already lost Ian Gillan, Gloria was furious. Roger has said since that he felt he *"was the least worthy bass player Purple could have had."* But while there may well have been technically superior bassists out there at the time, Roger had mastered the instrument over four years and brought a number of important elements to the table, song writing skills for one thing, together with an inate ability to help refine the rock riffs which were to become central to much of Deep Purple's material. And despite their offer they could hardly have known what an asset he would become in the studio. The others quickly nicknamed him the 'stinking hippie', thanks to a combination of his foreign cigarettes, long hair and the scruffy, rarely laundered clothes (Roger and Ian Gillan shared a pair of crushed velvet bell bottoms for 'best', Gillan had got to wear them the evening Jon and Ritchie came to call).

The arrival of the new members generated a number of problems for Deep Purple's managers, not the least of which was the fact that Nick and Rod were still working with the group and knew nothing of their impending dismissal. Having initially asked Ritchie, Ian and Jon to hold back from telling Nick and Rod they were out until the American tour had ended, the managers now asked them to keep mum for a few more weeks. During the rest of June and into July, Episode Six and Deep Purple had the task of playing out existing dates, ironically the first of which for both bands was in Cambridge for the May Balls there, albeit at different colleges, on June 10th 1969. Gloria Bristow began pushing for a settlement from Deep Purple's management company HEC. Both Ian Gillan and Roger were under contract so some agreement was necessary to free them from that. HEC were keen to avoid a drawn out legal conflict, and told Roger and Ian to keep as much from her as possible. Roger: *"We had terrible scenes with the management. All of a sudden from a guy that's got no money, earning £10 a week maximum, I'm involved in a court case involving about £3000!"*

John Coletta explained the problems: *"We had to break their contract, we had to pay a certain amount of money to the manager to release them, I think the group was breaking up anyway and had already got new ideas of what they wanted to do and everything, and so to her that was a little bit of a Godsend, to get a little bit of money anyway for something she was already going to do. To us it was important, so we paid up. I think it cost us £3000 in end, plus a lot of negotiations, but I think it paid off; I think you can say it was a good £3000 spent."* • Voxpop, 1972[4]

On June 12th Deep Purple with Roger and Ian returned to the studio to put some more time in on Hallelujah, working through the night. On the next day Roger and Ian played with Episode Six at De La Salle College in Manchester, the next day it was off to Dudley College, Roger still keeping his matter of fact diary entries: *"Leisurely drive down. Free meal at service centre due to fag end in Neil's meal. Good booking, Ian contolled fancy dress crowd well."* The same evening Deep Purple played the Mother's Club in Birmingham with Evans and Simper still blissfully unaware of what was developing. The whole situation had become quite Machiavellian.

E.M.I. launch Harvest Records on the UNDERGROUND GROOVE

Deep Purple were recording with new members, and began proper rehearsals with them on June 16th 1969, while still performing live with their original line-up. This degree of often quite calculated behaviour within Deep Purple and their management organisation would become a feature of the band's story over the years. Roger Glover went along with it because he had to, but couldn't help feeling bad about Nick and Rod and felt they should have been told. HEC need to keep a lid on things as long as possible, they were already facing one legal battle and didn't want to be landed with another. *"It was normal behaviour for Purple,"* says Glover. *"I became aware that the modus operandi for Deep Purple was if there is a problem don't talk about it. Management is what you rely on to sort things out; musicians tend to shed their responsibilities as human beings once they're in a band. You have this cotton-wool surrounding you."* RG to Kieron Tyler.

Roger finally signed a contract with HEC on Friday 20th June 1969. He celebrated by putting down a £2.00 deposit on a Spanish guitar. Even though he and Ian Gillan were now officially in Deep Purple, incredibly the old line-up (who had been playing in Belgium the day Roger and Ian were signing their contract) still had bookings, with Nick and Rod remaining unaware of the fact they had been replaced. On 24th June 1969 (a week after Mk 2 had started rehearsing), Mk 1[5] went into Studio 5, Maida Vale in Delaware Road and recorded three session tracks. They did two more shows, and another BBC session on the 30th June. It was broadcast on Chris Grant's Tasty Pop Sundae show on the 6th July, by which time Mk 1 had played their last gig and Mk 2's first show was just four days away.

Deep Purple had managed to keep a lid on the changes, but the music business in London was a small world. Outside the band and managers studio personnel, road crew and others were perhaps more prone to chat about the latest comings and goings. Nick and Rod reportedly first learned what was going on through a gossip column in the underground paper International Times. Nick dismissed the story but finally learned the truth just before that final Mk 1 gig which took place at the Top Rank in Cardiff on Friday 4th July. As he recalled recently, he told Rod the news after the show. *"I was becoming pretty unpopular after suggesting we use a small bus and motels rather than limousines and hotels. Jon Lord had become the band's spokesman, but I was always elected to tell the management when there was bad news. What finally happened was that I got a phone call from Jon, saying that the rehearsal one night was cancelled, because we had problems with the equipment. So I said "great I'll have the night off and go to the pictures". Then a mate of mine told me that he'd seen the band with a new singer and bass player, Ian Gillan and Roger Glover. So I phoned the record company in America, who told me that they'd been given a Purple single, Hallelujah, which had a session singer and bass player on it."*

As you might imagine Nick was speechless. *"I told Rod what had happened and he went mental. I can't tell you what he wanted to do to them. We drove down to John Coletta's house in Brighton. He realised we knew what was going on and took us out to dinner, where he explained that we were no longer in the band and that there would be a financial settlement if we came to his office the following Monday."* • Record Collector, Dec 2004. But when Nick turned up for the meeting he was simply told *"You're out. Goodbye. No financial settlement whatsoever."* Which was Coletta's way of trying to bully people into rolling over. In the end Nick sued HEC and they settled before it got to court *"for about 20 grand, which was quite a lot back then."* Nick's feeling was that he had ended up as the bad boy, so the managers were happy to see him go.

Mk 2 made their live debut on July 10th at the Speakeasy Club in London. At least the personnel changes were now out in the open. As agreed Gillan and Glover continued to honor their bookings with Episode Six. This meant them continuing to lead a double life for the next few weeks, playing Douglas House on the 13th July with Episode Six, then swopping hats to play the Redcar Jazz Club on the 18th and Birmingham Mother's on the 20th July with Deep Purple. Episode Six did their last gig with Ian and Roger at the Barn Club in Little Bardfield on the 26th July. After six years together it was an emotional event for all concerned, especially for Roger who had been with the group since day one and had known most of the musicians since his boyhood.

1 - Robinson and Underwood formed Quatermass not long after Gillan left.

2 - It is now demolished.

3 - This has been sampled a number of times, including for a dance single in Germany in 2013.

4 - From Roger's later comments it seems this was later recouped from his royalties.

5 - Rock historians use the designations Mk 1, Mk 2 and so forth to differentiate the line-ups.

2 • Hanwell Community Centre

"In a short space of maybe three or four weeks, we found that everything was possible, and it was all contained within ourselves." Ian Paice

Hanwell today.

While the reverberations of Simper and Evan's departure would continue to occupy the minds of HEC's managers and lawyers, Deep Purple began to look to the future. The four main areas to be addressed were clear; they needed gigs, rehearsals, new material and an album. These concerns were interlinked: new material would come from rehearsals, could be tried out on stage and be honed for the album.

If any one location could be said to have been the birthplace of *Deep Purple In Rock*, then Hanwell Community Centre on Westcott Crescent in London surely takes that honour. Indeed it might rightly be judged as the place where Deep Purple as they are known today really came into being.

Begun in 1856, the Central London District Poor Law School in Hanwell housed and educated disadvantaged and orphaned children from Central London. Most famously Charlie Chaplin was orphaned here as a child in 1896 for two years. Now a crowded suburb of West

DEEP PURPLE SPLIT

London, at that time it stood surrounded by open countryside. In 1930, the buildings and grounds were taken over by London County Council. They demolished most of the buildings until only the central administration block remained. The surrounding land was developed as an LCC council housing estate after which in 1945 the administration block was turned into the Hanwell Community Centre with some land retained as a park and sports field. Local groups, societies and sports clubs were able to rent rooms there. When we say 'local groups' it's not certain if the post-war administrators ever foresaw the use of the centre's facilities by the likes of Deep Purple, The Who, Uriah Heep, The Alan Bown Set (some of whom then formed Supertramp), Rod Stewart & The Faces, Marsha Hunt, Geno Washington and Led Zeppelin.

History doesn't record when the centre started providing rehearsal space for music groups. It seems with the rise of 'the teenager' during the fifties, local skiffle and jazz groups began renting rooms here, and word got around that Hanwell was a place where amateur bands could make a noise without causing problems for the neighbours. And you don't get any noisier than The Who. They used Hanwell to rehearse Tommy in the main ground floor sports hall, Spice (or Uriah Heep as they became) would sometimes rehearse in the room next to Deep Purple (though only once were they both there at the same time, with Heep working on their song *Gypsy*), while Led Zeppelin used the centre to rehearse for their fourth British tour around the time of their debut album. If anywhere deserves a blue plaque for services to popular music, surely this it it.

As for Deep Purple, they were certainly using the centre by June 1969. The rooms could be rented by the week or longer, enabling the band to leave gear on site between gigs rather than be continually moving it in and out. Photographs show them working in one of the smaller rooms at the front of the building, but they also had the option of using the gym if it was free. Thanks to Roger's trusty pocket diary we know that Deep Purple first set up here on Monday June 16th, the first rehearsal of Deep Purple Mk 2. *"Went over to Ian's and met him in Houslow, got a cab to Hanwell Community Centre where Deep Purple rehearse. Jon was late so just had a blow. Jon gave us £10.00 each."*

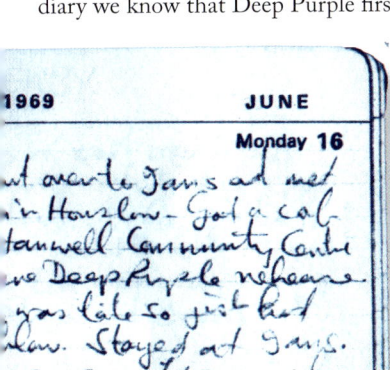

Jon was notorious for sleeping in (*"I was late for every practice"*) so the rest of the band just jammed and got to know one another, before rehearsing properly the next day. Jon: *"Deep Purple rehearsal sessions always started with a jam, that's how we came up with most of our stuff to be perfectly honest."* • JL to SC

Roger had never had a roadie before, and famously put his foot in it at the end of the first day's rehearsal when he started dismantling his gear: *"Ian Hansford, their roadie, ran over and told me sternly not to do his job for him, muttered on about job security, and then laughed!"*

Hansford was crewed with Mick Angus, and they were later joined by Ron Quinton - he was there by November 1970 - to form the basic Deep Purple crew (Ian's last gig with them was at Liverpool on Feb. 28th 1973, Mick left towards the end of 1970 but Ron stayed on as Ritchie's technician into 1975. He died that year in a car crash). With three Ian's now on board, they devised nicknames; Ian Gillan answered to Ian; Ian Paice was Little "E" and Ian Hansford was Big "E" (later sortened to Bige.)

The group rehearsed the next day with more success (*"Another rehearsal at the Centre. More work done this time. Feeling very pleased with progress."* Roger's diary) before driving over to De Lane Lea to do wrap up work on Hallelujah. Ian Paice remembers their time at Hanwell: *"It was always available, it was cheap and it was close to where we were all living at the time. In a short space of maybe three or four weeks, we found that everything was possible, and it was all contained within ourselves. We didn't have to look outside, and that was really exciting."*

For the first time he and the others could forget about trying to cover other people's material, something which no self-respecting progressive rock band wanted to do. Ian Gillan, standing slightly back from what was going on around him, quickly saw the potential as well: *"First of all, everyone could perform. There was a good balanced chemistry, a suitable amount of eccentricity and common sense."*

"When I joined Deep Purple, the members had multiple influences. One guy loved classical, another was into rock 'n' roll, a third into instrumental music and a fourth into blues. Our role models ranged from Beethoven, to Buddy Rich, to Bob Dylan, to Ella Fitzgerald, to Sonny Boy Williamson, to Chuck Berry, to so many others. So there were a variety of influences in the songs we wrote. In contrast, today's bands are only influenced by Deep Purple, Black Sabbath and a few other groups. Because of that, they do pretty much the same thing." • IG to Bombay Midday Newspaper, 2002.

During coffee breaks at Hanwell, the two new lads sat around listening, often in disbelief, to stories of life on the road Stateside from the more seasoned players, as Roger recalls: *"We were regaled by tales of touring America, of the girls, the diseases, the clubs, the bed sizes, the hotels, the people, the music, the bands."*

Dave Pring had a part time job at Hanwell at the time and his recollections help give a feel of the place. *"I was a tubby schoolboy of 14 who used to spend his time hanging around the centre, helping the caretaker do odd jobs and so on. I was hanging around outside the room that the bands used to use in the main - it was room A, first on the left as you went in through the front doors - when their roadie Ian Hansford asked me if I would like to give him a hand to load the gear on the truck as he'd been left on his own (their other roadie hardly ever used to turn up). I did so and after this I became a sort of honorary roadie and used to help Ian set up and then sit in the room while the band rehearsed. I also remember going with Ian in the truck to the Marshall shop in Ealing Broadway. I remember being asked to leave the room sometimes while the band had a meeting, also Ritchie would sometimes go AWOL from rehearsals and there would be some frantic phoning around to try and find him and get him to come over. I also helped Uriah Heep a few times, that is until I somehow managed to break off part of their organ lid!"* • DP to SR.

The first couple of rehearsals under their belt there was a mad couple of weeks with business meetings, shows by Episode Six and Deep Purple Mk 1. It was only come the end of June that they could knuckle down at Hanwell, with four days of rehearsals off and on before they were due to play that all important first Mk 2 concert. Some of this time was spent trying out Mk 1 songs they thought might be used until such time as new numbers came along. Roger remembers them practising *Help* (which the group had covered on their first album), *And The Address*, *This Bird Has Flown*, *Hey Joe*, and *Hush* while the mainstay of a Deep Purple show at that time were three lengthy (and mainly) intrumentals: *Wring That Neck* and *Mandrake Root* (from the Mk 1 albums) and *Paint It Black*. Did they do *Hallelujah*? *"Maybe, but if (we) did, it didn't stay long."* • RG to Tonny Steenhagen.

Ian Gillan wouldn't have an awful lot to do in these sections of the set but certainly Roger needed to develop his working relationship with Ian Paice in particular to be able to adapt to Purple's way of improvising within numbers live: *"When we joined Purple of course the first few gigs was all the Mark One stuff like Hush and things from the first albums that the band had done. I think both Ian Gillan and I, we kind of raised our game because I don't think we'd ever worked with such great musicians before where anything you could think of they could play. So all of a sudden your imagination just went nuts because you could actually play anything and they'd be with you."* • RG to Ultimate Guitar

"I remember one of the key thoughts, the key philosophies, of the band when I first joined, is if they love us, great, if they hate us, great. Some people are going to love us, some people are going to hate us." • RG to Martin Popoff.

For Ian Gillan and Roger, joining Deep Purple together helped immensely. They joined not just as an individual singer and a bass player, but as a songwriting team, and as friends.

Although Hanwell was the band's main rehearsal space they did try another venue once. On August 27th after an interview with a reporter from Prague Radio they went to St. Anselms Church Hall, in Hatch End, Harrow, to rehearse. Roger's diary notes that they *"Dropped St. Louis (Blues) and tried to write something new."* In a residential area, it is unlikely that they would have been allowed to play too loudly even during daytime. Nobody recalls why they went there, although it was known to Roger and Ian as Episode Six had gigged there in the past.

This grainy image shows the group inside the rehearsal room, around July 1969.

3 • Writing In Rock

"We throw out a lot of our material, if one member of the band doesn't like a number, then that's enough. We don't use it." Ian Gillan

Initially time spent at Hanwell had to be devoted to getting a set together for their first concert. The writing and recording of *Deep Purple In Rock* turned out to be a very lengthy process and while four new songs emerged from subsequent rehearsals at Hanwell, as gigging started to occupy more and more of their time, the remaining material would come from either the occasional song writing session or by getting ideas together in the studio. There just wasn't the budget to allow the group a fixed period off the road to get an album finished. Income from their initial American successes was drying up as the record label's financial problems grew. Playing concerts at least brought in some ready money and paid the wages.

"Deep Purple's method of composing is a rather unusual 'upside-down' affair. But it works, and works well with all five members contributing equally. A new number will perhaps evolve from a bass riff or basic theme and will gradually grow in stature as the others add their thoughts. In many instances the actual instrumental arrangement is set before the lyric and melody lines are finally written so that the lyrics more directly complement the sound rather than trying to fit an appropriate sound around a set of lyrics." • In Rock songbook, 1971.

This rather quaintly 'pop journalese' description of their song writing process (included - unaccredited - in a book of music and lyrics later issued to cover both this and the next studio album) wouldn't have been out of place on the back of a sixties album sleeve, but is factually not too far off the mark. The band would jam and get the music sorted, then Ian Gillan would write lyrics to fit in and around the tune. Ian's approach to lyric writing he describes as… *"All spontaneous. It's still the same with DP today, while they are jamming I use gibberish lyrics so I can concentrate on the phrasing, tune, etc. Generally one or two useable ideas pop up and I work on the words later."*

While this may give the impression that the songs were all the subject of equal contributions from each member, this was not always the case. Usually one musician's idea would be developed through jamming (and sometimes live work) to form the foundation of the song. Varying levels of contributions would come from the other band members during this process and give the finished number it's eventual overall sound. When the album was finished all the songs were credited to the whole band (an almost unique decision), regardless of who had the initial inspiration. They felt this was a fair way to recognise the unique development process. This five way writing split was agreed between all the musicians in the heady days of 1969 (it had not been applied to the Mk 1 albums) although it would become the source of friction a couple of years down the line when the band began to enjoy increasing album sales. Looking at the money coming in some members began to feel that they were due a larger share as they had contributed more. Eventually the five way equal split was dropped and they reverted to crediting just the main writers, but it would take a change in line-up before that could happen.

"All the stuff on the new LP is written by us, which is the only way really, because our music is more in the arrangement and the playing than in the writing - everyone puts more or less the same into it. Usually what happens is one of us comes up with a riff and we develop it from there. The melody comes last and poor old Ian has to put something over the top." •
RB to Zigzag, Aug 1970.

Jon Lord felt that the original concept was very valid. *"80% of the songs on our albums came from somebody with an idea and with jamming it, or, nobody with an idea and Paicey starting playing and just saying 'come on'. And Ritchie was full of ideas, teaming with ideas, as we all were. Paicey never wrote a note in his life. But if he hadn't been there, and if his input hadn't been there, this song or that song would not have happened. (On) some songs some people did more than others and in other songs other people did more than others. It was just right, I mean correct that it was done that way. Ian and Roger have said ideas came out on stage mostly in the long jams and that is true. Wring That Neck was a great sort of growing ground for ideas to come up on stage."* JL to SC.

Roger Glover in particular had a lot of input into the album but felt the equal split recognised the period as one of huge creativity and untold possibilites: *"In Rock was so easy, it was a new band, we were still finding out about each other, and I had just come from a group which didn't take my song writing very seriously, into a group which really wanted my song writing. All the ideas I came up with, they could play them, and usually did! So I probably wrote more on In Rock than any other album, a greater input, as I had so many ideas bottled up for years in Episode Six and Purple were looking for that, as they had been known basically for cover versions. Though they did do originals it hadn't grown at that point, so there was a hot bed of creative talent around In Rock time, so all the songs were very fresh, and had so much fire and aggression."*
• RG to SR.

"We didn't write; we played. Songs evolved and there was no thought

---

DEEP PURPLE SPLIT

TWO MEMBERS of Deep Purple quit the group this week. They are Rod Evans and Nicky Simper, who have been replaced by vocalist Ian Gillan (24) and bassist Roger Glover (24).

Reasons for the split — "diversity of musical ideas within the group." Rod Evans is also expected to go to America to be married.

Other members of Deep Purple are Jon Lord (organ), Ritchie Blackmore (lead guitar) and Ian Paice (drums).

They have a new single released on July 25 on Harvest called "Hallelujah" written by Greenaway and Cook, coupled with "April Part I."

The group appear tomorrow (Friday) at Redcar Jazz Club and at Mothers, Birmingham, (20). They will be at the Lyceum, London on July 25.

Plans are in hand for them to perform in concert with a symphony orchestra in London in September, and later in the month they tour America.

involved. Just someone started a riff, either Ritchie or me in those days, and people just joined in and say, 'Oh, we need the chorus. Where should we go for a chorus? How about Bb? OK, fine.' It was that simple and that instant and it kind of didn't really matter where you went because it was the feel of the music that mattered. All those early songs, they could have been slightly different choruses or different riffs here and there and it probably wouldn't have made a lot of difference. Because it was the time when music kind of spoke for people." • RG to Ultimate Guitar

Ritchie understood how the others could help put flesh on ideas he put forward, recognising his weaknesses. *"My failing is composing; I really fall down in composing. I can come up with riffs and I'm good at improvising, but I'm not very good at putting a song together."* • Trouser Press 1978. Ritchie also explained how the writing process on this album differed to that on the first three, when he and Jon would work out ideas together. *"We don't write together now like we used to, but we're not growing apart musically. We both like each other's stuff. He's happy now he's done his Concerto and happy just to play with the band."* • RB to Disc, June 1970.

"I contribute nothing lyrically or melodically, I just suggest rhythms and arrangements. And in any type of music the arrangement is important. It's always a five way thing for us." • Ian Paice, 1971.

Ian Gillan was asked about the way they wrote in early 1970 as the album recording was under way, expressing his opinion that the band's first three albums had been very classical in their structure; *"Since those albums were released, the group's changed. Our music now is much harder, our next album will be purely a group sound. The music has an aggression and a rawness now that it didn't have before but it has been a natural development, surprisingly enough. I think this happened when the group line-up changed, when Roger and I joined. We both brought new influences with us and I think the other members of the group were beginning to feel they wanted to move in a different direction as well."*

"Perhaps the biggest thing that's helped us to get to know one another has been the writing. We've all worked on the album and when you're all creating something together, that's when you begin to get through to one another".

"We throw out a lot of our material, if one member of the band doesn't like a number, then that's enough. We don't use it. Jon has been writing for a long time but then I suppose we all have. Roger and myself had about seventy-five songs published before we joined the group". • Music Now. 3rd January 1970.

Ian Paice agrees that the work benefitted from the touring they were having to do: *"We used to try things out on stage before they were really songs, so that by the time you got into the studio, you might not know exactly what the finished article would be, but you had a bloody good idea. And because you'd tried it on stage, if it didn't work, you changed it so that by the time you got it on tape you knew it was as right as it was going to be. In later days it got difficult, because you did not have that recording, gig, recording, gig situation, but it really did help cement those songs in our minds before we went into the studio."* Over forty years later it's impossible to be certain in exactly what order the album tracks were written but we can make an educated guess using contemporary documents, interviews and the evidence of live recordings.

Child In Time • Roger Glover feels Speed King was the first track they put together, but what evidence there is (including Roger's own diary) suggests Child In Time emerged a few days earlier (though the writing may simply have overlapped). It quickly became something of a classic for the band. A lengthy composition, it turned into a dynamic live showcase for the band and their singer and (as the album's side one closer) perhaps sums up this period of rock music more than any other track, thanks to the slightly spacey lyrics, gentle instrumental passages, blistering solos and the final climactic build up. A progressive blueprint for the seventies, yet one which unashamedly traced it's origins to another band altogether, It's A Beautiful Day, as Roger Glover confirms: *"One of the first things I did when I joined was go on holiday with Ian Paice and Ritchie. We took a boat on the Thames and listened to a lot of records by groups that we were into at the time."* One of the albums they took was *It's A Beautiful Day* by the American band of the same name. Legal issues had prevented It's A Beautiful Day cutting an album until mid-1969. They were picked up by Columbia and the album was topping US radio playlists come September (it didn't peak in the UK until May 1970 and then 'only' at number 58).

Jon says he had heard the album in America and was fascinated by the strings on the song *Bombay Calling*. Nick Simper remembered that Mk 1 did *"kick around"* the *Bombay Calling* riff at one time and Deep Purple had been on the same bill as It's A Beautiful Day at American concerts in late 1968 at the Fillmore West where they probably first heard the track. Then in April 1969 It's A Beautiful Day again supported Deep Purple on several more US dates. Perhaps they even gave the band a copy of their new album, which is thought to have been released there in May 1969.

During rehearsals at Hanwell on July 15th 1969, the band took a break and Ritchie raised the subject of this particular track. Roger again: *"There had been a lull in the jamming. Someone said do you remember that song Bombay Calling by It's A Beautiful Day? Jon started*

The band photographed outside Hanwell in 1969. The spot today, to the right of the facade's columns on page 12.

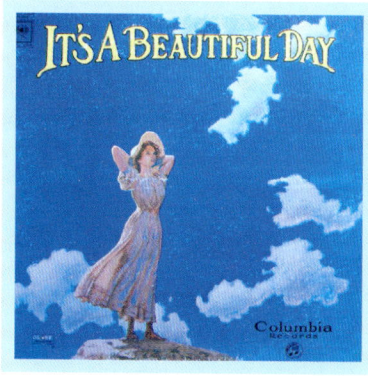

playing it for us. We all joined in, we slowed it down, Ian started singing something over it and it sounded like it could be interesting." The seeds of *Child In Time* had be sown. Or as Roger put it in his diary *"Routined Bombay Calling into our own way."*

Comparing the two album tracks today it is very clear that both the chord sequence and something like the first 20 seconds of the melody played by Jon derive from *Bombay Calling*. The original track is a 4.25 minute instrumental which features a violin as the main solo instrument. The main melody is repeated a number of times throughout and there is also a short guitar solo in the middle. Yet while Deep Purple had both been inspired by the track and borrowed the opening chords and melody (as well as some of the feel of the number), they took it into a new level, and creating an individual piece which achieves immense feeling, grandeur and an almost orchestral tension throughout.

These days of course such an obvious source of inspiration might well tempt a record label to consult m'learned friends but in rock music at this time there was an awful lot of creative ideas being bounced around from one band to another, reused, developed and reworked. A much more experimental and open attitude prevailed, and this cross fertilization of ideas was not unlike the sort of borrowing and referencing which had long been a feature of classical music. Let's face it, Led Zeppelin's debut album is so heavily laden with ideas lifted wholesale from the blues masters that belatedly the band have started credting the original writers. Yet few would argue that Zeppelin hadn't brought an entirely new approach to the material.

And before we become too disparaging of Deep Purple here, it's worth noting that there remains some controversy over who actually wrote *Bombay Calling* in the first place. Jazz Saxophonist Vince Wallace claims he penned the song back in 1962, and taught it to It's A Beautiful Day vocalist and violinist David LaFlamme. LaFlamme then played a version of the tune in a short lived experimental band called The Orkustra, who set out to blend symphonic orchestral music with rock psychedelia in 1966/7 but didn't release any records. LaFlamme then helped form It's A Beautiful Day. And while he did give Wallace a co-writing credit on *Bombay Calling* inevitably the song became associated with Its A Beautiful Day. In fact It's a Beautiful Day's version only references the first few seconds of the opening melody in the middle of the song and is otherwise completely different.

As a coda to the story, while It's a Beautiful Day's eyebrows were raised over Deep Purple's use of the riff they later chose instead to borrow one of Deep Purple's tracks, *Wring That Neck*, and base a track on that.

Jon recalled the day they started work on *Child In Time*: *"With Mk 2 we got a little bit more stream of consciousness and we just allowed things to happen and see what came out of that. I started messing around with that Bombay Calling thing, but much much slower, and Ian Gillan started. The first thing he started doing was the ooh's and then the aah's and then the scream long before the verse. We started playing it and it just goes round and round, and we just got louder and louder. Then it got to the point where it wouldn't go anywhere else because we had got nowhere else to go and that's where the bolero thing started. Then it was, I think it was, Ian Paice, being the thoughtful and sensitive man that he is, said "I've had enough of this", and he went into the shuffle and if you listen to it, the way that the shuffles comes out of the bolero, they are rhythmically connected and it just seemed like a good idea to just suddenly stop and go all the way back down again."* • JL to SC.

Ian Gillan has also looked back at his contribution to the song's development: *"Jon Lord was dicking around* (or 'extemporising on a theme' as it's known in the trade. Ed) *with a tune from the new album by It's a Beautiful Day. I started singing and the words came easily because we were all aware of the nuclear threat which hovered over us at this time, which was probably when the 'cold war' was at its hottest. Through the medium of Radio Free Europe this song and many others reached the ears and hearts of like minded people behind the Iron Curtain and as I found out many years later, it was of a great comfort to them when they understood that there were some peace loving friends out there somewhere."* • IG on his website.

Ian Gillan was the only one of the group who didn't know where the opening riff had come from: *"It sounded good, and we thought we'd play around with it, change it a bit and do something new keeping that as a base. But then, I had never heard the original Bombay Calling. The song basically reflected the mood of the moment, and that's why it became so popular."* • IG, 2002.

Exactly how Ian Gillan came to write such an insired song was a bit of mystery to Roger: *"Where Ian got those wonderful lyrics from I can't imagine; our song-writing prior to joining Deep Purple was not especially inspired and rather more in the pop field, although the period around the middle to late sixties, particularly music coming from West Coast, influenced us to write deeper and better stuff. It was a very exciting*

2154-A1

2154-A2

Thought to be the first Mk 2 photoshoot from July 14, 1969.

2154-A3

2154-A5

2154-A6

2154-A7

2154-A9

2154-A10

2154-A12

time for music." • RG to SC.

"We created this song using the Cold War as the theme, and wrote the lines 'Sweet child in time, you'll see the line.' That's how the lyrical side came in. Then, Jon had the keyboard parts ready and Ritchie had the guitar parts ready." • IG Interview, Bombay Midday Newspaper, 2002.

"I can see this being regarded as a social and / or political comment song in America. It's Ian's comment on the world and all the mentally blind people in it. But you can take it any way you want. It's up to you if you want to read any deep significance into the words. We like them very much." • IP to NME, June 1970.

Having laid out and developed the main body of the song together with the arresting sudden halt in the middle, they felt an appropriately epic ending was needed as Jon remembered: *"That was thought out in the van because we didn't know how to finish it and to try it, and Ian still hadn't written the words properly. It was Ritchie who said 'We can go to the tonic and go down to E and then just build up and up, and (then) what we did on stage, purely naturally, we just got faster and faster and faster and Ian said all that nonsense stream of consciousness yelling and screaming and speaking in tongues."* • JL to SC.

The very ending of the album track also tips its hat to The Beatles' song *A Day In The Life*. The end chromatic rising section and in particular the final chord from The Beatles song sounds very similar to the closing build up of Child In Time. Jon confirmed this was not accidental: *"We liked the sound of it, so we nicked it you might say."* • JL to SC.

We can't say exactly when it was first performed but it was certainly played at the Paradiso concert in Holland on August 23rd 1969, and is likely to have been premiered at one of the handful of shows prior to this. It quickly became a pivotal point in their live set.

Even though the structure of the song was pretty much established at Hanwell, on the Paradiso version the band experiment with some of the details which make this recording unique in a number of ways. Jon sounds particularly inspired during the introduction and moves well outside the quite introspective playing of later versions, while Ian Gillan sings with a great deal of passion and conviction. On the other hand the band's backing is very basic and lacks the dynamics they were to develop in later performances, perhaps a sign that this was quite an early rendition. The oohs and ahhs are tackled slightly differently too, with the last phrase of the final section sung as an alternating note instead of a straight scream, which actually works well.

After Gillan has finished the first verse the song goes into the bolero style section and it is Ritchie who takes the linking solo as opposed to (almost all) later live versions where it was covered by

The early Dutch release of Speed King, now one of the rarest Deep Purple singles.

Jon. Ritchie also plays in a style unusual for him at that time, lots of sharp notes and quick repeated phrases. We then arrive at the main guitar solo where Ritchie appears to be trying out runs, phrases and styles rather than working to something prepared. At one point he just stops and Jon fills in but then Ritchie returns with some aggressive phrasing that is very recognisable from later versions. He stops briefly again, returning with another few bars of experimentation. There is no defined structure to the solo yet, but he is clearly pushing at the envelope to see what works. Then we are into the arpeggios and Jon leads off into the second shorter verse.

Four weeks later Deep Purple were performing *Child In Time* at their biggest show so far. The occasion was as a prelude to the first of Jon Lord's innovative works with a rock group and orchestra at the Royal Albert Hall, London, September 24th 1969. There had been a lot of press interest and publicity surrounding this ground-breaking work, which had been set in motion by Deep Purple's manager Tony Edwards who more or less called Jon's bluff by booking the hall and giving him a deadline. The evening was carefully structured, opening with a classical piece by conductor Malcolm Arnold, a short showcase set from Deep Purple and then the main event of the evening, The Concerto itself (see page 35).

The band did three numbers on their own, closing with a twelve minute *Child In Time*. They sound nervous and even restrained, clearly a little intimidated by the occasion, especially in front of an audience which was far removed from a regular rock crowd. Ian Gillan is perhaps the exception; his vocals are impeccable. He provides the dynamics to the performance and his screaming is devastating. Jon takes the solo over the link to the guitar passage while Ritchie's three and a half minute solo has a measured start which rapidly picks up momentum but doesn't quite develop any particular direction or pattern (although it is more structured than Paradiso). Again he is trying out phrases and fast runs, but it feels as if he has yet to decide how best to sequence them. About halfway through the guitar solo Ian Paice starts bashing away a pattern on the drums but no-one feels confident enough to run with him and he soon drops back to the normal backing.

During the second verse it is again left to Ian Gillan to deliver a shattering performance. The band's discordant semitone chromatic build up then crashes into the song's end before Ritchie delivers some short, beautiful volume controlled phrasing over a fading organ chord.

The last surviving live recording before the album version was laid down comes from Montreux Casino, Switzerland on October 4th 1969 (yes, *that* Casino) at the start of a short tour. Only ten days after the Albert Hall outing, this performance is a very different beast, much looser and self assured, with the band starting to work dynamics into the backing during the introduction and verses which add enormously to the overall atmosphere and give Ian Gillan's vocals the support they deserve. *"Let that man out immediately"* cries Gillan in response to something happening elsewhere on the stage, before the track begins. Again the organ takes the link into the solo and Jon is really in control. Ritchie's solo starts off promisingly but has a guitar string out of tune and no matter what he tries, he cannot resolve the problem. Quickly he moves his solo around the neck and manages to pull off a four minute break that is becoming a little more structured.

The second half of the song is as good, and though the guitar

tuning cripples the finale quite a bit, the recording does show how the general dynamic phrasing within the song was building up in a live setting, something which would alter in later years: *"As the song has been played and played over the years, some of the dynamics and atmosphere on display here have sadly been lost in favour of a more obvious suckerpunch, but back in `69 Gillan could still scream and the dynamics were controlled rather than overwhelmingly elevated by the use of overloaded guitars and sheer brute force. Here we have what could be considered definitive Deep Purple, displaying on the one hand a measured calm and confidence towards their music and on the other that "teetering on the precipice" sensation as they pound away at the middle section, crackling with energy until the familiar run of triplets heralds the abrupt termination and return to near-silence, Jon continuing almost as if in a world of his own for a few bars after everyone else has stopped, before switching gear down to begin the final section of the song."* • Martin Ashberry, CD review.

Four weeks later they would go into the studio to record the album version. They had played this classic song around two dozen times before commiting it to tape but, as Roger would go on to say, it had been *"stage honed"* and they were ready to record it. It also helps explain the sheer quality of the studio performance, with everyone open to the possibilities of what could be achieved.

Speed King (aka Kneel And Pray, aka Ricochet) • The genesis of *Speed King* came simply from Ritchie who was after a powerful heads down, no nonsense new opening number for their live set, as Ian Paice explained: *"We wanted to do a frantic rock AND roll number, so we used all the standard cliches. Which turned out to be the most effective way."* • IP to NME, June 1970. The group knocked it into shape during rehearsals on July 24th. Roger's diary confirms this and he remembers how the song came about. *"As far as I can recall, Kneel and Pray was the first song we wrote. It came from a thought of Ritchie's that we could do with some sort of stop / start, rock 'n' roll type thing similar to Hendrix's Fire, whereupon I started playing the first thing that came into my head and to my surprise they all started jamming around it. It stayed as Kneel and Pray (from one of the lyric lines) for several gigs before it turned into Speed King."* • RG to SC. *"I stood there in the huge echoey gym. I just made it up on the spot. It was exhilarating."* • RG to SR.

His diary also noted at the time that the track sounded *"similar to I'm A Man"*, the Spencer Davies hit. However, listening to Hendrix's *Fire* having read Roger's comments it is easy to see why this would have provided Ritchie and Roger with inspiration. Both of them have said they were trying to write something that would *"convey a similar feeling"*. The final cut of *Speed King* bore little resemblance musically to the Hendrix track, other than perhaps harnessing a similar raw energy. Ritchie has also mentioned the Hendrix track *Stone Free* as an inspiration but if so, the similarities are even more remote[1].

It's important to understand what Hendrix's arrival in the UK meant to the music scene in September 1966. Based in London and playing the Marquee in early 1967, it's fair to say that his influence on our nascent rock guitar players was enormous. There was plenty of talent about without a doubt but Hendrix in many ways proved to be a catalyst for unleashing it. Ritchie remembers being told by some of his mates that he must see this new player who could get a tune out a Strat with his teeth, but wrote it off as hype at first. It was not all one-way traffic by any means. Hendrix had reportedly already heard Ritchie's work through his famously outlandish 1964 guitar solos on The Outlaws' manic single *Keep A Knockin'* (regarded by some as the world's first heavy metal record).

Deep Purple's original producer Derek Lawrence recalls that Ritchie was not one to accept many compliments, but relished a moment at an after-show party in California in 1968 on Deep Purple's first tour thrown by headliners Cream. Hendrix had been invited and complimented Deep Purple, before walking over to Eric Clapton to tell him (within hearing range) that Ritchie had blown him off stage that night...

The earliest known recording of *Speed King* was made for the BBC on Monday August 11th 1969 in studio 2, the Aeolin Hall (and aired on the Dave Symonds 'Symonds on Sunday' show six days later). BBC sessions, introduced primarily as a way of getting round needle time restrictions, proved to be important outlets for new bands at the time and could potentially reach a large audience. Championed by a few BBC producers and DJs nearly all the bands of the period, big and small, did them. The recordings where they survive (the BBC re-used many of the tapes) are an invaluable source of rare performances. Deep Purple by the way received a fee of £40 for their efforts.

The track was named *Ricochet* on this occasion, it seems simply due to a mishearing of the title *Kneel And Pray* by whoever was making notes for the BBC (certainly the word ricochet does not appear in the lyrics)[2].

There had only been three gigs between the first ideas for *Kneel And Pray* and the BBC session, but they clearly felt confident enough about their progress to give it this early radio airing (and may have wanted to do at least one new track). It is considerably shorter than later versions, played in the key of A instead of the lower key of G it would end up in. The track starts with a single sustained keyboard chord, two drum stick taps, snare and straight in on the first verse. Chorus, verse, and chorus follow with the link between them bridged by a simple arrangement of four chords instead of the more complex phrase that was later introduced.

The slightly eastern style guitar solo section is done using a violin effect tone (or volume) control technique over a simple repeated bass line, with the backing organ only coming in near the end of the solo. The song builds out of the solo with Ian Gillan singing *"You'd better turn around, look at the ground"* through a frenzied rising chord crescendo. It is at this point the structure of the song is shortened. Instead of going into another verse (as on the album), it goes straight into the chorus, repeated three times on the run out with a vocal scream in the break before the last chorus which ends abruptly.

Lyrically it is almost completely different to the eventual album version although some of the lines were retained for a time in a revised version of the track which they now added to the start of their live set, possibly at their show at the Revolution Club on August 8th. Still known as *Kneel And Pray*, the earliest surviving audio comes from a show at the Paradiso in Amsterdam, August 23rd 1969.

Having largely ignored the UK and Europe as Mk 1, wrongly assuming that American success would save them spadework back home (enabling the band to come back and march into big venues),

they had quickly taken a decision to reverse this policy with Mk 2 in order to build a following. The Paradiso was an ideal place to get the group noticed.

Again played in the key of A it starts off with the organ building up then into the verse and chorus. Technical problems are quickly evident and after the second verse and chorus they reach the solo section with Ian Gillan having to adlib vocals for a while, filling in whilst the equipment problem is sorted out. The roadies crack the fault and the guitar suddenly breaks through; the band goes into the crescendo leading out of the guitar solo then straight into the chorus. Instead of running out the song, it surprisingly shifts up a key and goes into another solo section. The band ease back and Ritchie gives the tremelo bar a good workout before Jon takes over the soloing. Ritchie then returns with a short solo which clearly points the way to the work he would put in on the studio version, although there is no sign yet of the keyboard / guitar interplay. The band hammer out the chords into the crescendo again, before Gillan hits the verse with what sound like more adlibbed vocals, chorus, a break for the scream, the chorus and close. It's astonishingly heady stuff indeed and clearly makes an impact on the laid back, pot smoking crowd.

Five days later on August 29th they recorded *Kneel And Pray* again for yet another BBC session - now lost - aired on the Stuart Henry Show (7th September). These sessions certainly helped get the word about and primed people for upcoming gigs by a band they might not otherwise have been aware of.

The next suviving live recording of *Kneel And Pray* comes from the 1969 Montreux Casino recording. Still in the key of A but now clocking in at nearly six minutes, twice the length of that first BBC version, it once more opens the set. Following what Martin Ashberry refers to in a review of the tape as *"the extended swell of Hammer horror-esque Hammond, ebbing and flowing for nigh on 45 seconds"*, the band kick in with four chords previously used as the introduction to the Mk 1 track *And The Address* (which often heralded the opening of Mk 1 concerts).

Key aside, the song has now developed much of the basic structure that was to appear on the album, as has the first verse. The second and final verses still appear to be partly adlibbed and the phrase "speed king" still doesn't appear in the chorus.

The solo section changes up yet another key (unlike the album). There's still no organ/guitar exchange, but instead there are more adlib vocals followed by the guitar phrase that would be recalled by Ritchie at the end of his solo in the studio version (and here duetted with Ian Gillan). A short ascending organ phrase builds up and leads out of the solo section as the band thrash their way back into the final verse. Chorus, chorus, break with a small scream and a final adlibbed chorus before the big ending. Ian Gillan announces the song at the end as *Kneel And Pray*.

Martin Ashberry compared this rendition to later versions: *"Some of the lyrical structures are familiar, as is the music (the references to Miss Molly, Lucille etc are there) but there's no "chorus" as such lyrically, and the break after the chorus rolls away with none of the crashing power that later developed to carry the chorus into the following verses. Gillan screams through much of the second verse, then the middle section is upon us, "you've got to kneel down, turn around, tell me what you found..." Much of the construction is still way off from the final brutal onslaught of the In Rock version but the ending is an exercise in controlled power; tight and to the point."*

The band now went into the studio to have a first go at recording the track (see page 64). It was transposed down to the key of G (where it would remain) and Jon Lord tackled it on piano. (with Roger and Jon doing backing vocals). This version, under the final title *Speed King*, was issued in Holland in early 1970 as an a-side (see sleeve on page 20), backed by another finished track, *Into The Fire*. Selling in very small numbers, this alternate take was forgotten about for years until a mistake at EMI saw what to most was a never before heard version slipped onto an otherwise unremarkable collection in the 1980s. Just a couple of weeks after this first studio recording, it was done at the BBC for the fourth time under the new title *Speed King* in Studio 4, Maida Vale on October 31st 1969 for the Stuart Henry Show (aired on 9th November).

Speed King was now three months old and Roger had come up with the final title after seeing a chain of launderettes called Speed Queen, and just changed the gender. The Speed Queen Company is still going (the world's largest commercial laundry company if you must know), specialising in the big industrial washing machines seen in launderettes. Maybe Roger was giving his crushed velvet loons a much needed wash.

The last known live recording before they laid down the definitive studio take dates from a TV special in Holland recorded on the

15th/16th January 1970 (but not aired there until July). Following the blueprint of the piano version, the version clocks in here at just under four minutes and keeps the same structure, albeit with organ not piano, opening with a rising swell from the keyboard before the four chord intro comes in. The lyrics are finalised for the most part although again the phrase *"see me fly"* is awkwardly harmonised (as it was on the piano version) by Ian Gillan, Jon and Roger. It sounds just as odd live and would soon be dropped.

Ritchie's solo consists only of the phrases he would retain for the end of the solo in the studio, with Ian Gillan matching his phrasing. The organ/guitar interplay is still not present, and as there is no evidence of them playing this section live, we think it was an idea which they developed during the recording session (see page 70.)

The inspiration for the opening segment of *Speed King*, the last part to be written, came from their live shows. At this time Deep Purple often shambled on stage at the start of their shows and laid down what can only be described as an unholy electronic (and percussive) din. The purpose of this sudden blast of noise was two fold; first it announced to the crowd in no uncertain terms that they had arrived but more importantly it sent the sound engineer's equipment into melt-down, and allowed him a couple of minutes to adjust levels and tweak the balance if they had been unable to do a sound check. Over time this routine developed a format and a life of its own and was the origin of the album opening to *Speed King*: *"That's what we used to do if we hadn't had a sound check. Say you had arrived at 8 o'clock in the evening and got there and had to be onstage in half an hour, and the roadies would rush the gear in and the guy who drove us and put the gear up would go out to the front, or the side, with his mixer and of course we had to go onstage dry with no sound check. So we used to make as much racket as we could so he could set his levels."* • JL talking to SC.

They became so used to this preceeding *Speed King* on stage that when they got to the studio they had the idea of replicating the effect, or something similar, when they recorded it in November 1969.

Livin' Wreck • Both Roger and Jon have confirmed that this short powerful track began life during the Hanwell rehearsals and was tried out at a couple of gigs soon after they'd written it. Jon: *"I remember a back room of a pub in East Essex, (or) East London, where we did Livin' Wreck before it was called Livin' Wreck. I'm pretty sure Livin' Wreck was played there because it was a riff that had come up at Hanwell, and because I had come up with (those) vicious organ swells which were meant to be like a scream. I think Ian Gillan had just made the words up."* Jon also recalls that their new singer suffered one of Ritchie's pranks on this occasion as well. *"The dressing room was behind the stage and the only way to get to it was across the stage. It was a tiny little place; we were getting changed in the back and Gillan, in his usual way, took all his clothes off to put his next lot of clothes on, and Ritchie pushed him out onto the stage, cos he thought that was funny! So Gillan's out on the stage with the audience waiting, naked except for a bandana around his neck. He took this huge bow and went back in and was about to hit Ritchie when he saw a big grin on his face and that's it!"* • JL to SC.

From Jon's understandably vague description of the venue, of the few shows they played before recording the track, the only pub venue which fits the description is Klooks Kleek (though admittedly 'East London' hardly gels with Hampstead). This rock night was held in the upstairs function room at The Railway Hotel on 100 West End Lane, West Hampstead. Originally a jazz club opened in 1966, Klooks Kleek adapted to the growing rhythm and blues (Jon played there with The Artwoods) and progressive trends of the late sixties. Just about every band of the era gigged there until they stopped holding gigs in 1970 (the pub survives). Deep Purple were booked there on August 26th 1969 (see the advert opposite), so if this is the venue it suggests a writing date sometime in the first half of that month.

Lyrically it was inspired by Ian Gillan's encounters with the opposite sex. *"This time the chatting-up tables were turned on him, when a young lady friend of his turned out to be the biggest groupie going!"* • IP to NME, June 1970.

Into The Fire • The origins of *Into The Fire* once again mix Hendrix and Hanwell, with an added dash of King Crimson. It is also the last of the *In Rock* songs which we can say with certainty came about at Hanwell (which doesn't mean that other titles didn't at least suggest themselves here), and was sparked off by a conversation between Roger and Ritchie: *"Ritchie said something about a riff he had heard that involved a chromatic scale. I just played whatever came into my head, almost as if I was imagining what he was referring to, and the band joined in and it sounded great. I loved the song, it was so heavy. Lyrically it was a vague warning about drugs."* • RG to SC.

Jon feels the riff Ritchie was referring to came off a King Crimson album, as they'd all been besotted by that band's amazing debut: *"I think that was inspired by 21st Century Schizoid Man and of course Hendrix is a big influence, those dramatic run ups, that's a bit Hendrixy. I remember the writing because when we started to do the verse in the same key which is B minor, I said why don't we go somewhere else and do that old trick, you know drop the fifth or up the forth or whichever you care to call it for the verse, so the verse was in E. Again I remember*

Another shot taken outside Hanwell in 1969.

it coming quite quickly. I think Ian wrote the lyrics overnight and we did it the next day at rehearsals." • JL to SC.

21st Century Schizoid Man was on King Crimson's *In The Court Of The Crimson King*, released on October 10th 1969. As *Into The Fire* was recorded just a few weeks later they must have been early purchasers. They may also have seen the band play it live, possibly at the Speakeasy, as it had been in the Crimson stage show for some months. In a contemporary article Jon was very clearly a fan and spoke about how many times he'd played the album just to soak up the sound.

Ian Paice recalled at the time of release *Into The Fire* being picked up by some radio stations. *"The story of someone who is making a mistake, taking the wrong plunge. This is the one that's getting the most airplay, I suppose because it's only three minutes long."* • IP to NME, June 1970. Perhaps this influenced the band when deciding to play it live.

Jam Stew • Deep Purple's earliest surviving recording of this embryonic song was made for the BBC's Stuart Henry Show on Friday October 31st 1969 (studio 4, Maida Vale) along with *Speed King* and *Livin' Wreck*. Mk 2 did five BBC sessions in all (and one complete In Concert performance) before the release of the *In Rock* album, playing just about all new material.

The BBC version was titled *John Stew*, again (as with Richochet above) someone was either taking notes wrongly, or perhaps the band hadn't yet come up with a title and told them to call it *Jon's Stew*.

Clocking in at 4.02, it does sounds very much like a jam session, and begs the question why they didn't record something a little more finished for the BBC. It opens with a bit of picking from Ritchie (which sounds like a clucking chicken!) with some overdubbed guitar then the band joins in, keeping the simple basic rhythm going. The vocals are clearly improvised and have something to do with a 'mean eyed woman'. The organ solo is first up, a straight forward bluesy affair, before the song breaks for a keyboard run and then the second verse comes in, more or less just a variation on the first. The guitar solo that follows is very typical of Ritchie's *In Rock* era style. He and Jon then run together before the organ closes out to the end of the song. The key and rhythm remain the same throughout, there is no real structure to the song, while the vocals and solos are nothing exceptional when compared to the other work they were doing around that time. It's quite possible that they were in the middle of getting this together when the session came up, and were going to do more work on it, but in the end although they did try a version during the *In Rock* album sessions it remained unfinished.

And Jon remained ambivalent about the first appearance of the unfinished track as a bonus on the extended CD edition of *In Rock* in 1995. *"It was a jam. Very simply that's all it was. And it's only really for completists you know, I wouldn't put it on an album. I've always been slightly wary of issuing stuff that you threw away at the time. Ok it may be fun now to look at but you threw it away for a good reason because you didn't think it was good enough."* Jon here raising the age old question of bonus tracks, but then going on to add: *"I love hearing the way the Beatles for example worked on something, or the way that Brian Wilson worked on something or you know any of my heroes. I love to hear how they fitted things together, but you can see why Jam Stew was not used, it was just a jam."* • JL to SC.[3]

Hard Lovin' Man • *"The story of Ian's life when he's not making music. Nice one!"* • IP to NME, June 1970. Arguably the most intense track on the album, *Hard Lovin' Man* was written in the studio while the group were working at De Lane Lea, but two members of the band recall the origin differently. Roger feels the song was kicked off by a riff from him, then the others joined in and transformed it: *"This was at a time when our live shows were getting increasingly wild and I often think that Hard Loving Man was really influenced by this and that the defining character of the band was forged here."* • RG to SC.

Jon Lord remembered it differently: *"Ritchie just started going chugger, chugger, four to the bar and then I was just kinda messing around with that vicious hard sound I had arrived at by then and played the keyboard opening line and the others said 'that's great, what is it', I said 'I can't remember'. What I used to do, you know, boring trained musician crap, I used to write it down, I always had a piece of manuscript handy, write it down so I didn't forget. We didn't have little tape machines in 1969."* • JL to SC.

Ignoring the fact that the cassette machine had been launched back in 1964 one wonders if Jon archived these scraps of manuscript?

Cry Free • The writing of this lost *In Rock* composition remains a mystery, although Jon confirmed that it was a finished piece intended for the album. Towards the end of the sessions it was dropped from the running order and then as they moved on, forgotten about. Jon explained where the inspiration for the song lay: *"There was an English rock band, I mean rock and roll band, they used to do My Baby Left Me, that was an Elvis song wasn't it, and we used to jam around on it and I used to play this little thing we used to do it in E, and I used to start it on the G hand to hand and up to the part in fifth hand to hand, and that turns up in Cry Free if you think. I am pretty sure that arrived on the stage."* • JL to SC.

Jon couldn't remember which band they'd listened to. The track was indeed covered by Elvis though dates back to the forties, written by Arthur Crudup, but Dave Berry & The Cruisers had a hit with it in the mid-sixties which might fit the bill. There is no recorded evidence of *Cry Free* ever being done live. There are however a number of occasions in the long instrumentals on stage were Jon used the technique he describes, so perhaps it was a blend of this and the cover which sparked the track off. Ritchie Blackmore may have recalled it from his time with Neil Christian & The Crusaders (and would himself cover it a little later on the Green Bullfrog session album; see page 93).

Flight Of The Rat • Roger feels this was the only track (other than *Hard Lovin' Man*) put together in the studio, at De Lane Lea. He remembers powering in with the riff, which in turn kick-started the writing. It was never played live or in session. The title came from one of Jon's musical jokes, playing *Flight Of The Bumble Bee* (from

Rimsky-Korsakov's opera): *"I used to play this joke thing in sound checks. I would play Flight Of The Bumble Bee as fast as I could and then I would, like, splat on the keys and kill it, and of course it was fun at the time! I think I had been messing around with that and Ritchie played the guitar riff and you know, the way you go, just getting in there and see what happens. I think the title came from out of that and I think the title came before the subject matter. It was just Gillan being daft, but then that gave him the idea for the lyrics."* • JL to SC.

Ian Paice came up with the title. *"I got the idea when we were fooling around at rehearsal and Ritchie played 'Flight Of The Bumble Bee', and I said 'Ah, Flight Of The Rat.' Ian picked up on the idea from there. This is yer anti-drug song. Or anti-booze, or ciggies, or bad temper or whatever your personal hang-up is. It's an anti-nasty song, about getting rid of all your badness."* • IP to NME, June 1970. Ritchie used to play *Flight Of The Bumble Bee* back in the days of his short lived but legendary trio The Three Musketeers in 1965 in Germany. He enjoyed playing the song really fast, but the audiences then who had come simply to dance didn't enjoy it anywhere near as much.

Bloodsucker • The final song prepared for the album, written around the beginning of April 1970 towards the end of the sessions. Unusually, unlike most of the album, this piece was written by Roger and Ritchie away from the rehearsal rooms or the studio. Roger: *"Bloodsucker originally came from a rare evening at Ritchie's flat in Acton, he and I writing together on acoustic guitars. It was later finished with the rest of the band in Abbey Road Studios."*

Jon confirmed that the writing process differed from the other *In Rock* tracks: *"I've got a feeling Bloodsucker came to the studio. I think we just worked that up in the studio and I don't remember doing that at Hanwell at all. I'm pretty sure what happened was, the riff was Ritchie and Roger's, then we tried it out at a couple of sound checks, not the gig but at the sound check."* • JL to SC

They had played in Cologne, Vienna and Chatham in the early part of April 1970 before going into the studio so maybe they tried it out at one of the sound checks there.

The lyrics also reflect the first (but by no means last) of Ian Gillan's run-ins with the band's management, which does give a new slant on the track when you know about it. *"Gillan had his first argument somewhere in the beginning of 1970 with John Colletta and this was a direct result of the way he felt he was being treated as I remember. I went into the studio at Abbey Road and everybody said 'all ready for this' and we said to Ian 'Have you got the words?' and Ian he went 'Yep', and we worked it up in the studio and recorded it."* • JL to SC.

The argument had arisen because Ian Gillan dared to ask John Coletta for an advance against earnings of £20. Ian vented his anger in the lyrics; *"Maybe in a while, and when I've moved around, I can find a way to pay you back your twenty pounds."* Ian Paice suggests an earthier slant to the lyrics. *"What we call a lump-blagging song. Ian wanted to get this one out of his system. About all the lines you give a girl when you're chatting her up."* • IP to NME, June 1970.

1 - Blackmore became less worried about paying homage to Hendrix in his band Rainbow. A couple of their early eighties tracks sound much (much!) closer to *Fire* and they even played a cover version as an encore in the 1980s.

2 - Surviving sessions are available on Deep Purple The BBC Sessions EMI set released in 2011.

3 - I was lucky enough to watch Jon recording keyboards for a session a few years ago. He did a couple of takes then settled on the final one, before asking the engineer to wipe the others 'in case someone wants to reissue them someday', before turning to look at me with a grin. SR.

4 • ON THE ROAD July to September 23, 1969

"This is it, man. What we have been waiting for..." Ian Gillan

As has been noted, Deep Purple's writing process was intrinsically linked to their live performances. Looking at the concerts undertaken during the period when they were working on *In Rock* helps to illustrate the pressures they were under and how closely linked their live shows were to the material, both before and after the album was completed.

July/August 1969 • Mk 2 played their first gig on Thursday July 10th 1969 at the famous (or perhaps infamous) Speakeasy Club on Margaret Street, near Oxford Circus in London, just a short walk from their manager's office. They took out an advert for the gig in the music papers proclaiming "Back from their second successful USA tour", ignoring the fact only 60% of the band had taken part in that tour (which had finished at the end of May).

A popular late night drinking club and haunt of musicians, booking agents, A&R men and dolly birds since it first opened in 1966, The Speakeasy was one of those clubs where people in the music business could mix on the same level and feel comfortable. Members of The Beatles were known to drop by and it was name checked by The Who on their *Sell Out* album in 1967, listing the venue's attractions in order of importance: *"Speakeasy, drink easy, pull easy"*. Deep Purple were in good company; The Jimi Hendrix Experience, King Crimson, Yes and Black Sabbath were just some of the bands who played there around this time.

Roger: *"The first thing I ever did with Deep Purple was in the Speakeasy. It was a famous musicians club, and in fact a great place – live bands on every night, and all the music biz people in there, so you'd get people jamming. I used to hang out there, and I changed from a nice innocent boy in a smart group* (Episode Six) *to a degenerate very quickly."*

Jon remembered his feelings of that gig vividly: *"Terrified, because we really hadn't enough rehearsal and Gillan was pushed on stage before he was ready. Of course in the Speakeasy a lot of our mates were in there and it was like 'Go on then, let's see what you can do and who's this new vocalist then?'. The stage was only six inches high so you were on the same level as them which is intimidating. But I remember as we got underway being just thrilled to bits with what was happening, we knew it was great, it was the right thing."* • JL to SC.

Not surprisingly Ian Gillan also still remembers the show: *"I shall never forget that. It was only a small audience of 35 or so. Stunning. I was moved to tears. It was the first time I started using the congas. I had to do something; I didn't want to bugger off during these extraordinary long instrumental bits."*

Ian Paice on stage in Denmark, early September 1969.

Ian Gillan had already had it explained to him how the guitarist saw the dynamics between them developing: *"I love working with people that push me, because I get a lot of energy. For example with Ritchie, I mean Ritchie when he's playing onstage he tries to blow everyone off stage. It's a kind of competition. One of the things Ritchie said to me when I joined the Deep Purple, he said 'you've got to bear in mind because I don't mean it badly, but I'm going to try and blow you off stage every night.' I said 'All right, in that case I'm going to do the same thing to you.' And he said 'Great, and that way we'll have a good band'."*

"It was and remains the highlight of my life. I said to Roger that night, 'This is it, man. What we have been waiting for.'" • IG to Chris Epting, March 2013.

Reaction from the small audience and within the band was good, and it was probably a relief for everything to be out in the open at last, given the rumours and bad feeling over the departure of Simper and Evans (and even though Ian and Roger still had a few gigs to play with Episode Six).

The band had put together a workable set list for the time being. As they had nothing new (apart from Hallelujah which they may have done, though if so there is no surviving evidence), it had to rely largely on the Mk I routine, with Ian Gillan learning *Hush, Wring That Neck, Mandrake Root*. While these titles remained for a while, some of the other Mk 1 songs they did at first such as *Help, Hey Joe* and *Kentucky Woman* appear to have only been performed by Mk 2 a handful of times before being replaced with new material and live recordings of Mk 2 playing them are rare or non-existant. Their cover version of *Paint It Black* also remained. The older material at least had the benefit of being available on record so there was merit in promoting it. Shows at the Redcar Jazz Club in the Coatham Bowl Hotel, Redcar on the 18th (with Thunderclap Newman on the bill), and on the 20th at the Mother's Club, Erdington, in Birmingham (with Caravan) followed that month and may have included the newly written Child In Time, though we cannot be sure.

Mk 2's debut single Hallelujah was released on Friday 25th July but was a resounding flop despite the NME giving it a positive review: *"Although it's had a couple of big ones in the States, Deep Purple has yet to register here at home. And it's just possible that this could do the trick - it's one of those numbers that could either be a smash hit or a massive flop! Penned by the Greenaway-Cook team, it's a medium-pacer with a strong gospel-revivalist flavour. Ian Gillan delivers the preacher-like lyrics effectively, though I could have done without the screams, while the bluesy organ and strident guitar maintain an atmospheric backcloth. A disc that's laden with mystique and compulsion, and which - in its more inspired moments - develops a rock-like quality."*

The band even got to perform it on a couple of TV shows but again we cannot be certain if they ever tried it out on stage at this time. Harvest did do some promotion, handing out flyers at gigs, putting adverts in the music papers, and doing a special promotional version in a unique sleeve. These all took the opportunity to plug the upcoming Concerto. No B-side had been recorded so it was backed by the instrumental section of *April* from the third Mk 1 album (a very strange choice.)

After their initial gigs Roger was poorly in August and ended up in hospital from the 4th to the 16th of August 1969. The few shows they had (at Newcastle, Birmingham and London) were pulled allowing Jon time to work on the Concerto project while Ritchie and the two Ians went boating on the Thames. The hospital let Roger out on the 11th August 1969 to fulfill a BBC booking, laying down *Ricochet* (aka *Kneel And Pray*, see above) and the Mk 1 track *Bird Has Flown*. Aired during Symonds On Sunday on the 17th the band were paid the princely sum of £40.00 for the session (the BBC retained the right to repeat the tracks forever).

They managed only one more show that month, having rescheduled the cancelled gig at the hip Revolution Club in London to the 20th, another regular venue for progressive bands, though Roger (sadly neglecting the crucial stuff such as set list!) merely noted in his diary that it was a *"lousy crowd."* (Newcastle may also have been rescheduled.)

Clearly that early elitist Mk 1 approach to UK gigging had been abandoned in favour of a concerted effort in the UK and Europe. The first of those European gigs took place on August 22nd 1969 when they were one of around a dozen bands booked for the the Bilzen

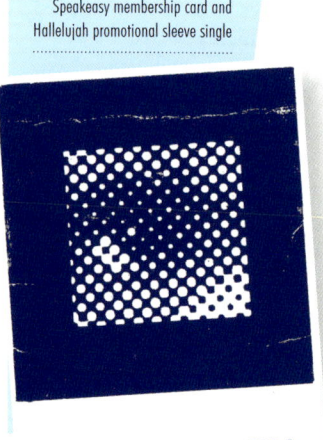

Speakeasy membership card and Hallelujah promotional sleeve single

Jazz Festival in Belgium (*"Blew them all off"* noted Roger). Incredibly, much of the festival was filmed by Tienerklanken WTN who edited highlights together some time later for a weekly Belgian teenagers programme. Chunks of *Wring That Neck* and *Mandrake Root*, along with a section of the drum solo in *Paint It Black*, survive[1], the earliest known live recordings of the line-up. And despite the editing, enough of the Bilzen set remains to illustrate the already powerful instrumental side of the band, a fabulous example of their improvisational core. If you went to a Deep Purple gig between July 1969 and right through to 1971, it was these three pieces that made up the 50-60 minute heart of the set. They show a band taking chances with their music as well as being technically brilliant, a little flash, even arrogant, yet giving audiences a show they could hardly ignore. *Deep Purple In Rock* was to be the future, but for now these tracks were the foundation of much of Mk 2's creativity.

Wring That Neck fades up into a solo from Jon. He works hard before Ritchie takes over with an amazingly fast flurry of notes before backing off a bit (he would still use his Vox AC30 mic'd up for this song). He engages in a short call and answer type session with Jon, then goes off again into more blisteringly quick guitar work. After everyone blasts back in with the song's main riff it's then Jon's turn and he changes between sections of chord work and runs, moving effortless around the keyboard, introducing classical phrases before leading into a jazzy section then swerving off into a dense darker sounding wall of sound, then bouncing back into the riff.

Mandrake Root also fades up into the song just in time for Jon's solo, so we miss Ian Gillan's verses at the start. Jon plays some short phrases before getting into his stride again, moving around the keys with total ease. The director then cuts straight into Ritchie's eastern style section which sounds very heavy. He eases into more structured phrasing and uses the tremelo arm in a way which was later harnessed for *Into The Fire*. Already we can see them using these tracks as a testing ground for ideas, either in a planned way, or simply by seeing what came out of the improvisation on stage.

From Belgium they drove to Holland to play The Paradiso, Amsterdam. Roger was very impressed with the Paradiso, especially after the small venues they'd done in the UK, and the atmosphere of the indoor 'festival': *"Fantastic club. Legal 'smokes'. Worked with some great bands. Another great job!"* • RG diary.

The Paradiso was a converted church near the Leidseplein, with a capacity of about 800. Painted in rainbow colours it soon turned into Amsterdam's 'Hippie Hotspot' (along with De Melkweg -The Milky Way). Home to many Dutch bands it soon became the venue for

Flyer for Hallelujah which was the first Mk 2 recording to appear, and one of the few reviews for the single.

upcoming UK and American groups to showcase in Holland. Deep Purple were only booked to play on the 24th, but when they turned up for their first gig in Rotterdam they found the venue closed. Arriving in Amsterdam a day early they talked the venue's management into letting them do an additional set on the 23rd.

"I saw Deep Purple for the first time as part of one of the many

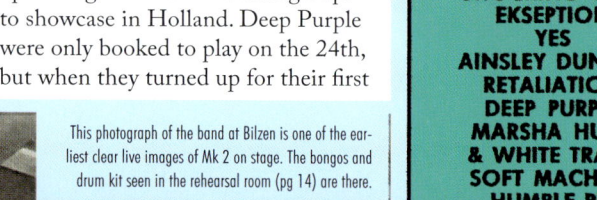

JAZZ BILZEN 1969
vrijdag 22 augustus
STEVIE SHORTER
& TILLY SET
VIPERS
SHOCKING BLUE
EKSEPTION
YES
AINSLEY DUNBAR
RETALIATION
DEEP PURPLE
MARSHA HUNT
& WHITE TRASH
SOFT MACHINE
HUMBLE PIE
zaterdag 23 augustus
CARRIAGE COMPANY
LIVING BLUES
GROUP 1850
BLUES DIMENSION
ROLAND &
BLUES WORKSHOP
(zondag)
BLOSSOM TOES
EIERE APPARENT
TASTE
BONZO DOG BAND
BRIAN AUGER & TRINITY
MOODY BLUES

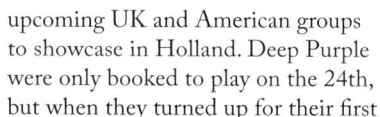

This photograph of the band at Bilzen is one of the earliest clear live images of Mk 2 on stage. The bongos and drum kit seen in the rehearsal room (pg 14) are there.

Ritchie Blackmore, on a short club tour of Scandinavia, Sept. 1969.

Clare Deniz has joined **Strawbs**. ● **Deep Purple's** concert with **Royal Philharmonic Orchestra** at London Royal Albert Hall on September 24 will be a charity event, presented by British Lion Films. ● **Deep Purple** playing concerts in Holland (this weekend), Germany (September 3-5) and Spain (27- October 1); group also appears at Montreaux Casino in Switzerland on October 4. ● **Vanity Fare** at Tottenham Mecca tonight ● Southampton group **Nite**

badly organised festivals of the time. I remember the long forgotten Dutch act George Cash setting up their equipment at least five times, and then having to take it all down again to make room for the late arrival of another foreign act. One of them was Deep Purple, and I have to be honest, they were the most successful of all of them. The 20 minute solos of Jon Lord and Ritchie Blackmore must have made a devastating impression, especially on those who ended up laying on their backs on the wooden floor, stoned out of their heads, (which must have been about 90% of them)." •
Dutch Journalist Jip Goldsteijn, 1974.

The concert was aired in part by a local radio station which was great promotion. Subsequently bootlegged it gives a fascinating glimpse of the new line-up as well as the earliest known versions of two new tracks *Kneel And Pray* and *Child In Time*. The recording is up and down, something Roger unsportingly blames on their roadies: *"Kneel and Pray is a mess, soundwise, (Ritchie) can hardly be heard until two thirds of the way through, the bass is loud and boomy in parts, not in others. It gets better after this. This would be sort of normal - the out front sound mixing in those days was handled by one of our two roadies, Ian Hansford or Mick Angus, neither of whom knew anything about what they were doing. The first song was always a mess while they sorted it out. We were nonplussed at the reaction to the first song - hardly anything - which led Ian to comment on the sight we saw as we peered out through the stage lights: the entire audience was sitting on the floor, a rare enough sight although not completely out of the ordinary (we used to get the audience to sit during the quiet parts of Episode Six's show), but it was the smell that wafted up to the stage that was so striking. We realised that we wouldn't be able to get much reaction from this crowd because they were all so out of it. That is why, a few songs later, it's good to hear them go wild for Wring That Neck, the song that really gets them going."*

Holland really took to the group (voted 'Most

popular band' there in 1974), with *Child in Time* staying at the top of the Radio Veronica Top 100 of All Time for many years.

Whilst in mainland Europe the band were also booked for a promotional slot on the popular German rock TV show Beat Club on August 25th, filmed in Bremen. Looking all moody in black and white they mimed to *Hallelujah* which had also been issued there as a single. Roger noted in his diary: *"Turned out great. Went to club afterwards and got sizzled with Carl Wayne, Ritchie and Ian Paice"*. It was aired on the 30th; a second track filmed, *Bird Has Flown*, was never screened.

It was then back to the UK where on the 26th August they played Klook's Kleek to what Roger noted in his diary were *"Record crowds. Lots of old faces. Great reception."* On Friday the 29th they were busy all day in London. Roger and Ritchie went shopping with roadie Mick Angus to get a strobe effect for their lighting. From there is was off to the BBC for a second session, recording *Kneel And Pray* again and for the first time *Child In Time*. Jon recalls the BBC sessions were a good test of the band: *"They didn't allow overdubs. I felt they were useful and challenging because they were live to tape."* The session (now missing) was aired on the Stuart Henry Show the 7th September. From there they made their way for an all-nighter at the Lyceum in London, second on the bill to Atomic Rooster, with fellow Harvest act Pete Brown opening. *"We blew them all off. Great night. Marquee Martin were raving. Got home at 6.00 a.m."* Roger noted in his diary.

On the 30th August they played the Kent Pop Festival which Roger simply wrote up in his diary as *"Not too bad"*. Held at the local football ground, the promoters had high ambitions but little experience, booking mostly unknown local groups (and Deep Purple were hardly household names at the time), with only the Freddie Mac Experience having any reputation. It made a loss for the promoters and it was not repeated.

September / October 1969 • Deep Purple travelled across six countries in September and October, upping their gig rate again. The period was clearly crowned by the Concerto show, but they began with a trip up to Scandinavia, which had seen the band's first ever live shows back in April 1968, for three shows (a couple of dates in German were also mooted according to Melody Maker, but seem to have been pulled). Two shows a night was not unheard of. For example on September 6th 1969 they played a 45 minute set in Sweden starting at 8.00pm, and then drove 70 miles or so to Denmark to play a midnight show.

The group returned for a few more UK one-nighters, including one at the Winter Gardens in Malvern supporting Rory Gallagher's Taste. Belatedly EMI now dropped the third Mk 1 album into the mix, and came up with the rather catchy "And so Deep Purple progress..." strap line on adverts for this and the Concerto concert.

Reviews were often positive as well ("A good album showing exactly how talented this little-hailed group are") but Mk 2 appear to have resolutely ignored the album on stage, which is a shame as some of these track would have translated well into the new act. Instead the set list for the time largely comprised *Kneel And Prey*, *Child In Time*, *Wring That Neck*, *Paint It Black* and *Mandrake Root*. For encores they had a blast through a couple of covers, *Good Golly Miss Molly* (perhaps at Roger's suggestion, it was a record which got him interested in the pop scene at the time of its release) and/or *Lucille*.

4B • CONCERTO For Group & Orchestra

"Our manuscripts consisted of 'wait for the silly tune, watch Malcolm and count to four'." Roger Glover

While the *Concerto For Group And Orchestra* was a project largely outside Mk 2's new direction, you could put a case for something like this being *exactly* what progressive rock bands should be doing, exploring avenues beyond the mainstream. The work involved did affect the rehearsals and recording of *In Rock* and perhaps more critically brought problems of perception within the group. The project was without doubt Jon's baby. With his musical knowledge, Deep Purple had grafted classical themes on to tracks on their first album, featured a string section on their second and then included a lengthy piece called *April* with a movement written for a small orchestra on their third; it was clear that Jon had a musical path he was good at and needed to follow.

Jon: *"I had just heard an album Brubeck plays Bernstein. It was the Dave Brubeck Quartet and the New York Philharmonic [Orchestra], conducted by Leonard Bernstein. I didn't think the album was that brilliant, it was just interesting, although I really loved Paul Desmond's saxophone and I was a fan of Brubeck's piano playing, but that wasn't very important either."* • JL to Modern Keyboard, January 1989.

The album, the full title being *Bernstein Plays Brubeck Plays Bernstein*, was released in 1960. The Dave Brubeck Quartet and the New York Philharmonic Orchestra came together to play the Howard Brubeck's (Dave's brother) composition Dialogue For Jazz Combo And Ork.

"It just gave me the idea. Why not try something like this with a rock band? Why don't we try to break the barriers between popular music and this so called "serious" music – in both directions? This was when I was still playing with in The Artwoods[1]. It wasn't the band I could have done something like this with; but a few years later I was with Purple, and I remembered this, and they had two managers who really had quite a lot of money in an old sock somewhere to pay the orchestra with. I thought: Here's the band, there's the money and I've got the idea!"

"I played him [manager Tony Edwards] the Brubeck record and he said 'What's this?' And I said 'A jazz band playing with a symphony orchestra. But I want to bring together a rock'n'roll band and an orchestra!' He said 'You don't

A press event was held at EMI in late August to announce the Concerto. The group did a couple of songs then posed with Malcolm Arnold [second from left] for photos.

The group were also photographed inside the Royal Albert Hall to publicise The Concerto, while their third album (below) also gained belated UK release.

mean Deep Purple, right?' And I said 'Who else?' He asked 'And who is going to compose this "symphony?"' and I said 'Me, of course'. And he said 'Do you actually know how to compose an orchestra?' I said 'Nope, but I'll find out'."

Tony Edwards: *"Jon Lord said to me at the end of the American tour that he'd always dreamed of writing a work that could be performed by a rock group and a symphony orchestra, I just said 'how long would it take?' I came home, booked the Albert Hall and he was appalled. Once he'd got over the shock, he thought it was wonderful."* • JL to Kieron Tyler, Mojo Magazine, Jan 2003.

John Coletta: *"We needed something to get them to the front, you know, and we thought that was one way to do it, I mean I know the group basically didn't want to do it because they felt it was diverting, diverging too far from the rock field, which in a way it was, but I don't think it did them any harm at all. In the long run it did them a lot of good."* • Voxpop,1972.

Having been given the green light, Jon worked hard at the project. Most of the musical ideas he wrote down straight from his head, rather than working them out on keyboards, something he admitted later had been limiting. Jon: *"Composing it wasn't easy, but it's been so joyful that I couldn't say it's been hard. It's bound to be derivative, but worked out in my own way I hope. Certainly it's got everything in it that I've been influenced by."*

Tony Edwards spoke to Ben Nisbet at Deep Purple's music publishing company, and with his help secured the services of conductor and composer Malcolm Arnold, a major boost for the event. Malcolm was also able to help Jon on a more practical level, that of scoring the work and showing him what each instrument was or wasn't capable of.

The pressure of trying to finish this ambitious classic rock fusion experiment was immense, and it interfered with the writing work on *In Rock* as Jon did miss some of the Hanwell rehearsals, much to Ritchie's annoyance in particular (a case of pot and kettle really!)

New boys Ian Gillan and Roger Glover were really thrown in at the deep end on the piece, Roger: *"Jon was very kind, none of us read music, so our manuscripts consisted of 'wait for the silly tune, watch Malcolm and count to four.' It was an awe-inspiring event. I'd never seen so many musicians in one room before. I quite enjoyed it, a real adventure, and it got us a lot of headlines, and was my first taste of publicity."* Copies of the Mk 1 album *Deep Purple* were given away as raffle prizes during the interval, which caused some bewilderment to Ian Gillan and Roger when they were asked to autograph them (Roger had already been out and bought *The Book Of Taliesyn* to check over).

The crowd gave everyone a standing ovation lasting some fifteen minutes and the event brought Deep Purple a whole new level of public awareness. Most of the newspaper critics missed the fact that it had been done for enjoyment which annoyed Jon. *"We weren't trying to break down the barrier between pop and classical music. If we'd tried to do that it would have been a disaster. I thought it would come together, though be quite opposite but still get along, which is what happened in the end"*, he patiently explained afterwards.

Jon was not the only person to have the idea either; a couple of weeks later The Nice recorded their *Five Bridges Suite*, written largely by Keith Emerson, which sought to merge orchestra, brass and jazz rock. The orchestral parts were fairly basic but interesting, though overall it was not as acomplished as Jon's work. The concert also included classical works by the orchestra with The Nice rocking along. It is a source of great disappointment that Jon and Keith never got to write, perform or record anything together, despite discussions to do just that following their respective efforts.

Released on vinyl in December 1969 (USA) and January 1970 (UK), *Concerto* entered the charts here on the 18th January at the number 26 spot for one week, but then slipped away. The event was filmed but not shown on TV in the UK until April, and sadly nobody thought to keep the cameras on for Deep Purple's own set. Though some of the band grumbled at the time, with hindsight they also realised just how important the event was in bringing them to people's attention. Ian Gillan was one who saw this: *"I was completely wrong about it. I think it focused people's mind on the band, and therefore they noticed the other stuff as well."*

Roger: *"The aftermath of the Concerto was we got tons of publicity, but in the band it didn't go down very well. Jon was getting all the plaudits for being the leader and this went right up Ritchie's nose. Ian Gillan felt pretty much the same. The split between the musical side of Jon and the*

Deep Purple's managers John Coletta (left) and Tony Edwards in 1969.

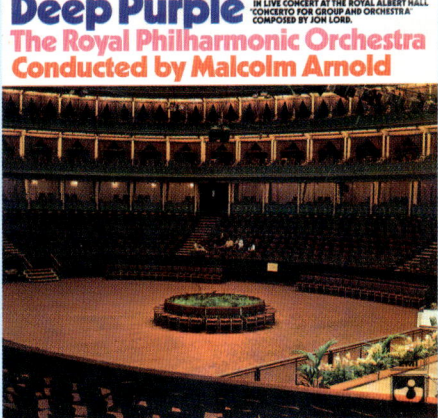

POP AND CLASSICS MIXTURE UNITED ALL

harder side of Ritchie came to a head when we started doing gigs after the Concerto. It did the Group a lot of good publicity wise, but not musically."

Ritchie: *"In Rock was my way of rebelling against a certain classical element in the band. Ian Gillan, Roger Glover and I wanted to be a hard rock band – we wanted to play rock and roll only. So off we went in that direction."* • RB to Guitar World, Feb 1991.

In fact as we've seen, the band had already been pushing in a rock direction, and the album was not a direct reaction to the event as Jon confirms: *"It's been perceived as that, yes. But in fact it wasn't quite as simple as that. We were actually already moving in that direction [of hard rock]. We had already that year, signed up Ian [Gillan] and Roger Glover and we were writing stuff that became In Rock."*

"It was a difficult time orchestrating and writing the Concerto. I was getting back at two in the morning, putting on a pot of coffee, and working through till first light. We had actually all already made a decision. And it was I hasten to add, a group decision. It wasn't just simply Ritchie's reaction to my Concerto." • JL talking at Sydney Opera House, January 2003.

Rumours also developed about more personal divisions within the band. Jon was increasingly perceived as the leader of Deep Purple, and it was being reported that the others started to resent. Jon: *"(The Concerto) got us labelled as a group who'd jumped on the classical/rock bandwagon. It was never intended to be part of the direction of the group. It was the turning point for us in this country but it caused a rift in the group. What they were afraid of and what I hadn't seen was happening, was that people weren't sure what we were all about. The group felt I was neglecting them. They thought we'd get railroaded into playing hundreds of Concertos, they thought I didn't want to play rock & roll".*

Things got so bad at one stage that it was rumoured Jon had made up his made to quit the band. In January 1970, Melody Maker's weekly Raver's Tonic column included the line, "Jon Lord strongly denies wild rumours of Deep Purple breaking up". He reassured the others of his commitment to Deep Purple but there were a few loose ends to tidy up, including another performance of the *Concerto* in America which they has agreed to do. Jon had also been commissioned to write a second orchestral/rock piece (which would become *The Gemini Suite*). The rest of the band accepted that it would go ahead, provided it was played down as much as possible and would be the last venture of this sort to be performed as Deep Purple.

Happily, the issues were worked through. It is difficult to see how they could have carried on and finished *In Rock* without Jon, there being few others around at the time who could match his technique. His input was essential to the Purple sound and it was the musical interplay between them all which was driving their new sound. And would the managers have been so keen to continue supporting the band if Jon had walked?

The American performance of the Concerto was originally going to be set up by Albert Grossman (Dylan's manager). The Royal Philharmonic were planning an American visit and were up for doing it (free of charge) while they were out there. It looked as if this would take place at the Carnegie Hall. *"We were going to fly out for just two days to play it, but it turned out that Carnegie had been advance booked."* • JL to Beat Intrumental, Sept 1969.

The US performance would finally take place in August 1970, with the Los Angeles Philharmonic Orchestra at the Hollywood Bowl. As at the Albert Hall, the band did a couple of their own numbers, *Wring That Neck* and *Child In Time*.[2]

1 - The band of Ron Wood's older brother Art Wood.
2 - Plans to perform it in Japan fell through. The Concerto was performed again on the thirtieth anniversary in September 1999 at the Albert Hall. It was then toured by the band with an orchestra. It is now performed by other orchestras and musicians. In 2011 Jon revised it for the debut studio recording.

4C • ON THE ROAD October to November 1969

"You develop a sort of telepathy, a conscious understanding of one another." Ian Gillan

After the big Albert Hall event on the 24th the band took stock as Roger recalls: *"We were so heavily in debt after The Concerto; there was a pressing need for work, so the recording was sporadic."*

The band finished the month with a couple more regular gigs, including Nottingham College on the 27th, and a little more rehearsal time before departing for half a dozen shows in Europe in early October, mainly headlining in Germany but including a support slot to The Nice in Amsterdam. As a live act they were going down well enough to secure repeat bookings.

Their first appearance at the Montreux Casino in Switzerland on 4th October 1969 was recorded although no one recalls quite why. Perhaps the venue recorded shows regularly and simply handed over the tapes at the end of the evening (Claude Nobs, organiser of many of Casino shows, certainly began recording and filming regularly in later years). Maybe the group and management wanted to capture a headlining show to evaluate a full performance and see how well the new line up was working in a live context. Whichever reason, the tape went straight to storage and would not be bootlegged[1].

The tape gives us what was by now the almost standard transitional set-list of *Speed King, Hush, Child in Time, Wring That Neck, Paint It Black, Mandrake Root* and *Kentucky Woman*.

"Kneel And Pray opens things up in what was probably one of its last performances before the final lyrics were nailed, and it became Speed King. The first verse opens with the familiar couplets even if the rest of the lyric wanders elsewhere. Instrumentally it bears a fair resemblance to the more familiar later takes, despite lacking the guitar vocal trade that became such a feature over the next twelve months." • Matthew Kean review.

Hush was there as a possible point of reference for anyone who might have heard the single (Switzerland being one country where it had been popular, it got to No. 7 on the 29th October 1968 in the Swiss National Radio Chart). Ian Gillan remarked later that the original band members disliked doing the song since it was a cover version. *Into The Fire* replaced it for a short while then *Black Night*. But as Mathew Kean noted in a sleeve note this was actually something of a shame, since it was developing into an exciting track (and much more so than was peddled around come the bands 1980's reunion.)

On stage at Leeds University Refectory Hall, November 1969, a show promoted by the students union. This is the stage where The Who recorded Live At Leeds three months later.

Child In Time we've looked at on page 21, while *Wring That Neck* sees Jon really stealing the show with some outstanding work: *"Blackmore and Lord (as ever in those days) spar for supremacy and in turn vying to outdo each other, flicking the switch between effortless jazz chords, particularly Ritchie's simple rhythmic work here, and then disappearing off with stratospheric roaring solos. You can only guess at the excitement at being witness first hand to this. Just under 6 minutes in, everybody backs off and Paice's shuffle and Roger's throbbing basswork underpin some nice noodling from Ritchie before the accelerator is applied again, some truly electrifying guitar work building to one of the many crescendos of the song. Eventually Blackmore backs off and it's Jon's turn to work, unaccompanied on one of his classically inspired outings, darting off all over the place before the reigns are handed back to the man in black for his solo spot."* • Martin Ashberry review.

We get a particularly fine version of *Mandrake Root*. Jon Lord even takes to rearranging The Beatles in his solo, and some fans have heard hints of both *The Mule* and *Grabsplatter* during the track. Matthew Kean again: *"It's moments like this that the critics tended to forget when accusing the band of being volume bound idiots. This is the 'rock-jazz' which Roger Glover speaks of when recalling his early years with the group. Coincidentally of course Miles Davis was approaching the same point from a different direction, as he laid down material for the seminal Bitches Brew album in August and November 1969. Canadian DJ Chris Meloche has played Davis and Purple discs from this era back to back on his Wired For Sound show, making much the same point."*

For the encore the audience is treated to what is now the only surviving Mk 2 version of *Kentucky Woman* (a Neil Diamond cover original included on Purple's *Book Of Taliesyn* album). If it sounds a bit unrehearsed, it was probably only played a few times (when they were supporting they would not have been allowed encores). Jon's keyboard solo here has been recognised as being used by him to introduce *Lazy* as recently as the late 1990s.

This European trip was notable for what was without doubt the band's strangest foray into film ever, the avante-garde P2 programme. Made by a German director, he appears to have tried to turn this film into an anti-capitalist piece. It's almost impossible to describe; but one slightly homoerotic sequence of the band being motored through the countryside in a bed, stroking each others arms (with manager John Coletta dashing about in a white nightshirt), is not to be missed. The three Mk 1 tracks performed are all mimed.

The group also did their first proper German festival, as part of an intense three day bill at the Essen Pop festival on the 11th October alongside name like Yes, Pink Floyd, The Nice and Taste. As at Bilzen some of the bands were filmed, though what remains of Deep Purple's footage are mostly grainy black and white clips of the two instrumentals again.

This busy tour over, on October 18th they were back in Britain to finally start the album, recording *Kneel & Pray* (this was the early piano-heavy version) and *Livin Wreck*. Apart from the occasional foray back into Europe for must-do bookings, Deep Purple now began to really knuckle down and essentially stayed in the UK to make sure *Deep Purple In Rock* was completed. During the recording period they still performed over seventy shows. At one of these, the group were surprised to turn up and find the promoter had booked a brass band, as he'd heard they played with an orchestra, but hadn't been able to find one...

After a headline show in Weston-super-Mare on the 25th, it was up the motorways and A-roads five days later for a support slot in Leeds

Teetering on the edge of a quarry in Stuttgart for a German film producer in 1969 (the Health & Safety Executive hadn't been invented).

at the University on the 30th. The band's fee more or less doubled post-Concerto, even for a support slot like this they were getting £150 or so when before they'd been averaging around half that. Sometimes HEC would let them go out for the old fee for smaller London clubs where little travel was involved, but those days wouldn't last much longer. The band ended the month with their fourth BBC session for the Stuart Henry show (aired on the 9th November 1969), laying down *Speed King* in it's largely final form, *Livin' Wreck* for the first time (missing from the surviving BBC tape) and *Jam Stew*. This was an ideal promotion opportunity for the band and a taster for the *In Rock* album rather than falling back on Mk 1 tracks as they'd done before.

November/December 1969 • As 1969 drew to a close, Deep Purple upped their workload still further, averaging a show every other day (sometimes up to five gigs back to back), a work load needed to keep things together and bring the wages in. Photographs of the group snapped at press events show their clothes to be 'tired and worn' and they clocked up over 3,500 miles across the UK over the last two months of the year.

It's obvious that the band were capable of cutting a new album in a couple of weeks if they'd been given time after *The Concerto*. Writing and rehearsal sessions had been very productive and Deep Purple Mk 1 had cut their first two albums in a matter of days (their first over a long weekend). Their management company HEC were in the red to the tune of just over £19,000 (around £250,000 in today's money) though. Added to this the managers were also having to sort out the problems caused by the collapse of the Tetragrammaton label in America. It's unlikely the managers would have wanted to extend the losses much further, so it appears that financial restraints

were the main reason for spreading the studio sessions. Whether it would have been quite the monster it became if they'd cut it quickly is open to question; with hindsight the slow progress appears to have allowed them to focus much more intensely on each track in turn. The other positive spin-off was that the extra few months of touring raised the band's profile still further, which would directly help the success of the finished album. Deep Purple kicked off November by appearing at the Teenpage Ball, a rock gig for 600 youngsters promoted by the Western Daily press in Bristol on the 1st, and heavily promoted by the paper. The band were slotted in between local acts voted for by the papers teenage readers, and also had to make way for a beauty contest by what the paper called "12 delectable lovelies". *"A great audience, baby,"* Ritchie reportedly told the paper's reviewer afterwards.

Then, in between gigs on the 2nd at The Lyceum in London (on the same bill as Yes) and 7th (the slightly more modest Kings Head, Romford) they slotted in the first of two album sessions that month (a month which would turn out to be their busiest of all in terms of the *In Rock* album). As well as putting together the intro to *Speed King* they did most of the work on *Child In Time* at IBC on the 4th.

The Kings Head gig turned out to be the gig when it all clicked into place for Ian Gillan, who was interviewed by Music Now magazine. He was very positive about the relationships that were developing between everyone and mentioned that particular gig:

"*Our music has become much freer now – and we all feel free as well. We're not hemmed in by tight arrangements any more – obviously that just destroys improvisation and spontaneity. Also, if you're observing the same arrangements on each number for every gig you do, the whole thing becomes stale.*

"*I only joined the group in about June or July of this year [has he forgotten already?! Ed] but now is the first chance we have to do some work in England. We're recording an album at the moment, and we also have the time set aside to do some concerts over here. I'm looking forward to it. No matter how successful you are abroad, there's nothing like making it in your own country. The thing is English audiences are very demanding, and force you to be good. Perhaps it was a mistake for Deep Purple to concentrate on the States, but then that was forced on the group by the success of Hush over there.*

"*Although we rely a lot on spontaneity, we just don't get up onstage and blow. We have six numbers worked out to run for one-and-a-half hours. Part of those are arranged – you can't rely entirely on improvisation or everything would end up in chaos. But we always leave a lot of room in our numbers for solos. And the thing is that now we've got to know one another.*

"*It's strange how you can work with a group for a while without really knowing what's happening and then suddenly it all falls into place. I remember when it happened for me with Deep Purple, it was one night in Romford. Everything clicked, and I started to communicate with the others. You develop a sort of telepathy, a conscious understanding of one another. Up until that night I think I'd been rather over-awed by the band, and it wasn't until I overcame that that it happened. Before I joined Deep Purple I'd always rated them – for me Ritchie Blackmore was streets ahead of any other guitarist. He still is. But it wasn't until I felt I was really part of them that I could let myself go.*

"*I suppose it's like when you're new anywhere – at work, in an office.*

Flyer for the band's show in October 1969 at the Montreux Lido, part of the Casino entertainment complex. Pictures of the new line-up had yet to reach the promoters.

And if you feel like travelling to **Essen** in Germany next month, there's a great treat in store from October 9-11 . . . The International Pop and Blues Festival 1969. Among those taking part are **Fleetwood Mac, Pretty Things, Spooky Tooth, Free, Aynsley Dunbar, Deep Purple, Pink Floyd, Nice, Taste** and **Champion Jack Dupree.** Why not take a week's holiday there?

Live in Leeds

Giving us some idea of finances on the concert circuit at the time, figures for a rock gig at Leeds Refectory in early 1970 survive. These show the hall cost £16.10 to book, the porters were paid £10 overtime and there was a £7 budget for publicity. After the gig, a late night disco was held in the hall and this cost another £20 to put on. Deep Purple's fee for their show as a support act on November 15th 1969 in Leeds was £100. The headliners were the somewhat ill-matched Bonzo Dog Doo Dah Band, we do not know their fee but might reasonable estimate £250. Nor do we know how much tickets cost for this show but for another similar concert around that time they were 10/- (50p) (while The Who tickets were 11/- a few weeks later for a show at the same venue). The venue normally held 2,000 when full, which means the Union would need to sell around 800 tickets to break even on this. Rock gigs at the Leeds Refectory were relatively new, there had only been four prior to the Bonzos and Deep Purple (Pink Floyd had played the previous weekend). There is a photo from the venue on page 39. The refectory venue was the main University dining room, and the long building was usually partitioned half way down the hall. The curved windows behind the stage are at the far end from the main entrance.

More shades of Deep Purple

"For the first couple of months you're terribly formal with everybody, until you gradually begin to feel at home. What's nice about Deep Purple is that we all dig one another both as people as well as musicians. I unashamedly would say that they are really great, and I consider myself very lucky to be with them." • IG to Music Now, Jan 1970.

Roger expressed his thoughts just a few years ago on the musicianship and early use of improvisation in the band at the time and seemed to mirror Ian Gillan's comments from over thirty years before: *"The band started as a musical band. The whole point was music made by really good musicians. When I joined the band I was the least worthy bass player they could have found because the standard of musicianship between Ritchie and Jon Lord and Ian Paice was stunning. I'd never heard anything like it. I came from the old school where you pick up a guitar, learn a couple chords and eventually make your way. These were musicians in the real sense of the word, and the band has always been about that, music. Real musicians tend to play like jazz players not cabaret players. So, every night, with Jon and Ritchie in particular, it would always be different. I'd come from more of a pop background and I thought they were playing it wrong every night. But, of course, I realized they were extemporising and having a bit of fun. A lot of the skeletal structure of the songs remains the same so people can recognize what it is. In fact, that's what keeps it alive."* • RG to Dennis Cook, JamBase, June 2007.

Extemporising or improvising had always been part of Purple's live sets but with Ian Gillan and Roger now fully settled in, the writing process starting to takeoff. Given the way they were reinventing Mk 1 tracks on stage, it would become the main-stay of Purple's operation as a band over the next few years. It was an approach which was often misunderstood by people who totally missed the point about much of the early progressive rock era. Ian Gillan: *"Other bands used the word to disguise incompetence, but in Purple's case it was actually pretty good. There was an abstract approach to the music, very radical in those days. Actually there's a particularly Purple approach to music, completely different to Led Zeppelin, Jethro Tull and Black Sabbath. The structures, the flair, the following key changes, the riffs, the arrangements, the dynamics –* tremendous dynamics, the texture to the music was light years ahead, or at least light years different, to what other bands were doing. Purple became a monster of the individual contribution." It was in the long instrumental passages that this really showed itself. Roger: *"It was almost like jazz in the early days, rock jazz, it had that freedom."*

Putting Ian and Rogers's comments to Jon about their core philosophy on improvisation elicited an interesting response: *"I think I had an easier job on that side of things because I could go where I wanted harmonically, and Ritchie certainly went where he wanted and it was one of his trademarks, wasn't it, you know, 'What key are we in Ritchie by the way?!'. I was given enormous freedom I felt because I was the founding member. I felt in a way we wrote the rule book, until I stopped certainly. And if you look at the early films you see Ritchie come across and I've got my head down and I just have a little look and see where we are. To me that was one of the greatest joys of it because, before the Artwoods really and in the Artwoods, I was in a band where improvisation was great. I tried jazz occasionally and I loved jazz and I loved modern jazz as well as you know. Quite funky modern jazz and I adored impro-*

Deep Purple were among guests invited to the opening of Alan Freeman's new record shop

ONE-NIGHTERS...

● Booked for Croydon Greyhound are Yes (this Sunday), Liverpool Scene (December 14), Keef Hartley Band (21) and Deep Purple (28).

vising, so in a way that had to be part of everything it had to be and I took that opportunity with both hands whenever I could."

"It's the value of improvisation because you are touching, the psychologists call it `place of imagination`, it's the posh explanation for it. It's the part of the brain that's not where the tutored part of your musical life lives, it's where your imagination lives. But because it's using your abilities as a musician that's when this wonderful random stuff occurs. Because the better you are at what you do, the better that is, the better your technique, the whole thing that you need to be a working musician the better your improvisation will be. But even so you can't learn improvisation, you just have to let yourself go, you have to have this open imagination, that part of the brain and trust it. I've improvised some nights on stage and I've looked at my right hand and gone, wow, and I've gone almost like what's it doing? It's doing something cool. So what we did in the early days is we all had pretty good memories and we used to remember what happened on stage and take it back into rehearsals sometimes, see if we could use it."

"You know what is wonderful is when you see somebody standing there with his eyes shining and he says 'you changed my life'. That's a big responsibility and I think that's one of the great things for anybody that's in any band that's had any kind of impact at all, because that's what music does to people. It defines a moment in time for them." • JL to SC.

Having brought those stage memories to the *Child In Time* recording, there was then another frenetic burst of one-nighters, kicking off at Leas Cliff Hall, Folkestone on the 8th, driving up for a rebooking in Leeds on the 15th by way of Bath, Wales and Birmingham, then on to Scotland supported by a band called The Shadettes (who would become better known before long as Nazareth). On the 22nd they played at Bradford University, supported by a North East semi-pro band called The Government. Their singer was a certain David Coverdale. He'd read in the papers about the band's line-up changes and gave Jon his number in case the new guy didn't work out (his band, would cover Black Night, Paranoid and T. Rex tracks at their shows the following year).

These and other gigs fired them up for their next studio session on the 27th where they laid down *Into The Fire* and *Jam Stew*. December was just as busy, with Melody Maker's Steve Peacock catching them at Manchester UMIST. Steve was clearly a fan, having already penned a longer piece for underground monthly Zigzag. Assuming Steve took it down correctly, it gives us a set list for the period, *Speed King, Hush, Child In Time, Wring That Neck, Paint It Black, Mandrake Root*. Of the latter, Steve was clearly blown away, especially by the set-closer: *"which lifted the group way above the standard of most of the bands that play in this country. Lord crouched over his instrument like an evil wizard, teasing out some beautifully tortured sounds and finishing up with him attacking it it with the might of a man possessed. He kicked it, he hit it, and he threw it around until it was groaning and screaming like a wounded monster, only to be pierced by some vicious guitar work from Blackmore. He danced in the strobe, weaving around and throwing his guitar all over the place. The noise was terrific and the spectacle was terrifying."*

You kind of get the idea, but then music journalism was struggling to keep up with the extremes to which rock music was going.

It's noticeable that the band's fee took another jump during December, rising to £225 for a regular booking, a little more if John Coletta felt he could get it. He later put this down to their increased profile following The Concerto. The month ended with a return visit to The Mothers Club in Birmingham and, after a week's rest over Christmas, a show at the Greyhound in Croydon on the 28th.

1969 had been quite a year. By December the band had properly settled in. Financially things were tight but there were no more Mk 1 studio releases to muddy the waters, new material was coming into the set and what remaining oldies there were had been so recharged as to have little resemblance to their forbears. Roger had more than pulled his weight while the new singer was coping magnificently. Gillan took stock of his situation and many years later would pen a track called '69 for one of the band's strongest albums of recent years, *Abandon*. It looked back on this momentous year as only a writer like he could, fondly recalling the names of clubs played or hung out in over thirty years earlier, *"Black Cat Woolwich, The Tiger's Head, The Cafe des Artistes. The Revolution and the Bag O'Nails, I'll see you down the Speak."*

1 - It was officially released as Kneel and Pray on the Sonic Zoom label in 2003.

5 • The Equipment and The Vision

"I know I play the ass off most guitarists. I am your original angry young man. I know I am..." Ritchie Blackmore

Ritchie on-stage at the National Jazz and Blues Festival, Plumpton, August 9th 1970.

This far removed from the time it's difficult to be precise about all aspects of the process, but it's worth taking a look at what we do know about how *Deep Purple In Rock* was recorded, what instruments the band were using and some of the techniques they employed.

DRUMS - Nick Lauro works in The Drum Shop in Liverpool, teaches the drums, has studied the technique of and met Ian Paice on a number of occasions. He offered us his take on the period.

"Ian Paice had grown up during a period in musical history when American Rock'n'Roll was the new upstart, threatening to usurp the old stars of Big Band and American/Anglo easy-listening crooners. Ian Paice's self-taught drumming technique was built on a background of listening to Swing-era players such as Gene Krupa and Buddy Rich, blended with the literally ground-breaking beats of the New Orleans pioneering Rock'n'Roll drummers like Earl Palmer and Charles Connor. These influences are clearly evident throughout Ian Paice's career in Deep Purple and still recognisable today. Because of the musical era that shaped Paice's formative years, he shares many similarities with his British contemporaries; John Bonham, Simon Kirk, Roger Taylor and Keith Moon in particular. By today's standards, his drumming could be viewed as slightly primitive in comparison to technicians such as Thomas Lang (clinic master) or Derek Roddy (Death-Metal supremo), yet it remains a style that few (if any) modern players can emulate with the authenticity and feel which comes from growing up in a time that would define the future of popular music as we know it today."

Nick contacted Ian for us to ask him what his drum kit was when In Rock was recorded. Ian replied that he was using *"a standard Black Oyster Pearl Ludwig 'Super Classic' (`Beatles`) kit with an extra floor Tom. The kit was - 22" x 14" Bass Drum (in around 71 he would use a 26" Bass Drum but only for live work), 13" x 9" Tom, 2 x 16" x 16" Floor toms, 14" x 5" Supraphonic Snare, 14" Zildjian hi hats, 20" Zildjian Crash, 20" Zildjian Crash-Ride and a 20" Zildjian Ride."* Nick adds: *"His kit reflected the standard Big-Band set-up made popular by the Swing-era drummers, one Rack tom and two Floor toms, paying homage to the past masters of the art.*

"It is impossible to know exactly how the drums were recorded. Paice, like Bonham, was an advocate of 'live' sounding drums, so it is likely that he would have fought any attempts by engineers to remove bottom heads and apply muffling tape. Judging by the drum sound (which differs in clarity from track-to-track), it hints at being close-mic'd rather than the ambient-mic sound favoured by the likes of John Bonham [the engineer confirms this - see below]. However, this may well be a result of post-production mastering to make the drums sound as though they were all recorded at the

A view of Ian Paice's kit in May 1970, also showing Ritchie's AC30 on the chair

DEAR DAVID J. MACHAM. I BOUGHT IT SO I'LL BLUDDY WELL BOOT IT — IAN PAICE OF DEEP PURPLE

Another view of the drum kit in 1970.

same studio. Because of the different locations used during the recording process, ambient room sounds would have varied from studio to studio, making it near impossible to capture a consistent room-sound for the kit. Even when they were cut in the same studio, differences between drum sounds are noticeable, such as between Speed King and Living Wreck (both done IBC) where the former struggles for true clarity, whilst the latter is clean and sits well within the mix.

"It is worth noting that during this period in studio recording, drummers were never under the threat of having to keep time with mechanical click-tracks dictating the tempos of songs. Therefore recordings of the era are often fairly sloppy tempo-wise by today's standards, which is by no means a bad thing, but certainly a trait that had been eradicated by the early 1980s (Drummers who couldn't play to click-tracks by 1983 either had to get with the new requirements or accept that their recording days were over). To his credit, Ian Paice has an impeccable sense of time for a drummer cutting his teeth on old-school recording techniques and it's rare to detect instances of shifting tempos. He is pretty much a rock-steady time-keeper.

"His feel and approach to the music is very much in keeping with that of his contemporaries of the time. He never overplays and has total respect for song-form, playing exactly what is necessary, avoiding the temptation of using the tracks as potential platforms for drum wizardry. In all, a very mature sensibility. This is not to say that his performances are overly safe, far from it. There are plenty of rapid-fire Buddy Rich-esque single-stroke rolls thrown in to the melting pot along with cheekily-quick Bonham style hand-foot Bass drum triplets. Had he been up against the stringent click-track recording requirements of today, he may well have had lose some of those elements of performance in order to produce a sterile take. Thankfully, the era has allowed his drumming personality to shine through the music in an organic way (an attribute sadly missing from modern recordings)."

Interestingly when one reporter tackled Ian Paice about wrecking his kit on stage some nights, Ian was defensive. *"It's not really wrecking. I bought that kit when I was seventeen and I've had it seven years now."* (IP to Richard Green, NME, Sept 1970). When others had a go about the destruction in the letters page of the Record Mirror, Ian Paice felt he had to reply, and did so in forthright terms. *"I've still got the same kit I'm reported to have busted up several times. It isn't just for display. The audience can keep their money and stay home if they think that."* • IP to Lon Goddard, Record Mirror, Nov 1970.

GUITAR - Ritchie Blackmore used two guitars on *In Rock*, his cherry red Gibson ES Thinline 335TDC for *Child In Time* (and possibly *Jam Stew*), a Fender Stratocaster for the rest.

The Gibson (serial number 26457) had been owned by Ritchie since 1961 and was bought second-hand in Jim Marshall's shop in Hanwell, London. Ritchie has told people that he had gone in with his heart set on a Gretsch but was talked into buying the Gibson instead. It was a semi-acoustic, with a solid wood block which ran through the center of the body and had hollow sides. The body finish was a striking cherry red colour and the mahogany neck had a rosewood finger board, with dot markings. The guitar originally came with a black scratch plate but this was removed some time in the mid sixties. The machine heads were made by Kluson and the bridge was a tune-o-matic. Ritchie's guitar also had a chunky Bigsby B5 vibrato bar which was not a stock item (it is not known if it was bought that way or he added it later). Ritchie used to raise up the pole pieces on the humbucker pick-ups to give it a bit more bite. They were controlled by four rotary controls and a selector switch.

According to Ritchie, he had picked up his first Stratocaster second-hand from Eric Clapton, but it had been fitted with a Telecaster neck and was considered almost unplayable due to intonation problems that could not be resolved (yet he can be seen using it on the Mk 1 video of Wring That Neck). It was also used, along with the 335, on the third Deep Purple album. He got his black and white maple fingerboard strat in 1968 (serial number 221737) and probably bought it in the US. Ritchie would go on to modify this guitar as he ventured into a harder rock style by putting in fatter Gibson style frets and ever thicker tremolo arms. Ritchie would only use the bridge and neck pick-ups on his Strat, the middle one was wound down so as not to get in the way. The tone controls would always be left up full (he would get his 'sound' by another route). He would switch between pickups regularly to change the tone within his solos. The volume as you would imagine was again left up full throughout *In Rock*. On stage things would be different as he would take the volume down for the quiet sections, sometimes almost to a whisper.

Ritchie explained the differences between the Gibson and the Strat: *"I prefer the Stratocaster because it has a more 'attacky' sound. At first I couldn't get used to the Strat after the Gibson. The necks are quite different. But now I can't get used to the Gibson again. A Stratocaster is harder to play than a Gibson, too. I don't know why. I think it's because you can't race across a Strat's fingerboard so fast. With a Gibson you tend to run away with yourself. It's so easy to zoom up an down, you end up just playing physical shapes rather than really working for an original sound."*
• RB to Martin K Webb.

Ritchie also owned a cherry red 1968 Gibson SG (serial number 524696) around 1968 - 1971. It was not used live or for any recordings to the best of our knowledge (both Gibsons were sold at auction in 1995 by his ex-wife Babs).

Ritchie had developed the use of finger vibrato over the years preceding *In Rock* to the point where he had a mastery of it which would be used extensively on the recordings, along with the 'whammy bar'. Ritchie: *"I liked the way Hendrix used his tremelo, though I don't think I use it the same way. A lot of guitarists think that a tremelo arm is for someone who can't play a hand vibrato. But the tremelo arm gives a different vibrato all together. It affects whole chords. I can do the old hand vibrato just fine, but I like attacking the strings and getting all those sounds. You can get a lot of aggression out with a tremelo arm. I've got a Bigsby on my Gibson, and it's a waste, because it's got too much leeway. You have to pull it back a half-an-inch before it does a thing. But the vibrato on the Strat reacts immediately. As soon as you pull on it, the strings start going back. I have a friend who balances the arm. He loosens the screws at the very front of the tailpiece and sets the whole thing at a different angle so it is in perfect balance. It's amazing; you just can't go out of tune. I never thought it would work. I just used to bolt them down and forget about it. I pull and push the vibrato bar - it goes down a whole octave when I push it.*

I use tortoiseshell picks, one end squared, one end pointed. I have them specially made for me because you can't get them at all. I use tortoiseshell because plastic is too soft. I like them brick-hard. I've used this shape ever since I was 11, and I just cannot play with those round things everybody plays with, because when you jump a string you tend to hit the other string on the way. With this pick you can be more nimble." • RB to Martin K Webb.

Ritchie also explained what got him into using the tremelo arm: *"I'd seen the James Cotton Blues Band at the Fillmore East, and the guitarist in the band played with the vibrato bar. He got the most amazing sounds. Right after seeing him, I started using the bar. Hendrix inspired me, too.*

"I went crazy with it. I used to have quarter-inch bars made for me because I'd keep snapping the normal kind. My repairman would look at me strangely and say, 'What are you doing to these tremolo bars?' Finally, he gave me this gigantic tremolo arm made of half-an-inch of solid iron [photo page 47] and said, Here. If you break this thing, I don't wanna know about it!'"

"About three weeks later I went back to the shop. He looked at me and said 'No - you haven't.' And I said, 'Yes I have!' In graphic detail I explained to him how I would twirl the guitar around the bar, throw it to the floor, put my foot on it and pull the bar off with two hands. He was a bit of a purist, so he wasn't amused." • RB to Guitar World, Feb 1991.

By the time of *In Rock* Ritchie had in many ways already perfected his technique and had the guitars he wanted. He had after all been playing for the best part of a decade, and professionally for nearly as long. He had the most studio experience of any of the musicians thanks to the hundreds of sessions he recorded from 1963 onwards for Joe Meek's studio, and been able to learn along the way, but in Purple there was a lot more pressure on him as a player.

Ritchie also became one of a growing number of rock guitarists who seldom played full chords (or even in his case seldom playing rhythm throughout a whole song). Rock guitarists had found full chords didn't work for the aggressive sound they were after. By just punching out the root of the chord they invented the 'power chord'.

On *In Rock* his songs are generally characterised by two note riffs, with the organ providing chordal tones and evolving harmonies as Jon thought fit. These modal (power) chords are neither major nor minor and use two notes - the root and the 4th/5th, allowing the melody to use both major and minor scales without dissonance.

There remains the question of the 'Blackmore sound' which more or less came to perfection at the time of *In Rock*. He achieved this in large measure through two simple methods, an overdrive effect and a boosted amp. He would have the bass turned down and the middle

and treble up a bit.

"A treble-booster with a variable control gives me sustain. Hornby Skewes made it, but I had it slightly modified, because I found that on some nights I had too much sustain, and on others I didn't have enough. So I had a variable control put on. Actually, using a Stratocaster, I don't really need any treble boost. I use the unit mostly for sustain." • RB in Guitar World Feb 1991.

"I have another (treble booster) made by organ and electronics expert Bill Hough, who looks after Keith Emerson's organs. The Hornby-Skewes booster unit overloads the input side and produces the distortion. I have the presence on the amplifier turned right off, the bass on to No. 4, the middle on to No. 5 an the treble usually on about No. 6." • RB to Melody Maker, Oct 1970.

Ritchie kept his Vox AC30 but his association with Marshalls also went back a good few years. Jim Marshall had opened a drum shop (Jim Marshall & Son) in Hanwell in 1960, where he also gave drum lessons. Musicians liked the helpful attitude of the shop and over time guitarists began asking if he would sell guitars and particularly amplifiers more suitable for the rock and roll market as well. His potential customers knew what they wanted from an amp; a dirtier, more aggressive and louder sound. Blackmore was always hanging round the shop, and Townshend and Jim Sullivan were also frequent visitors.

Jim Marshall wasn't sure he knew enough about amps but decided to give it a go so he turned to his repairman Ken Bran to see what they could come up with. Ken didn't feel he had to skills to design an amp from scratch but suggested they speak to a young guy called Dudley Craven who worked for EMI. Jim asked Dudley to join his team and made him an offer that he couldn't refuse. It wasn't until the sixth prototype (based around the Fender Bassman but with component changes including an ultra-linear output transformer), that they felt they had something close. The amp, still a collection of soldered components on a chassis, was put into the shop one Saturday in 1964 for people to hear. They took orders for 23 that first day, with Townshend, Blackmore and Sullivan amongst them. After that a 100 watt amp was developed in 1965.

Ritchie was always looking for improvements in his sound and as Marshall had modified his early 100 watt amp, naturally he looked to them when he wanted even more. The aim of the work was to make it sound more like Ritchie's

Marshall Standard Units — The Soundmovers

favourite Vox AC30 amp cranked to full volume, but with more treble. Ken Flegg was in charge of the electronic section and senior technician for Marshall in their new home at Milton Keynes in 1967. He worked directly with Ritchie on the modifications: *"Ritchie always wanted more treble (less bass) and more power. To accommodate this an effort was made to come up with a 200 watt amplifier. Rather than looking into the design properly and taking our time over this, we were pushed into basically copying the 100 watt output circuit but with the KT88 Valves, and with a completely different tonal network. It proved to be unreliable and too limited to modify, and without the sounds that people like Ritchie so much wanted. Hence it was nicknamed 'The Pig' (officially named the Marshall 200). However, Ritchie was still hassling us, or rather me, for something louder and with 'more treble', so I got together with Mr. Field from our transformer suppliers, and between us we designed a completely new 200 watt power stage that was reliable. To that we added the standard Marshall pre-amp stage (this was to become the Marshall Major in 1968), and for Ritchie we added an extra pre-amp valve stage with a bass reducing network and, of course, extra gain. By contrast the other members of the band were not as demanding as Ritchie, so standard Marshall units were used."*

Ritchie was virtually sworn to secrecy over the exact details of the changes at the time and told they would not be doing them for anyone else, but some years later he did say a little about the process: *"I saw the Marshall setup and liked the way they looked. The design I liked, but the sound was awful. So I went back to the factory because I knew Jim and I said, 'Look, I want this changed and I want that changed.' And I used to play in front of all the people that were there working, there would be women there assembling things, and I had the amp boosted. So I would be playing away right in front of all these people and they'd be trying to work. I'd go, 'That's not right, more treble,' and they'd take out a resistor. I had to play full blast or otherwise I couldn't know what it was going to sound like. The people hated me."* Ken recalled those tests: *"After realising what he really wanted, I sent him away whilst I sorted it out. On his return he seemed happy and he used that set up for many years after."*

"They're the loudest amplifier in the world on their own. I'm not saying I play the loudest, it depends on how many you use. But one on its own is the loudest. I don't like to use a lot of cabinets, I think just two cabinets is enough; otherwise the sound is all around you. I like to keep away from the sound, and that's why onstage I play to the left of it and point it the other way. Then I can get a perspective of what's going on; otherwise all you can hear is yourself. And you tend to get feedback and overtones you don't want."
Ritchie Blackmore

When the band got their first Marshalls, Ritchie is said to have asked Jim Marshall to have one cabinet stripped out and an AC30 fitted inside. Yet in late 1969 an AC30 can be seen propped in front of the Marshalls [photo page 48]. This unconfirmed AC30 experiment aside, Ritchie used two Marshall stacks for most of the time - a 1982 and a 1982B. They were not modified in any way. He used whatever speakers they came with and never experimented with other types as they did the job he wanted (at the Roundhouse gig in September 1969 he only had one stack - the size of the stage may have dictated this; see page 56.) In 1970 he moved to a 1960 and 1960a model cabinets (fitted with four 25watt Celestion speakers).

At some point in Spring 1970 he added a third stack to his set-up. This was a make-up set with a larger older bottom cabinet so stood a little higher than the others. A Marshall 2020 solid state (Hammond) reverb unit also appeared on stage often sat on a chair. He can be seen with this three stack set-up (and giving the reverb a kicking) on the footage shot at the Royal Festival Hall in July 1970 (and in photo on page 86). Some have suggested this was all for show, but Ritchie answered some technical questions from the Melody Maker on his gear in 1970 and said he did use them. *"(I have) six speakers, but only use four of these, except in very loud passages."*

They must have been set low according to experts. Only one cabinet is miked up as the sound engineer only needs one feed for the PA. The purpose of the stacks is to get the on-stage sound and volume right. Neil Priddy, who played 'Ritchie Blackmore' in the now defunct tribute band Deepest Purple, tried the three stack experiment. *"When you've got bass, Hammond organ and vocal monitors on you need a fair bit of volume. Running three stacks simultaneously means you can drive one amp quite hard and 'spread the sound' through the other amps and cabs. You'd be surprised how directional the cabs are. Stand right in line and you get a good level of sound, move to the side and the sound can easily get lost on stage. So running a wider 'wall' of cabs gives you a bigger on stage area where you can hear what you're playing."* This set-up didn't last too long, and by the end of 1970 he went back to two stacks.

Marshall also began using Deep Purple in press adverts in 1970, one of which can be seen on page 51. As an aside, The Who are credited with the invention of the Marshall Stack in 1965, combining an amp with an 8 x 12 Marshall cab (specially built for Pete Townshend). However the 8 x 12 cab was too heavy for lugging around and was changed to two 4 x 12 cabs, one with a sloping front to match the footprint of the amp on top.

Ritchie was also seen briefly in November 1970 playing a white bodied Fender Strat with a Telecaster neck, a hybrid sold by Fender

Jon Lord on-stage at the NJF festival August 9th 1970. The WEM cabinets are part of the festival sound set-up, Jon's Marshall Horn can be seen behind his Hammond.

at the time. This may have been in honour of one of the few contemporary players he openly admired, Jimi Hendrix, who had a similarly modified guitar.

On the early albums Ritchie seemed to be really experimenting in the studio; sometimes it worked superbly, at other times it was hard to see where he was going, and of course studio time was very limited. But things began to fall into place and by the time of *In Rock* Ritchie was able to give full vent both to the sound he envisaged for the guitar and the prominence he wanted it to have within each track. Recording the album Ritchie (like the rest of the band) played the same way as he was doing live, his guitar up full, his amp up full and the freedom to play what he really wanted.

"I know I play the ass off most guitarists. I am your original angry young man. I know I am. Basically I can't get across what I want to get across and I get very frustrated…" • RB to MM, Sept 1970.

ORGAN - Jon had soon realised in Mk 1 he needed to get a keyboard sound which worked with the guitar, and to do so he would have to 'toughen up' the organ. Jon talked about this challenge: *"From '68 onwards, I spent two or three years really working with Ritchie to find the best way to make our sounds work together. He and I started the band, and what we very much wanted was this synthesis of organ and guitar - a gorgon! I arrived there roughly about the time of Deep Purple in Rock; that's when I began to feel that I was learning how to integrate into what Ritchie does. I like to think that you often can't tell which of us is playing what."* • JL to Modern Keyboard, January 1989.

"The whole thing about that time and the way I was playing, the way I wanted to play, and I knew I didn't want to be the frontline instrumentalist but I knew I didn't want to be a sideline instrumentalist either. I had a vision (of) the organ as a rock instrument, and what I discovered, you know much to my intense happiness and joy and surprise, that you could tap into the back of the Hammond and take a direct sound out of it, rather than going through a Leslie. It changed my life because that was the sound that started to help to define Purple. Growling magnificent beast of the Hammond became almost a distorted thing, which was utterly adequate for standing up against Ritchie's guitar as he got louder and more as he started to discover his own tone. He started to get that really round deep intense sound that he got, it was almost cello like. I had to work really hard to be able to compete and that to me is where I saw Deep Purple at, it was the moments where you were on the rift you couldn't really tell which was which."

"I didn't use the Leslies very much at all (in the studio), mostly the Marshall 200, I kept the Leslie plugged in for the recording sessions and the direct out into the Marshall and just turned the Leslie down when I just wanted the Marshall."

"I didn't want that sort of jazzy Hammond, I wanted it to be right inside the thing. A lot of experimentation that was all done on stage, that's where we did our work. That's where the band discovered itself, not so much in the rehearsal studio." • JL to SC.

Roger shows off his Precsison bass backstage on the German tour in May 1970.

"I had a job on my hands to compete with this beast that was Blackmore. The great thing about Ritchie was that although he is a trained musician, he refused to be restricted by the harmonic considerations of where he might go. So sometimes his solos are way out there… I think that Hendrix was like a light coming on for Ritchie when he first heard him. That must have been an amazing moment for him. Saying oh, wow, of course you can do that … He kept getting louder and louder and stronger and stronger. He's also a lazy guitarist. He loves strict rhythm like on Highway Star, but would sometimes stop and go BLAM and let the feedback do the work for him. So the rhythm would go and I had to do that. Imagine rhythm keyboard instead of rhythm guitar. Then of course the sound I was getting was not competing with Ritchie. So I said to our roadie can we tap out of the amp in the Hammond and go into the Marshalls instead of the Leslie and several electric shocks later we had it.." • JL interview, Nov 2010.

"Ritchie didn't play rhythm guitar very often and that's really what formed Jon's sound—Jon started playing rhythm organ. To that end, he

wanted to match Ritchie's sound so he ditched the Leslies and went through a Marshall cab and that's what gives it that really harsh, edgy sound." •
RG to Steve Rosen, Ultimate Guitar, 2011.

Jon used his Hammond C3 (which he got on the 12th February 1968) through a 200 Watt Marshall Major amp, it was this combination that gave 'colour' to the Purple sound. Jon thought he paid around £850 for the Hammond, which he picked up from a Cambridge music shop where it had been used as a demonstration machine (the price was around £1400 new). As well as the Hammond, he used the studio piano for *Kneel and Prey* and the final chord on *Child In Time*. Marshall's did use Deep Purple for trying out new cabinets and Jon was the first to use Horn cabs.

BASS - Roger played a Fender Precision through a 200 Watt Marshall Major Amp and 4 X 12 Marshall stack throughout the In Rock recordings (he would go on to sell the Precision in the early 70's). Roger and Jon's Marshalls were placed together to form a bank of six. Roger quickly defined his role in the group and seemed to know what to play and when almost instinctively: *"There are very few people who can make a bass guitar into a lead instrument, McCartney and Jack Bruce can, but a bass player should be an anchor man and stand back and let someone else get the glory. Deep Purple is a difficult group to play bass for because there is so much happening all the time. I have to be very careful what I am playing because I could easily mess up someone's solo."* • RG, 1971.

PA - Although not relevant in the studio, it's worth mentioning that the band's PA at the time was listed in Melody Maker as a Marshall 1000 watt, comprising ten 100 watt slave amps linked together through a Marshall 8 channel mixer. Speakers were four 2X15 horn cabinets, two 2X12 horn cabinets and four open-bake 4X12 columns.

Early shot (inset) of the band at their first Roundhouse gig in September 1969 (they returned in 2013) and from behind Ritchie's amps in Kiel in May 1970.

Purple: Speed kings

The vision for In Rock • Looking at the principles behind the recording of *In Rock*, it was Ritchie who had set the work-ethic for the album very early on when he told the others *"if it's not dramatic or exciting, it has no place on this album."* Uncompromising as always, it became the band's enduring mantra over the following months. This was the first Deep Purple album where the band were able to properly decide were they wanted to go with the music, rather than just pulling together disparate ideas as they'd often had to do in the past. They went into the recording process with the intention of performing each track as if they were playing to an audience in the studio. The basic live kit was used and set at full volume (though stacks were not doubled up). They wanted the album to have a live feel. Given that studios were still discovering what was possible at the time they came as close to that goal as was possible.

The inability to plan too far ahead meant that they had to take pot luck when it came to booking a session. Grabbing a few days here and there, they sometimes found the studio they'd used last time booked by somebody else, and have to look elsewhere. In all they recorded the album in three different studios.

They also decided to dispense with the role of producer. Instead they would produce themselves and use studio engineers to get everything down on tape. Mk 1 had used Derek Lawrence on all their albums, and they would use producers again in the future, but for now they wanted more control. The decision did cause some chaos in the control room, as Ian Gillan remembers: *"Everybody leaning over the desk going 'I can't hear this, I can't hear that', and Blackmore saying to me when I said I can't hear the vocals 'Who do you think you fucking are, Tom Jones?'"*

Ian Paice likewise recalls the conflicts: *"Hundreds of hands all over the board. Everybody was looking after their own. If I had a drum fill I wanted everybody to listen to, then the faders went up. If there was a bit that I didn't play too well, the faders went down!"*

It's a wonder they didn't end up with white noise, but it certainly accounts for the album's full on sound, which often comes close to overload. Roger summed up the whole studio experience for the band recently: *"When we got into the studio and tried to capture what went on onstage, where things were pretty wild, we'd rehearse but nothing seemed to be anything like the concerts. People would just stop in the middle of songs and go off on a solo tangent then come thundering back in. It was chaotic and crazy and very exciting. There was a feeling of trying to play your instrument to its utmost limits."* • RG to Dennis Cook, JamBase.

"We were playing our instruments as hard as possible. Amplifiers and speakers were being driven. The sound was saturating the tape. If I had to pick one image that sums up Deep Purple In Rock, it would be the VU meters on the consoles bent hard over to the right, always in the red, always pumping. There was a sort of unconscious focus that the album was getting harder. And because the album was done interspersed with gigs, or live experiences, and finding ourselves as a live band, that kind of dangerous attitude that seemed to happen on stage was getting into the studio. The album got harder along the way because we were working in between, and finding ourselves." • RG to SR.

"It was a piecemeal record – we were doing gigs and then going into the studio for a day or two and then going out and doing another five days on the road and then coming back and doing another day in a different studio. It was a slightly awkward record to make but I think what had happened in the writing process is that the band had transformed live to this much more aggressive outfit than they'd been before. Before they were a bit more controlled and arrangement-oriented whereas now it became live-oriented; it became freeform; it became almost jazz. Hard rock jazz if you like." • RG to Ultimate Guitar.

"Generally, there was a business-like attitude towards recording but that doesn't mean to say we didn't have fun. There was quite a lot of horsing around. However, when the red light glowed, it was down to business. Interestingly enough, we hardly ever commented on or critiqued anyone else's musical parts; there was respect for each other's abilities." • RG to SC.

Roger's comment about the tracks getting harder reinforces the point made earlier about the album benefitting from being cut over a longer period. Even before you know the order in which the tracks were done, it's easy to pick out *Hard Lovin' Man*, *Speed King*, *Flight Of The Rat* and *Bloodsucker* as the hardest tracks on the album. Sure enough, they were the last four to be recorded. That this gradual build up of power came from the band's progression on stage was also confirmed by Roger: *"That didn't translate in the studio at first until we got to Hard Lovin' Man and I think was when the live experience started infiltrating itself into the studio experience."* • RG to Ultimate Guitar.

There is often a tendency to include one or two quieter tracks on an album but the band made a decision not to ease up. Ritchie explained why: *"Every now and again we thought 'this is going to be too hard, will it be too hard?' If there had been one track lighter than the rest a disc jockey might have taken it and played it and people would have taken that to be representative of the whole album, and it would have spoiled the effect. So we had to make each track as hard as the other."* • RB to Richard Green, NME, April 1971.

Roger confirmed this single minded attitude a couple of months later: *"We were determined to prove ourselves. Everything we did had to be within the limits of hard rock, or what we thought was hard rock. We really disciplined ourselves. What we wrote and what we recorded were within a very narrow margin."* • RG Oct 1971.

6 • The Studios

"The band knew all about theatre and dynamics ... to create great recordings and performances. For a heavy rock band they were really subtle." Andy Knight

The In Rock Studios • IBC • Deep Purple would record a total of ten complete tracks (or versions thereof) during the *In Rock* sessions and IBC played a pivotal role in the recordings. Two tracks were done at De Lane Lea, one at Abbey Road. All the rest were laid down at IBC's Studio A : *Speed King, Living Wreck, Child In Time* and *Into The Fire* (along with the early piano heavy version of *Kneel And Pray / Speed King* and the two out-takes).

The IBC (Independent Broadcasting Corporation) studio was at 35 Portland Place, a handsome Georgian town house in an area of the city laid out by the Adams brothers. IBC had a long history, starting back in the 1930s recording commercial radio shows in London, then broadcasting them from mainland Europe to get around the UK government ban on radio commercials. IBC eventually changed direction and became a fully equipped recording studio.

Joe Meek worked at IBC in the 1950s and learnt his craft there. With the boom in popular music in the 1960s most big British labels established their own studios, places like IBC taking up the slack. However in an era when there was still a lot of old-school snobbery in the industry, some engineers understood pop and rock music much better than others. As they got a reputation groups would ask to work with them, and this was the case at IBC. Indeed even more groups would probably have recorded here except they were slow to introduce stereo cutting. The Beatles and The Stones for example both used IBC for early jobs but didn't return. It was The Who that became IBCs most important early customers, Hendrix mastered tracks here and IBC also had an outside broadcast vehicle which was hired to record Bob Dylan live amongst others. The studio also generated the notes used by Mellotron, based in the same building.

Andy Knight worked for IBC and was the engineer on all the *In Rock* tracks recorded there. Kevin Barry acted as his tape operator, and it is their two names which appear on the tape boxes. Stephen Clare asked Andy to recall the routine during his time at IBC.
"The sessions were usually one day or booked for a series of days. (They) mostly took place on weekday evenings with at least one taking place on a Saturday afternoon from 2.30pm. The weekday sessions started about 7.00pm and went on until 2 or 3am. The band knew all about theatre and dynamics and they used that knowledge like so many bands of that time to create great recordings and performances. For a heavy rock band they were really subtle."

"Most of the work in getting the master take was done in getting the basic track right, even if that meant recording things over and over again. A recording studio is unlike anywhere else for a musician. If you put a microphone in front of someone who has never recorded before you can guarantee that they will make mistakes. When the red light goes on that is 'pressure time'. If you make a mistake live it is gone in an instance, if there is something an artiste doesn't like on a record they will spend their lives dreading hearing that bit there forever, which is why some artists don't listen to their recordings."

The microphone also is totally unlike (your) ears which hear in stereo and hear all the ambience that can make or break a performance. Somehow bands like Deep Purple had to overcome the sterile nature of the microphone and perform at peak performance to reach a compromise. They did this on In Rock by the sheer exuberance of their playing and going for a dynamic sound and performance".

"I remember them as a superb bunch of musicians who wanted to make a great album which they did, they were easy to work with and knew what they wanted and knew how to get it. They didn't appear to be at all egocentric and were all working to get the best recording they could. Deep Purple came to the studio to work and that is exactly what they did. I enjoyed working with Deep Purple" • AK to SC.

Denis Blackham also worked at IBC back then and described the studio geography: "The ground floor had the reception, main office, the caretaker's room, and toilets. At the rear of No. 35, there was another building that almost backed onto it, about a six foot gap between the two. The two buildings were joined on the ground floor only by a walkway. The ground floor of the other building contained the tape library and tape store room, stereo and mono disc cutting rooms, and a tape copying room. The back door opened onto a mews, and directly opposite was the Dover Castle pub, extensively used by the engineers and the artists using IBC Studios." A studio and a pub within yards of each other, it sounds like band heaven.

"Studio A was large enough to accommodate a 40 piece orchestra (this had been achieved by removing some of the original walls to open up the space), so there was plenty of room for a band. It was situated on the first floor, and the control room was on the mezzanine floor between the first and second floors."

"The control room was high up near the ceiling of the studio (see picture on next page), with a large window looking down onto the studio, and a stairway leading down to the studio. As well as a large open area, there was also a closed in vocal booth. This was a small room under the control room, with a window looking out into the main studio area. There were several movable acoustic screens which could be positioned anywhere in the studio. These could be used to form separate areas for the musicians and their instruments, amplifiers and microphones. The acoustic screens would form a barrier between the amplifiers and microphones. This helped cut down the amount of sound spill between the instruments in each area. There was also a small room behind the control room which housed an Ampex tape machine for tape echo. This was remotely controlled from the control room."

"In the late 1960's Studio 'A' had a custom built mixing desk, designed by Denis King who was the chief maintenance engineer of IBC, and built (our) own workshop. The monitoring was Tannoy 15 inch `Reds` speakers in Lockwood cabinets powered by Radford Valve Amplifiers. The control room had air-conditioning, and a variety of coloured spotlights to obtain a comfortable atmosphere to work in. There was an Ampex 8 track one inch tape recorder, an Ampex quarter inch stereo tape recorder, and an Ampex quarter inch mono tape recorder."

"Recording in the late 1960's was basically no different to today. The principles were exactly the same, except for the limitations of the amount of tracks and processing equipment available. Sometimes when you listen back to a track from 1969 it sounds so powerful, and often has more feeling than a recording made (today). This is usually because the old recordings were just the band with only a few overdubs. A band in the 1960's and 70's would often need to be able to play much better than some artists today as they would need to be able to play the particular track perfectly from start to finish. This created a real and powerful performance, which showed. There is a huge difference to the way bands often record today, one instrument at a time, and sometimes only a few bars at a time, no performance, and often no feeling either."

Andy recalled the limitations of the technology on him and the band: "Recording on limited number of tracks did concentrate the mind, but musicians worked with what they had at the time. There were many stereo recordings made transferring tape to tape whilst adding vocals and other instruments. What is perhaps lacking today is the atmosphere of performance where a band is getting off on what the other musicians are doing and the song/track developing as a group thing.

"I'd say musicians today are generally more technically gifted but the 60's and early 70's bands will never be beaten for the feel and atmosphere and originality they brought to their playing and compositions. The dynamics of analogue recording are still prized by certain musicians."

Deep Purple as we know never had the luxury of a long stay in any studio, but preparing was the same whatever the stay as Denis recalls: "When a band was booked in, usually the recording engineer and his assistant would set up the studio floor ready for the band's arrival. Sometimes the record label would have booked two weeks on a 'lock-out' basis. This meant the whole period was for the sole use of the band. The advantage of this meant everything could be set up and left in position for the two weeks, or however long the lock-out was for.

"There would be different areas laid out, separated by acoustic screens. The group members would set up their amplifier and speaker cabinets in the individual areas. The engineer and assistant would position a suitable microphone on a microphone stand very close to the speaker cabinet. All the musicians would usually wear a set of headphones, which had a mix of all or some of the instruments. This meant they could hear the other members of the band easily, even if they could not see them properly due to the acoustic screens."

Jon recalled how the band actually set themselves up within the studio for these sessions: "We recorded with a similar set up to our stage

Mixing desk in IBC Studio B, and IBC's 8-Track, marked up in-house to help the engineer (and a clearer view of a similar machine).

IBC Studio A in 1970 and exterior view of No. 35 today.

backline. We had to separate or it would have been a mess, but we had sightlines. A lot of what we did was on the nod so it was totally important to see each other. (I) didn't like recording that much with headphones, (I) would record with headphones but with one on and one off, I had to hear what the others were doing." • JL to SC.

Andy Knight could still remember how they set up in the studio: *"Bass left of the drums, next to each other on the end wall of the studio. The drums in the corner behind high screens with windows in them – Ian could see into the studio. Next to Ian on his left was Ritchie's screens around the amp and then Jon's set up with Leslie cabinet and amp. Ian Gillan would do guide vocal tracks in the vocal booth 2. They would all be able to see each other and there would be quite a bit of sound leakage from the instruments into the studio. Headphones were usually worn with just one mix going down to the studio, so that was a compromise but didn't cause any problems."*

Denis adds: *"When the band had set up they would then play their instrument while the engineer adjusted the recording volume and sound coming from the microphone. He would often ask the assistant to move the microphone a little if required. This was done for every microphone used for the recording. The close microphone technique was, and still is used for recording a band with loud electric instruments. This means the microphone is picking up 95% of the instrument it is intended for, and very little spill from other instruments. This allows for a more accurate and separate recording of each instrument onto the multi-track tape.*

"The bass player's speaker cabinet would be mic'd up, and there was often a direct injection feed from the bass amplifier as well. This gave a slightly rougher sound from the cabinet, and a clean sound from the amplifier. The two signals were then mixed together and recorded onto one track of the multi-track tape. The guitarist would usually be in separate screened off areas and would have a microphone set up close to the speaker cabinet. Probably less than two inches from one of the speaker cones behind the cabinet grill cloth.

"The drummer would have several microphones positioned around the drum kit. This varied enormously depending on the size of the drum kit, and the engineer's recording preference. Some engineers would have a microphone on the bass drum, a microphone close to the snare drum, and another two microphones a few feet apart above the drum kit. Other engineers would have a microphone on every playable part of the drum kit, to give total freedom for balancing the volumes and sound of each drum or cymbal. Sometime the front skin would be removed from the bass drum, and a large blanket placed inside. This often gave a good solid sound to the bass drum."

Andy explained how Ian Paice's drums were set up for recording In Rock: *"The drums were recorded with as live a sound as possible. Each drum being mic'd and the mix of the drum recorded on a stereo track usually recorded on tracks 1 and 4 of the eight track. We used Neumann mics U67 on the kit and U47 on the bass drum. When we mixed the master tapes, the drum spread was left and right as you looked at the drums but not full right and left. I didn't like the sound of the kit spread across the stereo as it loses the impact and in cases where the speakers are miles apart it sounds like the drummer has very long arms!"*

"On a mix drums can lose clarity as other instruments and vocals wrestle with them for the frequencies and the digital age has given us drum sounds that are enhanced and don't really represent a bloke hitting a drum with a stick. The worst thing that ever happened to music was the click track! Bands like Deep Purple would have sounded like The Carpenters if they had played to a click track. Rhythm and tempos are the things that made a band like Deep Purple exciting to watch and record."

Andy was very impressed by Deep Purple's drummer: *"Ian was a brilliant drummer and as good as any drummer that recorded at IBC. Other drummers who recorded there were Keith Moon, Ginger Baker and John Hiseman and I would have no hesitation in mentioning them in the same breathe. Ian was easy to work with and very professional."*

Ian's vocals and Roger's bass needed their own set-up, as Andy explained: *"The vocals were recorded using a U67 Neuman microphone. He used to sing in the middle of the studio. He had a very powerful voice, he was a great singer and I don't remember having to do a lot of dropping in to get the vocals. Most singers liked to do their vocals with the overhead lights out and the coloured spots on and Ian was the same. Roger was probably the quietest member. The bass drives the band when it is rocking and when it needs sensitivity he does it just perfectly. He also had a great sound immediately, I don't think we had to spend much time getting a bass sound as it came with his playing."*

Andy sort of confirmed Roger's memories of the VU meters being "always in the red" for the recordings: *"Technically speaking it's a bit*

De Lane Lea Music Limited   producer   DEEP PURPLE

like 11 on the Marshall amp. If the levels are in the red all the time then you are heading for distortion, tape can only bear so much signal after which it distorts. The secret is for the process to be giving the maximum it can - load the tape and then transfer the tape to vinyl at the maximum level. The band played at live levels in the studio and luckily that original sound was the basis for the rest. I have no doubt that we used limiters (a process which can raise low level sound and reduce high level to a preset parameter i.e. that is to stop the equipment from blowing up!) to keep the sound within the limits required for a good recording. If you over limit the sound too much you get what you sometimes used to hear from the Radio Live shows when it sounds like the band are playing backwards!".

Denis remembers that the organ players needed special attention: "The Hammond organ has a Leslie cabinet, a large box containing loud speakers that spin around at different speeds, which created the 'Leslie' effect. There were usually two microphones positioned close to the grills of the Leslie cabinet. Depending on the tracks available, and the sound required, the Leslie cabinets were recorded either in stereo across two tracks of the multi-track tape, or mixed together into mono using only one track".

In Deep Purple's case, the musicians had one track each for the backing track except, as Andy correctly recalls, the drums which were split across two tracks, with bass and rhythm guitar on one each. Once the backing track had been recorded, it was time for the overdubs. The multitrack tape is played back to the musician via headphones, enabling them to put down the extra instrument or vocal onto a spare track. IBC were using 8 track, at the time in Britain about as good as it got (16 track arrived in the country in 1970, shortly followed by 24 track). With five tracks already used up, and the sixth needed for the vocals, it wouldn't leave much room for double tracking or adding solos.

The technique if you needed more tracks was to do a partial mix or bounce down, mixing some or all of the backing tracks in stereo, freeing up more room for overdubbing. Sometimes this would be done back onto the existing reel if the budget was very tight, or perhaps onto fresh tape. If the former, the original tracks then had to be wiped to make room for the overdubs. It was crucial to get this right as Denis explains: *"you were stuck with the stereo bounce down and balance of those original instruments. In those days, you had to make a decision and stick with it."* If you had wiped the rest of the tape, there was of course no way to go back and change anything - short of starting from scratch.

And this was with 8 track; for their first album the band had been restricted to four track which would sometimes be bounced down twice to make enough room for all the parts. In fact the tape boxes show very little evidence of bouncing down except on complex tracks. Mostly they just used the two spare tracks for organ and guitar, or sometimes recorded organ and guitar on the same track 'live' and used the eighth track to double up the vocals.

Deep Purple were using a 1" Ampex AG 440-8 8 track machine (launched at the end of 1967), with recording, sync, playback and erase heads split into eight separate sections. This enabled recording onto each of the eight sections of tape separately or together and simultaneous playback. The tape speed was 15 ips (inches per second), standard at the time (domestic machines ran at half or a quarter of this speed, and only used quarter inch tape). *"As IBC used American Ampex machines they were set to a NAB standard. NAB[1] was the American recording standard."* • AK to SC.

Having rehearsed the song, perhaps with a dry run in the studio, Deep Purple would attempt to play it straight through whilst the engineer recorded the performance. They had to work hard to get that one perfect take but this approach helped give the live feel to the album. This first run through with the tapes 'rolling' would be Take One. From there they would have as many goes at the backing track as they felt was necessary until they reached a point where the band had done a take which captured what they wanted. Frequently they would start a take but have to stop due to a mistake, wrong note, or other reason. The engineer would label this as a separate take to help them find the spot on the reel during playback (and like a film clapper board) would voice each take number into the microphone. It was not an easy process and the *In Rock* tape boxes show how hard they had to work sometimes: *Cry Free* held the record with 31 takes. There was a studio shorthand to describe the various mistakes, Denis: *"The label has T1, T2, T3 etc. It was the job of the assistant or tape operator to operate the machines, and write the information on the box labels. So he or she also added information like FS for a False Start, CP for Complete Take, and BD for Breakdown."*

If everyone was certain a paricular take was 'the one', it would often be circled on the tape box label. Sometimes they might try a few more and occasionally on playback, they might decide they preferred an earlier take. Depending on how they were working, they might transfer this take to a new tape, bounce it down and do the overdubs on that. There was also the opportunity to splice sections of two or more takes together to make a composite master.

Once the recording was complete with vocals, overdubs and solos, it was time for the mixing. The engineer played back the track and got the correct balance of instruments, adjusting the eq (equalisation) of each track, sometimes adding a little reverb and echo. He

Deep Purple inside De Lane Lea, filming the promo for Black Night.

would also adjust the panning of each track to create a stereo image, guitar panned to the right, organ panned to the left. The skill was in remembering where during each playback the levels needed to be tweaked up and down at certain points in the song. The master would then be played back using these levels and recorded onto a clean stereo quarter inch tape. Each stereo master was then spliced out and reassembled onto a new reel to build up the album master copy. With eight-track machines, generally it was not very difficult to mix if the actual recording and playing was good.

Denis recalled how the whole process was drawn together to produce the final master reels. *"When completed, the take would be labelled 'Master Leadered'. The engineer or tape operator would splice in some (usually white) leader tape before the master take, and often some red leader tape at the end of the take. This made it easier to wind through the reel to find the correct take. The final master mixes would then be compiled together in the running order of the release. They would usually be on two reels – side one and side two."*

These reels (one is shown on page 100), often labelled 'production master', were the culmination (certainly in Purple's case) of months of work and generally the first job was to copy them to provide a duplicate in case of loss or damage. This master would then be delivered to the record company and usually a handful of acetate discs would then be cut, enabling band, managers and mates a preview of how it would all sound on disc (and also to spot any glitches). Cutting a vinyl disc is a skilled art and many collectors hunt out particular pressings done by specific cutting engineers as they have a noticeably better sound.

The In Rock Studios • De Lane Lea

The De Lane Lea studio came to be closely associated with Deep Purple in the minds of many fans. The group cut their second and third albums at the studio, as well as tracks for *In Rock* (and later *Fireball*), and filmed their first ever promo there in 1970 for *Black Night*.

De Lane Lea began in 1947, taking the name from its French founder, Major De Lane Lea, who set up his studio in the late 1940s to dub French films into English (what sort of films we don't know!). The studio took off and moved into music, with premises at 129 Kingsway, used by the Beatles, The Who, The Stones and Pink Floyd. Jimi Hendrix recorded Hey Joe here. Later they opened further studios and when they shut the original down in 1973 Ian Gillan

bought it. It operated as Kingsway Recorders for many years.

Two tracks for *Deep Purple In Rock* were done here, *Hard Lovin' Man* and *Flight Of The Rat*, as well as the single *Black Night*. Ian Paice was not too happy with the studio as far as recording his drum sound: *"De Lane Lea was weird; it was not a great studio for drummers. The sound was very flat, but it was convenient. It was difficult to get any studio that was good for drums in those days, the best was Abbey Road because that was the big one."* One curious point which nobody has been able to explain yet is why the two tracks recorded here have the guitar on the right and the organ on the left (which is the way audience would hear them on stage), while on the others it is usually the opposite way round.

De Lane Lea had one other connection with the band which would resonate for a long time; engineer Martin Birch. Working at the studio he was already known to the band having worked on the recording of *The Concerto*. Martin impressed the band during the *In Rock* recordings and by the time they came to do *Machine Head*, Martin was almost a sixth member of the band. He would go on to engineer all Deep Purple's albums up until the split in 1976, moving on to work for both Rainbow and Whitesnake in the late seventies.

All the band took to Martin very quickly. Roger remembers the first *In Rock* session with him: *"The chemistry between the band and Martin was instant. He felt like one of us. The studio itself was a bit small but Martin got us a good sound. We really liked the tracks done there. It was only when he came into the picture that we found our true selves. He had a sense of humour very like ours and was technically very adept. We immediately felt comfortable with him."* • RG to SC.

Jon was impressed as well: *"He always took more time over the keyboard mike placement than pretty much anything else; he was very good with keyboards. He found Ritchie very easy to record because Ritchie would say 'This is what I want,' and Martin would go 'Ok, then that's what you've got'. Ritchie was always very strong about his sound 'No that's not right, that's not what I've got in the studio, I want what I hear in the studio'."* • JL to SC.

Ian Paice was similarly enthusiastic: *"Martin was a great engineer. For his time he was streets ahead of anybody in England. I think eventually you ended up with Martin's sound rather than your own, but initially it was such a good sound you didn't mind."*

Ian Gillan made it unanimous: *"Engineers elsewhere were all stuffy idiots who just seemed to devote their entire time to destroying everything you were trying to do, either by incompetence, forgetfulness or sheer bloody mindedness. Martin was the only engineer (other than Alan McKenzie at Pye) who ever bothered going out into the studio to hear what the band sounded like before he actually attempted to reproduce the sound on tape. When we called him a catalyst [footnote - the band did this on the credits to Hard Lovin' Man on the sleeve], I think that was very true."*

The In Rock Studios • Abbey Road Finally to perhaps the most famous British studio of them all, Abbey Road, to complete the album. It is now the only studio Deep Purple used for the album still working as such (the De Lane Lea site was demolished some years ago for a supermarket and offices, IBC is now offices), and was given listed building status a couple of years ago.

Here (in studio 3 it is thought) they laid down *Bloodsucker*, engineered by Philip McDonald. Philip had joined Apple the previous year, working as an engineer on the *Abbey Road* album. He'd done a couple more Beatles solo projects before the Deep Purple booking, so it was something of a departure. Jon Lord worked with him again a year later on his first solo album, *The Gemini Suite*.

Abbey Road was opened in 1931, like IBC in a converted Georgian house. Following the merger of record labels, EMI took it over and it was formally known as EMI Studios until they relented and renamed it Abbey Road in 1970, the year Deep Purple were there. Considerably bigger than either De Lane Lea or IBC, it had been designed to handle full orchestras, and bands had a choice of studio depending on budget or ego.

Tapestock would vary between studios and each had their own preference. IBC used Agfa tape, De Lane Lea preferred Scotch. Bloodsucker was done (perhaps not surprisingly given who owned it) on EMI tape. In general these tapes have kept well, and have not suffered any of the issues associated with slightly later Ampex tape formulations.

1 NAB (National Association of Broadcasters) set a standard playback equalisation (EQ) for open-reel equipment in the U.S. to cope with limitations on tape to cope with treble. Set in the studio, it requires that the tape be played back on the same standard to produce the sound the producer wanted. Europe later set a higher standard.

> "Ian Gillan was probably the only guy who could sing that... That's him at his best." Ritchie Blackmore

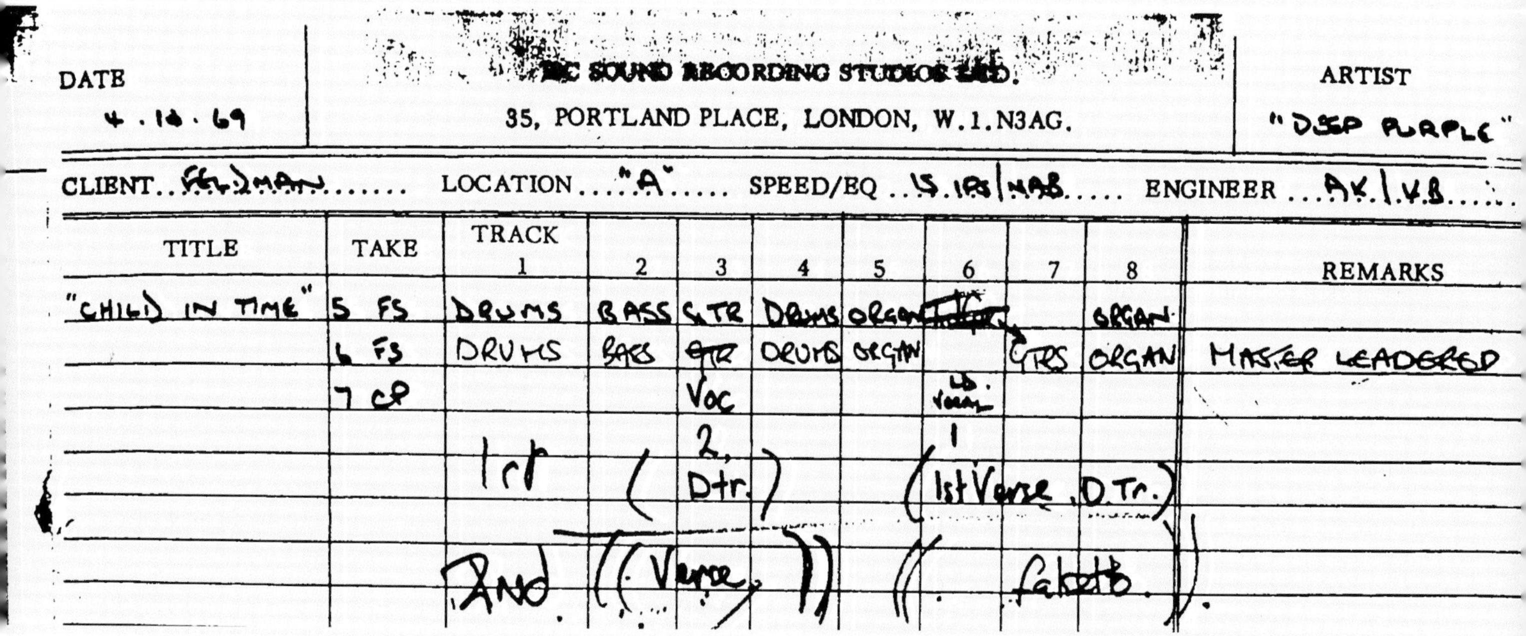

DATE 4.10.69	IBC SOUND RECORDING STUDIOS LTD. 35, PORTLAND PLACE, LONDON, W.1. N3AG.							ARTIST "DEEP PURPLE"	
CLIENT FELDMAN	LOCATION "A"			SPEED/EQ 15 IPS/NAB			ENGINEER AK/VB		

TITLE	TAKE	TRACK 1	2	3	4	5	6	7	8	REMARKS
"CHILD IN TIME"	5 FS	DRUMS	BASS	GTR	DRUMS	ORGAN			ORGAN	
	6 FS	DRUMS	BASS	GTR	DRUMS	ORGAN		GTRS	ORGAN	MASTER LEADERED
	7 CP			VOC			LD VOCAL			
		1st	(2. D.Tr.)				(1st Verse, D. Tr.)			
		2nd	((Verse))				(Falsetto)			

From the time Ian and Roger joined, it took Deep Purple Mk 2 almost exactly a year until their first album was released. But while the recording sessions were spread out over a six month period, they appear to have only spent a total of two weeks of that time actually working in a studio, little enough time to cut a rock masterpiece. And during that same half year period they played over seventy live concerts. The tracks are here documented by studio but the recording order (as best as we can determine it) was as shown on the right:

Kneel and Pray (aka Speed King / Piano version) • *Kneel And Pray* was recorded on October 18th 1969 at IBC, a session slotted in between shows in Hamburg on the 14th and Ipswich on the 22nd.

The song had been in the set for two months, worked and reworked on stage and in rehearsal before they got into the studio. However, even though on stage the track was as an out and out heavy rock piece (designed as we've seen as an in your face set opener) the first studio version of it was much less up front, recorded with piano instead of organ. The question has to be, given the direction the band were now going in, why did they decide to try it so differently in the studio? The reason is they were trying to cut a version suitable for a single: *"There was a thought it might be a single. The guy from the record company wanted something more pop orientated and I think that's why we did the piano version. I quite like (it but it's) nowhere near as raw."* • JL to SC.

IBC Studio
Kneel and Prey/Speed King	18/10/69
Living Wreck	18/10/69
Woffle (Speed King intro)	04/11/69
Child in Time	04/11/69
Into the Fire	27/11/69
Jam Stew	27/11/69

De Lane Lea Studio
Hard Lovin' Man	01/01/70

IBC Studio
Cry Free	13/01/70
Speed King	29/01/70

De Lane Lea Studio
Flight of the Rat	11/03/70

Abbey Road Studio
Bloodsucker	13/04/70

De Lane Lea Studio
Black Night (single)	04/05/70

Another major difference saw them transposing it down to the key of G (from A). There was a thought that Ian Gillan would find it easier to sing the quick-fire lyrics in a slightly lower key. Jon agreed that this may well have been the case and also that it *"felt slightly better in G, and blusier"*.

The tape box shows ten takes of the backing track (two are false starts) and is labelled *Kneel & Pray*. A second log sheet taped over this has the title *Kneel & Pray* scribbled out and *Speed King* written below. They marked the tenth take as the final one, and this became the master. It seems as if the title change came about during the actual session. Some of the studio chat from the recording was included on the EMI CD[1] The engineer clearly announces into the microphone in the control booth *"Kneel and Pray take five,"* which starts off fine but then falls apart after a duff note from Jon, who tells the studio that he had *"Dropped a real beaut'. I don't mean I farted, I played a wrong note."* (In the background you can just hear Ritchie's laugh!). On the second bit of chat the engineer says *"Speed King take 1"*, and they then launch into another take of the piano version. This also comes to an aprupt end with Ian Paice gleefully telling people *"I smashed a microphone!"* (if you listen carefully this can just be heard). The control room calmly asks *"Are you going to hit it again?"* to which he replies *"I don't think so"*...

What had been introduced on stage and at the BBC as *Kneel And Pray* now took it's final title, *Speed King*. It bore little resemblence lyrically to the first tentative live versions.

It's perhaps Ian Gillan who had been forced to keep up more than anyone else, driven by the band as he later reminisced when talking about the last stages of the song's development: *"I had never been in such an exciting and dangerous situation. Thrilled as I was, it became immediately obvious that I had to respond without delay, either that or become overwhelmed by it all and maybe not survive the initiation. I since found out that Roger felt pretty much the same about this new concept of blindfold-jamming at the Chancellor's residence.*

"There was no time to think, so – purely in self defence – I yelled back at them, screaming extracts from the first things that came to mind - Little Richard, Elvis Presley and Lonnie Donegan. Each of the aforementioned came to my rescue with the verses, but the chorus was all my own – Ha! Often misunderstood, it's not about drugs/speed, etc. In fact it is quite simply about fast, desperate singing." [IG on Caramba website]

Although never released in Britain, the piano version (4. 14 long) ended up as an a-side in Holland and Germany (backed by *Into The Fire*) when it was decided to push out a quick single there shortly after Christmas 1969. A new mix of this master (by Roger) was included on the EMI CD. It crashes straight in to the first verse and most of the lyrics are as they would be on the final album version, except in the last verse where Ian recycles lines from earlier.

The organ/guitar solo interplay is still absent, instead there are some gentle piano chords before the guitar plays a phrase very similar to that at the end of the solo section on the album cut. After the solo they introduce the drop down to D and bash away at this for a bit before the chromatic build up back into the verse, chorus (twice), break with a manic Ian Gillan laugh, and a final chorus leading into the noisy crash landing at the end.

Although this early version was unknown to most people until rescued for the EMI CD, the foundations of the album opener *Speed King* had been laid. All it needed now was a brilliant introduction and a stunning solo section. In the end they would ditch this early rendition and record the final LP version from scratch later on.

The BBC version followed the early piano take quite closely. Nearly a minute shorter, on the line "See me fly" the last word is harmonised which is something a bit unusual for Purple at that time. The words *Speed King* appear in the chorus but the phrase *"Kneel down and turn around, tell me what you've found"* heard in live versions is used over the piano lead in to the guitar solo.

Livin' Wreck • This IBC *Kneel And Pray* session also saw them make a start on *Livin' Wreck*. Interpreting the data suggests that they only managed one full take on this occasion, with the organ split over two tracks, perhaps indicating separate feeds for the Leslie and Marshall sound (see below).

The tape box simply says (probably written on later) *"master on reel 2"*. Perhaps they just ran out of studio time.

The group appear to have returned to the track on November 4th, with two more takes listed on *"Reel 2"* making three in total. The third was designated as the master. It is possible that these two further takes were also done on October 18th, and on November 4th they laid down the solos and vocals.

Roger and indeed the others felt the track wasn't good enough at first for the album. *"It was shelved for a while. We listened to it again towards the end of the album, and we suddenly thought 'Actually it's not that bad, is it?'."* Ian Paice was initially in a minority, and loved the sound on the track: *"One of my favourite drum sounds was on Living Wreck, really live and metallic and hard and nasty."* [IP to Modern Drummer, Dec. 84]. He later returned to the theme: *"It was a good drum sound and I thought the feel was right. There were some interesting fills in it"*.

It is difficult to see now why the band initially felt ambivalent about the track. It may simply have been that as they had only played together for a short period they were still unsure of what they really wanted to sound like. Whilst it is not quite as immediate a track and lacks the twists and dynamics that many of the other tracks possessed, it is nonetheless a very solid heavy rock song and provides a little balance to the album.

Woffle (aka Speed King intro) • The short but dramatic instrumental section which opens the *In Rock* album was cut during the second session at IBC on November 4th after they'd finished *Livin' Wreck*.

As we mentioned on page 25, the inspiration for this was taken from the ear-splitting racket the group would generate right at the start of their gigs to test the mixer desk (and shake up the audience if needs be). For the album they added a bit of finesse to the proceedings via a little of Jon's classical playing (played through the Leslie speakers alone). Roger recalls what happened during the recording of Jon's part of this piece: *"Halfway through he made a mistake, and an ugly discord made him pause. I expected him to stop and do another take, but he lingered on the discord for a while, played a clever discordant scale down, resolved it and ended with an expectant pause. He'd made it work for him."* However Jon recalls it differently: *"I thought I improvised that, I don't remember a mistake, I think Roger may be romanticising the story! Again that was the whole ethos of the band to see how much you could take from purely and simply what happened in the moment."* [JL to SC] The discordant pause is one of those magical Deep Purple moments that serves both to elevate the introduction and surprise (and perhaps delight) the listener. It's part of what made the band different to everyone else. However it came about, listening to it now it is impossible to imagine the introduction any other way. Unless you live in America. Over there, Warner's insisted the whole section be left off as they felt it would *put people off the start of the record...* (our italics). Clearly the Brits were made of sterner stuff, EMI even left it untouched when the track was used as a b-side[2]. They gave the 1.30 masterpiece the name *Woffle* simply to identify it on the tape boxes. Andy Knight confirms they only did two takes. As he put it, to try any more would have driven everyone crazy, and leaving it as it was also avoided lengthy discussions on whether the din was right.

The only puzzle remaining is why *Woffle* was laid down before the album version of *Speed King* itself had been recorded. Might they have done it initially to append to the earlier piano version of the track which was already in the can?

Child In Time • Given the complex structure and changing dynamics, it's hardly surprising that the album's anthem involved some serious work in the IBC studio on November 4th 1969. Two tape boxes survive and are marked *"Reel 3"* and *"Reel 4"*, which sequences them after *Speed King* and *Livin' Wreck* (Reels 1 and 2 above). Studios often numbered tapes in order to help keep an album session together, so you would know if one was missing.

Deciphering the tape box labels, it seems the group did four takes of the track to begin with. They only managed one complete run through, clocking in at nearly ten and a half minutes. The tape box has these four takes ruled out, which indicates that they were wiped. A further four takes were overlaid on the same reel. A 1" tape can only hold so much music (with 2,400 feet of tape on it, the normal length for studio use, it can hold approximately 32 minutes running at 15 ips), so this makes a lot of sense. Of the new takes, they completed the second (which was later marked up as 'master leadered'). Two of the others broke down and one was a false start.

Setting this tape to one side, a new reel was put on and they decided to try for another take. After two more false starts, they achieved a second complete ten minute plus take, later marked 'master leadered'. More tracks were then overdubbed, indicating this was the version used for the album.

The organ sound on *Child In Time* was crucial to the overall feel of the performance. Jon: *"Both the Leslie speakers and the Marshall sound were recorded but we ended up using what came through the Leslie."*

This is confirmed on the tapebox. Andy Knight explained how he recorded Jon's sound: *"We used two Neumann U67 mics on the top horns and two U47 Neumans on the bass, we would have used a U67 on*

the Marshall stack. The stereo track was panned left and right to give the space and movement as the notes move in the stereo picture (most sound engineers 'see' the sound as a visual picture). Child In Time seemed to mix itself. The thing about being a sound engineer is that you are there to get the mix the band wants, if it's a bit of a bun fight and the mix is terrific then who cares." Andy feels that Roger's bass sound was also an integral part of the *Child In Time* sound and remembers that Roger's part was *"perfectly played"*.

Coming to the studio the band had worked through the ideas for the song as a whole in rehearsal and on-stage, so by the time they began work at IBC they'd mapped it out. The only substantial change was that Ritchie took the solo spot that led into the main guitar solo rather than Jon who had taken on that role live.

The solos in songs like these ideally need to be laid down in a live atmosphere. The guitarist has to bounce off the band, while they in turn feed back off the solo to get the right dynamics and build up for the various phrases within the solo. Clearly this was not possible, so while the band played the backing live in the studio, the solos had to be overdubbed afterwards. It was inevitable that the recording process would subdue to some degree the powerful work achieved on stage, even so they came close to perfection. Ritchie spoke about how he laid down his solo on *Child In Time*: "I think the guitar solo is relatively average. I did it in two or three takes. Back then, whenever it came to guitar solos, I was given about 15 minutes. In those days that was enough for the guitar player. Paicey would be there tapping his foot, looking at his watch going 'How much longer?' And I'd be like 'I've just got my sound together', and he'd go 'You going to be much longer?'" • RB to Guitar World, December 1996.

Average? In the view of many[3], this is one of the greatest rock guitar solos *of all time*, perhaps only lacking wider recognition as it exists within the confines of an already lengthy and epic performance. Andy Knight's recollections of that day in the studio are still etched clearly in his mind and confirm the frankly astonishing fact that the solo really was adlibbed by the guitarist: "Ritchie recorded the solo for *Child in Time* from the control room, using a long lead down to his amp in the studio. He did a first take which was good but not as good as the second, which is the one that is on the record. We put echo on the guitar so that he could hear what the guitar would sound like in the mix. This take was recorded live without any later drop-ins. The whole band was in the control room while Ritchie was laying down his solo and we all knew that one of the great guitar solos of all time had just been played. It literally made the hairs on the back of your neck stand up."

And for a lot of listeners it still does. Andy paints a wonderful picture of Ritchie in the control room[5] surrounded by the rest of the band, pulling this masterpiece off in one pass on just his second attempt. An era defining solo.

After the second repeated verse, *Child In Time* ends in perhaps the only way it could, with a resounding power chord that was grafted on to the end of the final studio mayhem. The tape box indicates that Jon did nine takes of this final piano chord, which didn't phase Andy: *"It is possible to do nine takes of something as simple as a piano chord. There are many things that can go wrong. Noises from somewhere else, the wrong amount of pressure on the keys, a sniff from the pianist as the note fades away, or it just not sounding right."*

Kevin Vanbergen is a studio engineer who worked on the Child In Time tapes for a Guitar Hero type-project recently. These require separated out instruments to enable people to 'play along' with the original, but mixed to match the album. He is one of very few people to have heard the original masters since they were committed to tape. The project required a match-mix and initially Kevin had the difficult job of finding the right take, but when he did he remarked: "Sonically it was identical to all of the others but what it had over the other takes

is the indescribable "moment" when four guys suddenly click in a room together. They became a unit and recorded history".

"Its clear that the basic backing track was semi improvised as each time it varies slightly. Then they chose the best one and worked on that. I had to match all levels, eq automation and effects. I thought "this is gonna be easy to recreate the mix with only 8 tracks". I was wrong. I had done a lot of this kind of work, much of which were 48 track recordings, but this was so much more challenging in a completely different way. As I tend to do I cleared out all of the dead silence and tidied up as much spill as I could. I got the eq's and levels as close as possible to the original, but it didn't sound right. I played further with eq and started going around in circles. At that point I stopped and wondered what was I doing differently to the original session? The answer was "spill". I reinstated all of the open tracks, dead silence and spill, and at that point it clicked. Back then they wouldn't have cleaned up the hiss - they embraced it. There is a certain beauty to imperfection. Ian Gillan's raw vocals would nowadays have been tightened and tuned to death, leaving no room for a performance of this kind to breathe and have a life of its own. The timing of the drums would have been 'beat detectived' to a grid and all imperfections removed. Sadly this kind of magic is rarely captured these days as engineers all rely so heavily on technology to get themselves out of a tight spot. I noticed that the smallest clashes of tuning and timing were a massive contribution to the overall sound of the original". Whilst Kevin was only working on the one track, his comments clearly apply to the recording process of the whole album. Surviving snippets of earlier takes also show Jon improvised his intro each time. We asked Kevin about the individual organ track: "The organ sound was already there, it didn't state what was used but it would make sense that it wasn't a Marshall as the tone, whilst distorted, wasn't overly aggressive and required minimal eq to match the sound. The organ percussion on the lighter moments sing right through and you can clearly hear the movement of the top cones. It is highly unlikely you are going to get that kind of clarity through a Marshall."

Our last query was about Ritchie's first solo and whether it survived: "The original solo is not on the tape any more, the guitar track left on the tape was a compilation of the main guitar track and the overdubbed solo. The original guitar was replaced by a vocal. If you listen closely you can hear an overlap from the rhythm guitar and the solo, this overlap is on the same track of the tape and includes the sound of Richie muting his guitar at the point of the solo start. They didn't bother cleaning that bit up, it was the sound of a band, it didn't matter."

Jam Stew • On November 27th 1969 the band had a third session at IBC, again slotted in between shows, though this time both a little nearer to home, being at the Groovesville, Epping on the 23rd and Imperial College London on the 29th. The group were now about half way through the album. Two more reels of one inch tape were used and the group appear to have first had a go at *Into The Fire*. Of four takes only one complete backing was done. They then decided to have a go at *Jam Stew* instead and did this in just one take.

Jam Stew was recorded as an instrumental, a full studio jam with solos and everything played on the fly as on stage. Although the band cut a version for the BBC four weeks later with some improvised lyrics (see page 27), they never went back to that first studio take. It was left in the can, and only surfaced as a bonus on the EMI CD. Here a bit of studio chat captured on the take was also included. Ian Paice sounds a bit frustrated, suggesting to everyone *"Let's get through it without stopping you know."*

Into The Fire • Blasting through *Jam Stew* enabled them to let off some energy and fired up, they then went back to work on *Into The Fire*, doing ten more takes (the earlier attempts were wiped), six of which were complete. It was the tenth which they decided caught the moment, quit while you're ahead. The work went roughly along these lines; take one lasted 4.20, with the band doodling about for 45 seconds before kicking into it. Take two ran for approx 3.28. Having got these two full takes down, the next few attempts foundered, two collapsing within less than half a minute. Pulling themselves together a little, they got to two and a half minutes at the next attempt before it fell apart, then broke the three minute barrier before Jon cocked up. It's clear why the band regard these abandoned takes as of no merit, but they do provide a fascinating glimpse of the group at work. Finally the band all clicked into gear and laid down four more complete takes including the final album backing. Lead vocals and two lead guitar tracks were added later.

One of the surviving tapes lands us with a bit of a puzzle, a

---

From the letters page of the Melody Maker! You're never too old for your mother to come to your defence...

HAS ANYONE noticed the similarity between "Bombay Calling" on the album "Its A Beautiful Day," which was issued in 1969 and "Child In Time" on the album "Deep Purple in Rock" issued in 1970? — PHILIP KRAMER, 15 Firshill Avenue, Sheffield 4, Yorks.

REGARDING PHILIP KRAMER'S letter in MM, Deep Purple performed "Child in Time" publicly at their concert at the Albert Hall on September 24, 1969, and had played it at their gigs for several months before that.

Is it not within the bounds of possibility that Philip Kramer is putting the cart before the horse? Quite without malice, of course. — MRS. M. LORD (mother of Jon Lord), 120 Averil Road, Leicester.

powerful take of *Into The Fire* which is suddenly transformed into a version of *Jam Stew*. It's either the band having a play about or just a coincidence, the result of laying down the latter without having fully erased an earlier recording.

Cry Free • It was another six weeks before they could get back to IBC, on the 13th January 1970, having played Reading University on the 10th. Although it was recorded only about a week and a half after *Hard Lovin' Man*, it has to be said that *Cry Free* does not share any of that track's fire and conviction. That they were struggling is perhaps indicated by the laying down of no fewer than *thirty one takes* of the track, but completing only six (the first master reel box - below - shows the takes piling up. Solos and vocals were added to that thirty first take. Then after all this effort it was left off the album.

The group clearly felt it was worth persevering with as Jon recalled: *"We thought it was a real contender that's probably why we did thirty one takes of it to try and get it right. I don't think that we bothered to change it to the right key for Ian to see it properly. Maybe because we had in our minds that he would see something different. He had in his mind what he wanted to sing on it and never the twain shall meet."* • JL to SC.

A rare instance of studio block really. With the band's permission the finished out-take was included on the EMI CD along with another snippet of studio chat. The engineer announces *"Take Five"* but they don't get beyond a few notes before it falls apart with Ian Paice heard saying *"Oh shit!"*. To save tape, the engineer would stop recording once a track had clearly run it's course. He would hit record again once everyone indicated they were ready, but often something would crop up which delayed the start a little, and this is where the fragments of studio chatter were preserved.

Speed King • The day before the group played an important Royal Albert Hall support slot, Deep Purple returned to IBC to try and nail *Speed King* on January 29th 1970. The earlier piano take (see above) which had kicked off the album sessions was ignored in favour of starting afresh on what they regarded as an important track, designed to make as much impact at the start of the album as it did on stage.

The song's format had by now been well worked through at gigs for six months or more, and apart from cutting a heavier version, the only part that needed any real development was the solo section. It is here that the first example of Deep Purple's organ / guitar duel came to be recorded. Jon thinks the idea for this came from their work on stage: *"Ritchie and I used to swop licks onstage, and I think what we did in the studio was say we've got to do that, so we did the 8, 4, 2, 1 you know, so maybe that came from (work) in the studio and we thought give that a whirl."* • JL to SC.

Compared to the struggle they'd had with *Cry Free*, their confidence in this track shows; of the six takes there was only one false start and one break down. They went with the last take for the album. Once the backing was laid down, they began building up the recording. Jon and Ritchie did the guitar / organ duel live together on a separate track. The vocals took a lot of work, double tracking, adding backing vocals, then double tracking those. By the end of the session they had a 4.21 master. It was the band's last session at IBC for *In Rock*.

Hard Lovin' Man • What would become the album's closer was recorded on 1st January 1970 (despite what the engineer wrote on the tape box - right!) at De Lane Lea; what a way to bring in the New Year (or even the new decade for that matter). In many ways *Hard Lovin' Man* would become the defining track on the album, and summed up the group's hard rock style to perfection. It always seemed destined to close out the album, how you could follow it goodness only knows.

The tape box cover survives and immediately throws us a curve ball. It is marked up as *Hard Lovin' Man*, but this is done over the heavily scribbled out title *Blood Sucker*. There are a couple of possible explanations; Martin may have made a mistake, though this being

the first session with him, he must have been given the title for the backing track by somebody. The other possibility is that Ian Gillan had already been working on the lyrics to *Bloodsucker* for this riff. Sometime during the session (or later) he came up with a new idea and the track was retitled *Hard Lovin' Man*, leaving the *Bloodsucker* lyrics needing a new riff.

Whatever the reason, this is most definitely *Hard Lovin' Man*. Driving the track is an aggressive and all encompassing organ sound which just fills the studio, with a powerful solo which starts half a step down from the key of the tune as well.

Jon recalled his inspiration for the solo: *"I think what it was I'd said what I would love to do on this one is do an organ solo like I would do on stage with the madness and the freedom of being on stage, which is what I proceeded to try and do and throw the rule book out the window. I think that we had tried it once in Hanwell, I think like that you know, just wild and free and no real limits as to what anybody was doing and I think it just came from that that. It seemed like that was the only way it could end, and to try and capture that on tape was a huge challenge and I don't think we could have done it without Martin Birch who said 'just do it lads, and I'll catch up'."* • JL to SC.

Jon: *"The guitar is doing this galloping kind of rhythm and I play a solo that goes just about anywhere but in the chord that Ritchie's playing. You want to do whatever you can to slightly pervert that rather jolly German beer-barrel rock you might end up doing. I'm very proud of Hard Loving Man, I really dragged the organ all the way through the studio."* • JL to Modern Keyboard, January 1989.

Watching Jon at work on the track left a lasting impression with Roger: *"I remember Jon's great solo where he incorporated a few tricks from the stage, switching the Hammond off and then starting it immediately, thereby enabling him to bend notes like a guitar, rocking the organ back and forth so that the built-in reverb would crash and scream, adding a sense of danger to the solo. It was thrilling to watch."* • RG to SC.

Ritchie also brought together all the wild technique and sound tricks he'd been developing on stage over the last few months, and threw them into this track, a hugely personal statement of exactly where he was at that moment in his career. Not everyone was quite ready for it: *"One of the engineers who originally worked on that album was this stuffy bloke who didn't like rock and roll music. While I was recording the solo on that song, I got this urge and started rubbing the guitar up and down the doorway of the control room to get all that wild guitar noise. So this bloke looks at me, and he's got this expression on his face as if I'd lost my mind. Another time, we were listening to a playback and I went 'I can't quite hear the guitar'. And this guy's going 'Guitar? It's deafening, it's absolutely deafening! I can't take it, it's too loud'. And I'm going 'Y'know, I can't hear it. I really can't hear it'. And this guy's going 'You can't hear the guitar? It's fucking deafening, man. What's wrong with you?' And then Martin [Birch] goes 'Oh, wait a minute, and he pushes the fader and the guitar had been completely off. So the guy went 'Ooops!' And then he had me thinking it was me, that I had lost my senses or something."* • RB to Guitar World, December 1996.

You do also wonder whether had the band been trying to cut the whole album in one go, they might have begun to lose it delivering track after track like this. By going in with the purpose of laying down just one or two tracks at a time, they could give it everything, and walk away.⁴

Flight Of The Rat • It was back to De Lane Lea's Kingsway studio a second time to cut another really driving track, the fearsome *Flight Of The Rat*, on March 11th 1970. They were on the home straight now, with just one more album track to do after this. As the remarkably fluid and single-minded performance here shows, the almost constant stream of live work was having a clear and growing influence on the band's writing, performing and recording abilities.

They did four takes, the second and forth being complete, and went with the latter. The eight tracks on the tape were allocated as follows; track one - drums (left), two - bass, three - guitar, four - drums (right), five - organ, six - lead vocal, seven - organ / guitar live solos,

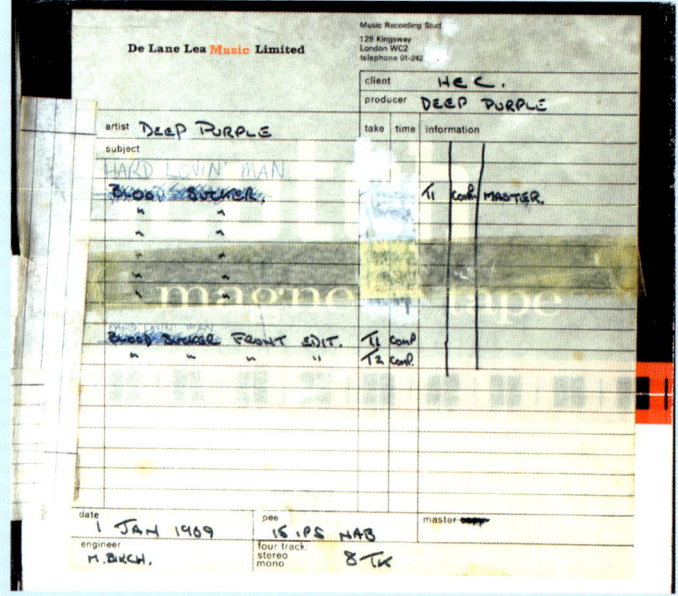

Ian and Ritchie backstage in 1970, venue unknown

eight - double tracked vocal.

The two vocal performances do not differ in any substantial way, Ian is simply repeating the same vocal line without any attempt at harmonisation. However by layering the two together and spacing them out across the left and right channels, the end effect is of opening out the vocal and giving them more depth within the overall track. Whether this idea came from Gillan, the band or Martin isn't known. It may have been a happy accident. It sounds fantastic.

As they'd done on *Speed King*, Ritchie and Jon did their solo work together for maximum live effect - and only did it the once. The raw energy and sheer madness of Jon's solo was a direct inspiration from the concerts: *"That was because I was doing that onstage. Again I said to Martin I want to do what I do onstage, he just said 'Just do it and we will see what happens.' It was the only take, we didn't do any others."*

During work at EMI a tape log came to light for this session which hints at a hugely complex set of overdubs that never made the final cut. Martin Birch carefully listed all these instruments in order on the sheet: Irish Knees, Lemon Lip, Rupert's Y-Fronts, Peruvian Log, Ford Escort, Big Noise (well, perhaps they left that on), Rolls Royce Harp, Andalusian Feet, Left Nostril Trumpet, 2nd Tympani, 36" Bongos, Fuck All, Blah, Esharp Thumb, Oxtail Soup, Rhino, The Mafia, Brass Chicken, A Punch In The Dark, Swollen Boil, Lino, Blackpool and (last but certainly not least) Martin's Left Sock.

Clearly De Lane Lea was much better equipped than many studios of the day.

Bloodsucker • Again sandwiched between live shows, this time at Central Hall, Chatham on the 11th and the Technical College there on the 18th, *Bloodsucker* was recorded on the 13th April 1970 at Abbey Road. EMI being a bit of an old-fashioned organisation, paperwork for this session survived. It shows they were booked in for eight hours, from 2.30 to 6.30pm, then 7.30pm onwards. Once the track was laid down, they mixed it in the early hours, and dropped the stereo take onto a quarter inch master. Cost to HEC? A little over £300 (not far off £4,000 in today's money). Bills for the other sessions don't survive but Ritchie told Record Mirror that in all they'd spent close to £10,000 on the recording (which comes in around the £120,000 today).

As before it was a no nonsense approach to the work, get in and blast through eight takes until they found one they were all happy with. Unlike other studios, engineer Philip McDonald appears to have gone back and erased any false starts or breakdowns as they went, leaving a reel with four complete backing tracks lasting some 28 minutes (any more and he'd have run out of tape). It's worth pointing out that these backing tracks are just that, and lack any solos or vocals.

Again in a repeat of previous tracks, once the four instruments were nailed, Jon and Ritchie laid down their solo work together, and Ian Gillan did a double tracked vocal. There is a reminder on the box to fade the track when it came to be mixed. *Bloodsucker* ran for 5.50 but was faded back to 4.13 on the album. This doesn't mean that they hacked one and a half minutes off the track, as generally the group would play through to the end of the song then carry on for a few bars and gradually stop in a random fashion.

The album was, as they say, 'in the can'.

1- The phrase *EMI CD* in this chapter refers to the 1995 25th Anniversary Edition 1CD release. It included gentle remasters of the whole album and single, plus new mixes of selected tracks by Roger Glover and some unreleased material.

2- It certainly worked for me. Nipping up to a little local electrical store during school lunchbreak I purchased Black Night, but when I got it home I was utterly unprepared for the adrenaline rush of Speed King, and remember hearing that intro for the first time as if it were yesterday. Instead of forty-odd years ago. SR

3 - And I'm one of them. SR

4 - At school when the album came out, there was one lad who kept claiming he'd made love to his girlfriend with this track playing on the hi-fi. We never knew whether he was bullshitting us, or just had extraordinary stamina...

5 - Ritchie would work like this on a number of guitar solos on future albums.

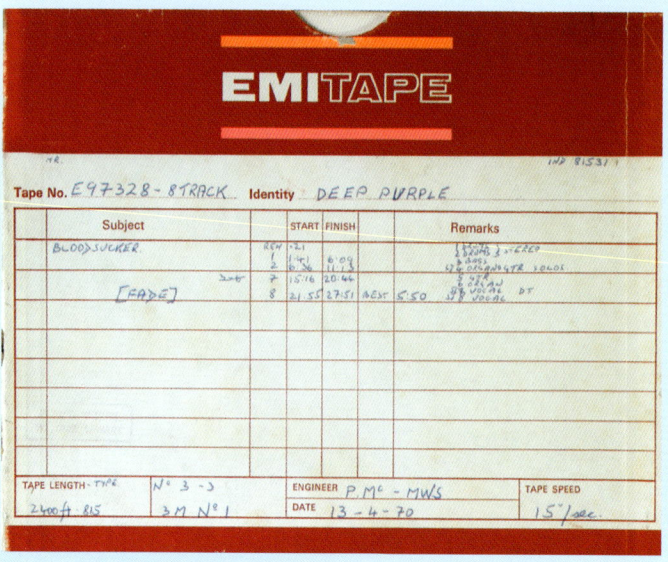

8 • Black Night and Top Of The Pops

"Roger and I then worked out the lyrics, which was difficult considering the condition we were in. What on earth was 'a dark tree and a rough sea'?" Ian Gillan.

With the album finished, the band's managers were quick to raise the question *"where's the single?"* As Coletta has already indicated, they left the music very much up to the musicians, but felt something was needed to help market and promote the new album. The single was still the best device for this, crucially because radio was geared to the format. Initially the group did not particularly want to do one. In the early 1970s there was a lot of debate amongst progressive bands, journalists and fans about getting involved in the singles market. Many musicians saw themselves as part of an underground movement which wanted no part of the commercial radio scene, and releasing singles was just pandering to a medium they despised (and which largely ignored the rock scene). The most famous example were Led Zeppelin, who made much of their 'no singles' policy in Britain (then promptly issued singles in every other country on the planet). There was also a concern in Deep Purple that if they issued a 45, people would mutter darkly about the band 'selling-out'.

On the other side of the argument there was pressure from EMI who insisted on a single, so a compromise was reached. Deep Purple wouldn't use an album track, which was seen as short changing fans buying the album, but record something new. Another recording session was booked for May 4th 1970 (sandwiched between gigs on the 1st (Art College, Bath) and 9th (Roundhouse, Dagenham).

Going into De Lane Lea, with Martin Birch engineering, Deep Purple had absolutely nothing left over from the album sessions to work on (having dismissed the two left-over tracks) and no particular inspiration either. Writing music on demand for any band is not easy. Sometimes no matter how hard you try you cannot come up with anything worthwhile, let alone commercial. For the early part of the session nothing seemed to work. Having spent most of the afternoon and early evening fruitlessly jamming around, they all retired to the pub. Roger recalls how they finally got it together: *"We went back at two in the afternoon and searched around fruitlessly for a riff which never came. Around eight we went to the Newton Arms and got plastered. Ritchie and I left the others and went back to the studio and he picked up his guitar and started playing. It sounded pretty good to me. Ritchie said it was borrowed (from Ricky Nelson's Summertime) so I said 'You can't use that' and Ritchie said, 'Why not? Have you ever heard of it? I said 'No', so he said 'Fine.'"*

Ricky Nelson was a rock and roll star of the late 1950's and early 60's, second only to Elvis in popularity for a time. *Summertime* took the Gershwin lyrics and dropped them over a riff written by guitarist James Burton, which ran through most of the song. It was recorded in 1962 but only appeared on a little known b-side (Nick Simper has claimed he showed Ritchie the riff during Mk 1 days).

Deep Purple were not the first to borrow the riff either. The Blue Magoos, a psychedelic band from the Bronx, had done so for *(We ain't got) Nothin' Yet*, released in 1967 (and charting at number 5 in the US. It also appeared in the film *Easy Rider*). The Blue Magoos' vocal line followed the guitar riff exactly, although they put in a few extra chords for the chorus.

Back to 1970. When the others came back from the pub (full of scotch and coke) [we don't have their bar tab! Ed] Ritchie and Roger played the idea to the rest of the band, Jon recalled how the band then put together the pieces of the song Heath Robinson fashion: *"Ritchie and Roger started playing it like the Rick Nelson song which just goes around and then someone said, I don't know it might have been me but god knows who it was (said), 'why don't we chop it up with the breaks' and Paicey said 'Yeah I can play this' and played an unplayable break which has nothing to do with anything, it's just pure Paice."* [JL to SC]

The idea was beginning to come together at last. A bass/drum intro, backings for the verses, chorus and solos were all roughed out quite quickly on the *"that will do there"*, or, *"this will work here"* approach to composing. As for the tempo, Ian Gillan recalled that *"We stole the tempo from Canned Heat."* Specifically *On the Road Again*, a UK top ten hit two years earlier. In all the whole process seems to have taken about 30 minutes (although Ritchie seems to

The UK sheet music; printed music for individual tracks was popular with musicians who wanted to cover hits. Often in print for years they were sold through specialist sheet music shops.

Black Night : Holland. The single got to Number 11 in the Dutch charts on November 13, 1970.

remember it only took 10!). Roger fondly remembers the experience as being: *"Instant, drunken and fun"*.

Instant? The band had eight goes at laying it down, filling up an entire tape reel, bashing away at it in their slightly inebriated state until they got a version laid down they were kind of happy with. They put on a second reel of tape on and started off again and after a string of false starts and breakdowns finally nailed it on the fourteenth attempt. It was done and dusted in just one 3 hour session.

After the structure had been worked out, Ian and Roger sat around to try and come up with some lyrics. Ian Gillan: *"We borrowed the title from the words of an old Arthur Alexandra song. Roger and I then worked out the lyrics, which was difficult considering the condition we were in. Trying to write the most banal lyrics we could think of. What on earth was 'a dark tree and a rough sea?' I remember laughing at the stupidity of the lyrics."* The image of the band sat around hunting for phrases which rhymed with *Black Night* still remains with Roger to this day: *"One of us said 'Don't feel too bright', probably an accurate description of our physical state at the time, but it would do."* Jon remembered that there was also a discussion about the spelling of Night, is it with a K or just an N? It depends whether it was about a chess piece, or a cloudy English evening, but no one knew which. In the end Night won, though for all the times it has been spelt incorrectly over the years... they left the studio in the early hours, thinking 'job done'.

In the cold light of day the band thought it had all been a wasted session that they might just get away with as a B side. The rough mix was sent round to the HEC office, who called up the band the next day and congratulated them on the track. They insisted, despite what the band thought, that it was just right for the singles market. It turned out that the management were on the nail, although it would be a while before this was to be proved the case. The track was probably mixed on the following Thursday, the 7th.

"The song starts with Ian Paice and Roger kicking proceedings off with a unison triplet fill to bring the band in. A steady but loose quarter note Hi-Hats dominates the back-beat making up the basis of the groove. The interesting bit is the quasi-triplet feel during the main riff drop-out sections, where Paice quickly slips to 8th notes on the Hi-Hat to set-up his syncopated off-beat Bass drum part before returning to the quarter note groove for the main riff. The song has a text-book 70's sloppy-good-time feel throughout it. Roger remembers the session for this track as "drunken" so maybe that had some bearing on Ian Paice's drum part!" • Nick Lauro.

Ian Gillan's vocal line is minimal and single tracked (the tape log shows two vocals tracks offering the possibility of a complete alternate vocal still in the can) but he still manages to breath life into the hastily thrown together lyrics and has a nicely executed if a little clichéd touch of mirroring the guitar's slow vibrato on the end of the chorus. Ritchie's solo is first up and he really lays into the tremelo arm and follows this with some deliberate phrasing. Change of key and into Jon's solo, more chord based than Ritchie's. *"Ian Paice also manages to throw in some cheeky drum parts that would probably defy the draconian rule of today's studio click-tracks. Check out the 'big fills' at 2:26 when Ian Paice brings the band powering into the last verse (and then refer to Paice's own comment on the track: "What wouldn't you play there!")"* • Nick Lauro. The final solo on the run out is by Ritchie and this time he uses the tremelo sparingly and goes for the rocky melodic lines he is famous for.

Overall the song has an easy feel to it that does not quite fit the really heavy nature of the album, which probably explains why it was more accessible to a broader audience. That's not to say it isn't a great track, because it is, but it does have a very different atmosphere from the rest of the album.

So, a day in the pub, a borrowed riff, lyrics no one can understand and around 30 minutes creative writing would give Mk 2 a certified single hit right across Europe, and a 'must-have' set list inclusion. Even so, Ian Paice was a little dismissive of the importance of having a hit single: *"Singles aren't really important, they're an asset, but not the first thing I'd jump at. A hit single might push our price up by a hundred pounds but that's nothing when it's split between the group because it all gets eaten up. It might make the billing a bit better. It's as confusing to us as everyone else why this single was so slow selling. We went to America and thought it was*

> The band originally had a different title for the single!

TRACK SHEET	DE LANE LEA MUSIC LTD.	129, KINGSWAY,	LONDON W.C.2.	tel: 01-242-2743/01-437-4252			
EIGHT-TRACK ✓	FOUR-TRACK	NAB ✓	CCIR	30 i.p.s.	15 i.p.s. ✓		
ARTIST DEEP PURPLE		CLIENT HEC		DATE 4-5-70	ENGINEER M. BIRCH		
MAIN TITLE THEME.	TRACK ONE STY	TRACK TWO MB.	TRACK THREE DOM.	TRACK FOUR TASTE	TRACK FIVE AY	TRACK SIX LIST.	TRACK SEVEN UALLY	TRACK EIGHT TRED.
1 FART (iii) (???)	(STEREO) DRUMS.	BASS	ORGAN ② SOLO	(STEREO) DRUMS.	GUITAR.	VOCALS	LEAD VOCAL	ORGAN ①
2 (BLACK NIGHT)								
3								
4								
5								

Ritchie on Top Of The Pops for Black Night, with his black and white Stratocaster.

another Purple miss in a long line of flops but we got a Top Of The Pops on it while we were away and a lot of plugs and that was it.

We think Ian Paice means 'got offered', unless it appeared during the play-out one week. Roger Glover was also circumspect. *"There was a bit of managerial pressure and although we would never go out to write a chart single this thing came up at just the right moment."*

"In fact," Ritchie responded, *"it's a nick from various other things which we've converted into a smash hit!"* • RG and RB to Record Mirror, July 1970.

With the demands of touring, they realised they couldn't fulfil every offer to appear on TV so in October it was decided to make a promotional film version of *Black Night* to supply to European television stations. This was filmed inside De Lane Lea studios, the band simply miming to the single. It was shot on 35mm film, although the original print seems long since lost. A number of slightly different versions do survive on video; one seems to run fast, another has shots of various antiques cropping up. As well as the film, the band were photographed and images from the shoot have been used on singles and elsewhere in later years.

Released on the same day as the album, the single took several weeks to make any inroad into the UK charts. They weren't a very well-known name to most DJs and producers, who were always conservative in what they would and wouldn't take a chance with. Eventually however it began to get airplay. Sales grew, more airplay followed, and it was eventually headed slowly up the charts. On the 7th August the band went back into to De Lane Lea to record a new audio track for *Black Night* to qualify for an appearance on Top Of The Pops, even though the single only just entered the top 50 that week. Any act who appeared on the popular weekly BBC TV chart show were supposed to re-record the song to satisfy strict Musicians Union rules, dating back to a time when they were trying to protect the livelihood of big band and orchestra players. Deep Purple would mime over this rerecording on the show. (In later years bands began to get fed up of these MU rules and often cheated, just doing slight remixes rather than redo the entire track.)

Their first ever appearance on Top Of The Pops was the 10th September 1970. Filmed at the BBC Lime Grove Studio in Shepherds Bush, the band are fairly subdued, there was a certain amount of embarrassment in doing this sort of miming (though they'd done their fair share, both early on in the US and more recently in Europe). Ritchie said afterwards that he just put his head down and tried to get through it. He 'plays' his black and white strat (and sports the pilgrim hat he had taken to wearing at the time) while Ian Paice wears a Superman t-shirt. The show's director even manages to catch most of the mimed soloing (the show was famous for close ups of the wrong instrument, showing a bass player during the piano solo, etc.). The song is very close to the single though the short guitar fills and both solos are different.

The band were touring Scotland when *Black Night* rose to the number 2 spot on the 11th October. The success helped keep sales of *In Rock* strong and it was at the number 10 UK album chart spot on this date (even *The Concerto* sales picked up, making a final appearance in the UK album charts at number 62).

On the strength of this Top Of The Pops aired a repeat of their appearance on the 15th October (Deep Purple were playing the Caird Hall, Dundee that night) which helped the song stay at the number 2 spot the following week. (The Top Of The Pops appearance is now on DVD and is used so often whenever the group are mentioned on TV it has almost become a cliché.)

Black Night was also recorded for BBC Radio on the 23rd September 1970 at Studio T1, Shepherds Bush. Along with *Grabsplatter, Into The Fire* and *Child In Time*, this was not a regular radio sessions, but was done specially for the BBC's transcription service and pressed up for distribution to BBC affiliates around the world.

Black Night was mentioned as early as May 17th in a review of a show in Bristol, raising the possibility that they used it to replace *Hush* almost as soon as they'd recorded it. It stayed until around October 1970 before becoming a regular encore until July 1971 after which it came and went (it was done at the *Made In Japan* shows).

Originally performed much like the single, when it became an encore the band would tend to jam around a shuffling rhythm, building the tension slowly before hammering into the bass and drum line, then into the song. The solo structures again lengthened a bit and there was also the introduction of a call and answer section between Ritchie and Ian (with Jon occasionally joining in). This was a little like the later guitar / vocal section in *Strange Kind Of Woman* although never developed to quite

Charts from the monthly Best Magazine, France, Dec 1970, Record Mirror October 31. 1970 and New Musical Express week-ending October 28. 1970.

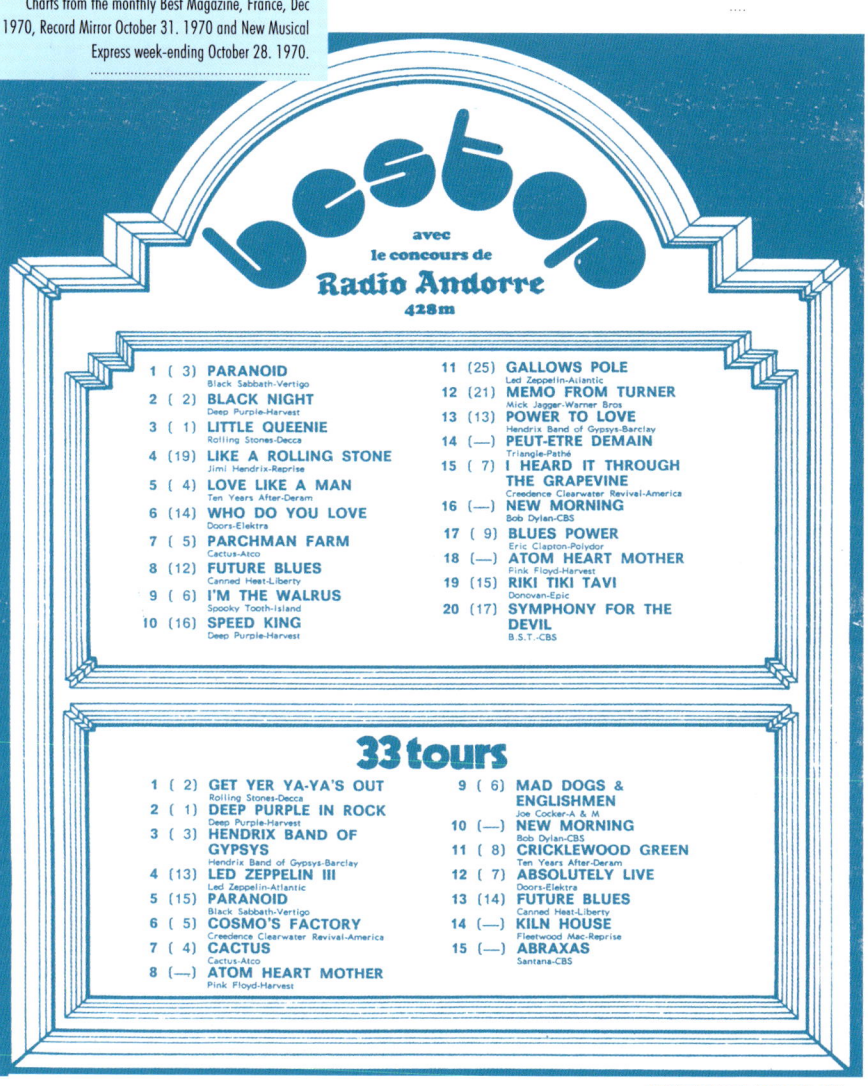

best avec le concours de Radio Andorre 428m

1 (3)	PARANOID	Black Sabbath-Vertigo
2 (2)	BLACK NIGHT	Deep Purple-Harvest
3 (1)	LITTLE QUEENIE	Rolling Stones-Decca
4 (19)	LIKE A ROLLING STONE	Jimi Hendrix-Reprise
5 (4)	LOVE LIKE A MAN	Ten Years After-Deram
6 (14)	WHO DO YOU LOVE	Doors-Elektra
7 (5)	PARCHMAN FARM	Cactus-Atco
8 (12)	FUTURE BLUES	Canned Heat-Liberty
9 (6)	I'M THE WALRUS	Spooky Tooth-Island
10 (16)	SPEED KING	Deep Purple-Harvest
11 (25)	GALLOWS POLE	Led Zeppelin-Atlantic
12 (21)	MEMO FROM TURNER	Mick Jagger-Warner Bros
13 (13)	POWER TO LOVE	Hendrix Band of Gypsys-Barclay
14 (—)	PEUT-ETRE DEMAIN	Triangle-Pathé
15 (7)	I HEARD IT THROUGH THE GRAPEVINE	Creedence Clearwater Revival-America
16 (—)	NEW MORNING	Bob Dylan-CBS
17 (9)	BLUES POWER	Eric Clapton-Polydor
18 (—)	ATOM HEART MOTHER	Pink Floyd-Harvest
19 (15)	RIKI TIKI TAVI	Donovan-Epic
20 (17)	SYMPHONY FOR THE DEVIL	B.S.T.-CBS

33 tours

1 (2)	GET YER YA-YA'S OUT	Rolling Stones-Decca
2 (1)	DEEP PURPLE IN ROCK	Deep Purple-Harvest
3 (3)	HENDRIX BAND OF GYPSYS	Hendrix Band of Gypsys-Barclay
4 (13)	LED ZEPPELIN III	Led Zeppelin-Atlantic
5 (15)	PARANOID	Black Sabbath-Vertigo
6 (5)	COSMO'S FACTORY	Creedence Clearwater Revival-America
7 (4)	CACTUS	Cactus-Atco
8 (—)	ATOM HEART MOTHER	Pink Floyd-Harvest
9 (6)	MAD DOGS & ENGLISHMEN	Joe Cocker-A & M
10 (—)	NEW MORNING	Bob Dylan-CBS
11 (8)	CRICKLEWOOD GREEN	Ten Years After-Deram
12 (7)	ABSOLUTELY LIVE	Doors-Elektra
13 (14)	FUTURE BLUES	Canned Heat-Liberty
14 (—)	KILN HOUSE	Fleetwood Mac-Reprise
15 (—)	ABRAXAS	Santana-CBS

RECORD MIRROR, October 31, 1970

NME TOP 30

(Week ending Wednesday, October 28, 1970)

LAST WEEK	THIS WEEK			WEEKS IN CHART
2	1	BLACK NIGHT	Deep Purple (Harvest)	8
5	2	PATCHES	Clarence Carter (Atlantic)	4
4	3	WOODSTOCK	Matthews Southern Comfort (UNI)	5
1	4	BAND OF GOLD	Freda Payne (Invictus)	8
5	5	ME AND MY LIFE	Tremeloes (CBS)	6
7	6	PARANOID	Black Sabbath (Vertigo)	6
3	7	CLOSE TO YOU	Carpenters (A & M)	7
11	8	BALL OF CONFUSION	Temptations (Tamla Motown)	6
14	9	RUBY TUESDAY	Melanie (Buddah)	3
8	10	AIN'T NO MOUNTAIN HIGH ENOUGH	Diana Ross (Tamla Motown)	8
13	11	STILL WATERS	Four Tops (Tamla Motown)	6
20	12	WAR	Edwin Starr (Tamla Motown)	2
10	13	YOU CAN GET IT IF YOU REALLY WANT	Desmond Dekker (Trojan)	9
16	14	GASOLINE ALLEY BRED	Hollies (Parlophone)	4
9	15	MONTEGO BAY	Bobby Bloom (Polydor)	9
12	16	BLACK PEARL	Horace Faith (Trojan)	6
17	17	TIPS OF MY FINGERS	Des O'Connor (Columbia)	3
25	18	THE WITCH	Rattles (Decca)	2
26	18	IT'S WONDERFUL TO BE LOVED BY YOU	Jimmy Ruffin (Tamla Motown)	2
15	20	WHICH WAY YOU GOIN' BILLY	Poppy Family (Decca)	9
28	21	INDIAN RESERVATION	Don Fardon (Young Blood)	2
22	22	NEW WORLD IN THE MORNING	Roger Whittaker (Columbia)	2
24	23	OUR WORLD	Blue Mink (Philips)	5
20	24	GET UP I FEEL LIKE BEING A SEX MACHINE	James Brown (Polydor)	4
●	25	SAN BERNADINO	Christie (CBS)	1
●	26	JULIE DO YA LOVE ME	White Plains (Deram)	1
18	27	STRANGE BAND	Family (Reprise)	8
29	28	THE WONDER OF YOU	Elvis Presley (RCA)	17
●	28	HEAVEN IS HERE	Julie Felix (Rak)	1
●	30	MY WAY	Frank Sinatra (Reprise)	14
●	30	THINK ABOUT YOUR CHILDREN	Mary Hopkin (Apple)	1

Britain's Top 20 LPs

●	1	LED ZEPPELIN VOL. 3	(Atlantic)	1
4	2	MOTOWN CHARTBUSTERS VOL. 4	Various Artistes (Tamla Motown)	3
1	3	PARANOID	Black Sabbath (Vertigo)	6
9	4	ATOM HEART MOTHER	Pink Floyd (Harvest)	3
2	5	BRIDGE OVER TROUBLED WATER	Simon & Garfunkel (CBS)	38
5	6	DEEP PURPLE IN ROCK	(Harvest)	19
3	7	GET YER YA YAS OUT	Rolling Stones (Decca)	8
10	8	CANDLES IN THE RAIN	Melanie (Buddah)	5
8	9	COSMO'S FACTORY	Creedence Clearwater Revival (Liberty)	9

the 50 record mirror singles albums

1	(10)	6	WOODSTOCK Matthews Southern Comfort	Uni UNS 526
2	(3)	4	PATCHES Clarence Carter	Atlantic 2091 030
3	(1)	9	BAND OF GOLD Freda Payne	Invictus INV 502
4	(4)	8	ME AND MY LIFE Tremeloes	CBS 5139
5	(2)	12	BLACK NIGHT Deep Purple	Harvest HAR 5020
6	(5)	10	PARANOID Black Sabbath	Vertigo 6059 010
7	(9)	7	BALL OF CONFUSION Temptations	Tamla Motown TMG 749
8	(11)	10	MONTEGO BAY Bobby Bloom	Polydor 2058 051
9	(7)	8	AIN'T NO MOUNTAIN HIGH ENOUGH	

1	(4)	MOTOWN CHARTBUSTERS Vol 4	Tamla Motown STML 11162
2	(1)	ATOM HEART MOTHER Pink Floyd	Harvest SHVL 781
3	(2)	PARANOID Black Sabbath	Vertigo 6360 011
4	(3)	BRIDGE OVER TROUBLED WATER Simon and Garfunkel	CBS 63699
5	(14)	DEEP PURPLE IN ROCK	Harvest SHVL 777
6	(6)	LED ZEPPELIN 2	Atlantic 588 198
7	(9)	CANDLES IN THE RAIN Melanie	Buddah 2318 009
8	(11)	EVERLY BROTHERS ORIGINAL GREATEST HITS	

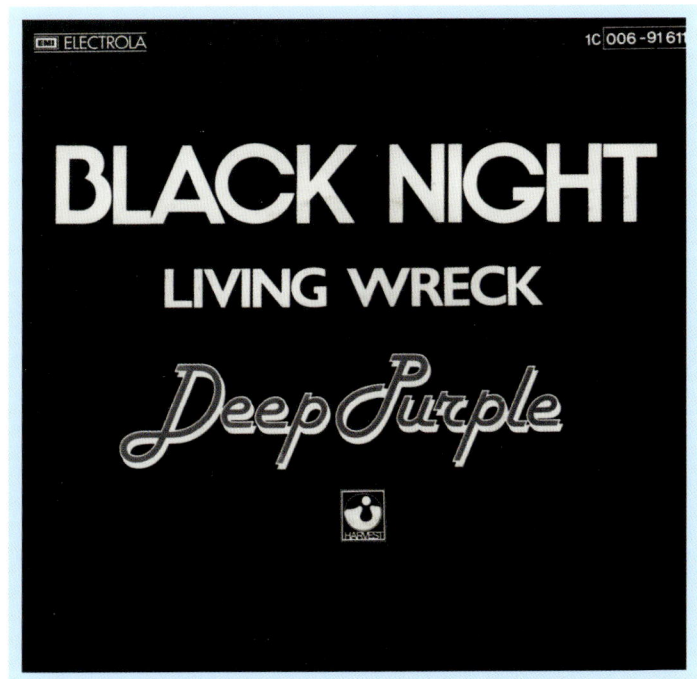

the same degree – probably because everyone was pretty shattered by that part of the show.

On the Anniversary edition of *In Rock* we get to hear the full original version of the song (4.47) with the run out and close (faded and edited on the single - the 1970 American edit of the single was slightly different to the UK by the way). The band keep playing the end run out rhythm until they begin to get bored. We have a section of ad-libbed guitar from Ritchie over an increasingly haphazard backing. He calls the song to an end with a twangy low E note and it then falls apart.

EMI decided to publicise the 25th anniversary album release by reissuing *Black Night* as a single, backed with an otherwise unavailable match-mix of *Speed King*[1] This came out as a smart looking 12" numbered edition in a picture sleeve[2] on coloured vinyl and a 5" CD single. Whilst not scaling the heights of the original chart success it did manage to register an entry on the 18th June 1996 at the number 66 spot in the UK.

It was to be EMI's last ever full UK Deep Purple single.

1 - This wouldn't fit on the CD. Roger had done a number of match-mixes, taking the 8 track tapes and mixing them as close to the original as possible but improving the clarity and fidelty.

2 - I remember spending hours recreating the missing letters of the In Rock cover typeface to make up the single title... SR

Black Night came in the simple sleeve design [top left] in Germany, but an eye-catching psych look on the Japanese original release [a rarity as it was soon replaced by the album art version below].

9 • ON THE ROAD January to June 1970

"There are so many places we want to play – we just haven't had the chance yet…" Ian Gillan

The dawn of a new decade and one in which the band both developed and prospered. Whether it was beyond any of their wildest dreams or not is a difficult one to answer, but within four years they would be one of the biggest rock bands on the planet. Nor should Deep Purple's success be seen in isolation. There was an out-pouring of classic rock albums in 1970 from emerging acts such as Black Sabbath, King Crimson, Jethro Tull, Genesis, Led Zeppelin, David Bowie, Emerson, Lake & Palmer and Free, all of whom had spent the sixties learning their craft, gigging like crazy and developing their own sound. We must not forget to mention important offerings from some of the old guard either, including Pink Floyd, The Beatles and The Doors. It was an astonishing time to be a rock fan, even if most almost took it for granted that it was the natural order of things and would always be like this. You got your weekly fix from one of the many music papers and if you were a teenager it all belonged to you; your parents largely hadn't got a clue, while the mainstream media mostly ignored it.

The heavy concert schedule Deep Purple had let themselves in for was proving a bit of a double edged sword. Whilst it allowed the band the freedom to experiment and develop their craft in the testing environment of a live setting, it also meant that the recording sessions for the album were being dragged out. Inevitably this could have resulted in an album which didn't hang together but as the group were feeding back ideas from the stage into the recording (and vice versa), they were able to keep focused. There was a clear synergy here, and far from diluting the album, it just got heavier and more intense as time went on.

Ian Gillan spoke about the coming year; *"There are so many places we want to play - we just haven't had the chance yet. It's great fun being on the road. I love it. It's very hectic, gigging around, but very exciting - and I find it very satisfying."* • IG to Music Now, Jan 1970.

January/February 1970 • Deep Purple started the New Year with their first recording session on the 1st January 1970 when they cut *Hard Lovin Man*. What a way to begin the year. This is the first album track where the line between studio and stage was almost obliterated, the band conjuring up what almost sounds like a live performance within a studio environment. It was a moment in their development which saw all the work of the previous six months come together. Whether the change of studios from IBC to De Lane Lea was forced on them, they simply fancied a change, or went in search of Martin Birch (who had coped perhaps as well as anyone could recording the Concerto live) we can only speculate. After a couple of one-nighters (including a foray across the channel to Paris) they went back to IBC on the 13th to record *Cry Free* so it looks like a chance move. Either way they were lucky; Martin was already gaining a reputation as a great technical engineer and in late 1969 Fleetwood Mac were citing him as the only engineer they wanted to work with.

Two days later they were back in Europe, this time for a live performance filmed for the Dutch TV show Doebiedoe in Amsterdam. But although photographs from this show survive, the film (aired in part in February, the rest in July) doesn't[1]. Which is a huge shame as poor cassettes hint at an amazing no-holds barred twenty five minute tour de force which must have had a huge imact on any Dutch teenagers who happened to be watching. *Speed King, Mandrake*

Roger and Ritchie during rehearsals for the Doebie-doe television show in Holland.

ROCK ALBUM SOLVED DEEP PURPLE RIFT

Root, *Wring That Neck* and *Into The Fire* were squeezed into the slot. A Dutch dancer called Penny de Jager (co-presenter of the Dutch music show Top Pop) and two of her dance troupe 'spiced up' the show! Quite who secured the band for this booking remains a mystery, perhaps a producer bowled over by one of their Paradiso concerts.

January provided the first tangible evidence of all the band's hard work when *The Concerto* sneaked into the UK album chart. You needed to shift a good few units at this time for a top thirty album, and despite reservations about the project artistically within the group, it did at least show that their name was getting about. Then after a couple more one-nighters it was back into IBC to record what would become the final version of *Speed King* at the end of January. Ian Gillan spoke to Rodney Collins about the progress that month *"(It) should be ready by the end of next month. It's the best thing we've done and the group is thoroughly satisfied with it. I think it's probably the first time you could say that about one of our studio LPs. There's a more definite direction than before. The main thing for any group is the get truly representative material. The group are just not happy with their earlier albums - they were just messy."* • IG to Disc, Jan 1970.

Progress on the album then had to take a back seat again, with another concentrated round of live shows, something like 17 gigs across the UK, starting at the Royal Albert Hall on the 30th January where they took second billing (or 'special extra attraction' as they were listed in the programme) to Canned Heat. It was a useful gig, reaching a far larger London crowd than they could have done on their own at the time. The rest of the shows were mostly more modest University and Polytechnic venues where they headlined, and once more HEC's new years resolution was clear, the band's fee had gone up again to £300 and £350. It was a sure sign of the band's reputation that college Ents managers felt it was worth it, though some club promoters resented the University circuit and felt they were driving up fees. There was one exception, Deep Purple played The Mothers Club again for £70, a favour to the venue they had probably appeared at most since their formation. Whether the band offered to pay for the cost to the ceiling damage when Ritchie drove his guitar through it at one of these shows we don't know! Sadly it was their last show there. While the group might have been willing to play again, they were simply getting too big and there was a danger ticketless fans might try to get in.

During the tour the band were also booked for the BBC's In Concert radio programme, taped on the 19th February 1970 at the famous Paris Theatre (which with a low stage and 400 seat capacity ensured plenty of atmosphere). If the BBC sessions were useful exposure, the newly inaugurated In Concert (Deep Purple's was only the seventh edition) was more targeted, aimed at the growing audience for underground music. Lasting an hour, the show either featured two up and coming acts or one bigger one.

It was just as well there was no support, they'd have been lucky to squeeze in two numbers if they'd been held to a half hour slot. In fact the group's appearance was providential. Joe Cocker and The Greaseband had been booked but at the last moment had to cancel. Perhaps remembering their excellent session slots, the show's producer Jeff Griffin quickly contacted Deep Purple. They had already built up an incredible live reputation, particularly in the London region, but the new studio album was still more than four months away at this stage; for the moment Deep Purple could still lay claim to being truly an underground band.

It was transmitted on the Sunday Show on February 22nd at 4.00 pm (and repeated the following Wednesday). The band were paid just £80 for the show. The live acts on this first In Concert series were introduced by Radio One DJ John Peel, an early champion of the group (who had featured them already on his Top Gear radio programme). In typical Peel fashion he lost interest as the group achieved a degree of recognition, and later that year there was a much publicised slanging match in the columns of the Melody Maker between the two sides.

For now though the band stuck to the core of their stage show with the forthcoming *In Rock* tracks *Speed King* and *Child In Time*, alongside the stage improv vehicles *Wring That Neck* and *Mandrake Root*, the latter being particularly blistering. They simply ripped into the closing sequence. Normally this was as much a visual experience as anything, with Ritchie making full use of migraine-inducing strobe lights. Mindful that on this occasion they were working for radio, the passage is here much shorter than was usually the case.

Although the group do seem slightly nervous in places, especially in *Child In Time*, the set still has some breathtaking moments and it isn't hard to understand the stunned silence before the audience erupts into wild applause at the end of *Mandrake Root*. [2]

The group's solid month of touring ending at the Philharmonic Hall in Liverpool on the 28th February, possibly their biggest venue outside London to date, reflecting the area's big appetite for rock music [3]. Prestigious though this show at Liverpool was, some of the crowd got a little bit carried away and one of Ritchie's guitars was liberated by an over-enthusiastic fan. The problem was that Ritchie did quite a bit of customising to his guitars and they were keen to get it back, placing adverts in the music papers offering a reward. Roadie Ian Hansford remembers the event: *"During Mandrake Root Ritchie would sometimes smash up an old guitar which, if there was any left, would be put back together and used next time. That night Ritchie was at the front of the stage rubbing the guitar up and down during the strobe section, it was in his hands, not around his neck and the lead came out (of) the jack plug. He came running back towards me as I ran towards him, with the strobe lights flashing and we crashed into each other. By the time he had picked up his other guitar and I had gone to the front of the stage*

Ritchie with the three Marshall stack set-up in Berlin, 1970

Photographs taken in Berlin, 1970

BLACKPOOL COLLEGE OF TECHNOLOGY & ART
present

ARTS BALL 1970

MARCH 13, Empress Ballroom, Winter Gardens
8 p.m.-2 a.m. Bar till 1 a.m.

DEEP PURPLE
FLIRTATIONS   FREE
INTERSTATE ROAD SHOW   GRISBY DYKE

Nova Express Light Show & D.J. Cabaret, Folk, Jazz in the Planet Room
Late transport. Tickets 12/6 obtainable from Students Union, Palatine
Road, Tel. 28328, Record Salon, Church Street, Blackpool, and
Winter Gardens from 10 a.m. on the day.
ALL PROCEEDS GO TO LOCAL CHARITIES

CENTRAL HALL – CHATHAM HIGH STREET
Asgard present in concert

Saturday, March 28th

BLODWYN PIG   with MORNING

Saturday, April 4th

LIVERPOOL SCENE   with MR. CHARLEY

Saturday, April 11th

DEEP PURPLE   with GENESIS

Tickets 10/-, 14/-, 17/-, 20/- (send S.A.E.) from Central Hall Box
Office, High Street, Chatham, Kent, Medway 43930, or at door on
night. Doors open 7 p.m.

'People began saying we had no direction'

for the (first) guitar it had gone. We tried to find it at the front of the stage and even in the streets outside but it was gone. After that we had a couple of days off and then went onto Switzerland. The lad who had the guitar had taken it home and when his parents (found out) they got in touch with the hall, who then got in touch with the promoter, who got in touch with the office and eventually the guitar found its way back to Ritchie, who was then very happy." [4]

March/April 1970 • Apart from half a dozen shows in Europe over the next two months the group were again largely anchored in the UK, where their concerts were attracting ever more people. A couple of the shows survive on poor cassettes [5], and show them juggling the set around. They tried *Into The Fire* from time to time after set-opener *Speed King*, but went back to *Hush* as nobody knew it.

After three gigs in Switzerland (which drew a combined fee of £1200), they returned to De lane Lea to record *Flight Of The Rat* on the 11th March, before another two week UK tour which began on the 13th at the Winter Gardens in Blackpool and ran through to the 28th at the Roundhouse, Dagenham [6] including six consecutive shows across Scotland. Venues like the Winter Gardens and Kings Hall in Stoke again show the group's increasing pulling power. Brian Smith went to the show in Aberdeen: *"What sticks in my mind is that I was shocked at the amount and size of their amps. They were without doubt the loudest band I had ever heard and the balcony of the Music Hall was literally shaking!"* In contrast at Hamilton, the place was only half full thanks largely to a strike by the local bus company. It was the show in Edinburgh Odeon on Match 20th that 17-year-old Prime Minister to be Tony Blair broke boarding school curfew to watch. He and several fellow pupils enjoyed what one of them later recalled was a 'fabulous concert', but had to climb the wall to get back into school. They were found out and later summoned to the headmaster's study for a caning, though somehow Blair escaped this punishment. [7]

Jon also got married in March, which meant his days of sharing a £25 a week flat with Ian Paice in Parsons Green (at the end of the King's Road) were over. He and his new wife Judith moved out to a rented house in Putney soon after. Ian Paice then began sharing a third floor flat with Roger Glover in a back street of Fulham. Ian Gillan moved from a two bedroom flat (with the curtains always drawn) to a Georgian style house near Pangbourne in Berkshire. Ritchie was to take on a five bedroom property in Camberley in London with his wife Babs.

Deep Purple returned to Europe for another mixed assortment of regular gigs, festivals and media slots in Germany and Austria. The Peace Pop World Concert at the Sportpalast in Berlin on the 30th March featured four other groups including headliners The Nice, Keith Emerson joining Deep Purple on electric piano for an encore of *Movin' On Down The Line* (reports of Ritchie and Ian Gillan jamming with The Nice during their set remain unconfirmed.) Talk of doing a double album, The Nice plus orchestra on one, Deep Purple with orchestra on the other (possibly at a special Albert Hall concert in early 1970), came to nothing. *"The financial problems would have been ridiculous. But I'd like to write something for him."* • JL to Disc Oct 1970.

The second German gig at the Mulheim Sporthalle, Cologne on the 4th April 1970 was another two day event with Yes, The Kinks, Free and many more. These rock festivals became very popular in Germany at this time, enabling music fans to catch several biggish UK acts together, often with top-flight German bands on the same bill. Deep Purple suffered equipment issues during their set, so prolonged that they dropped into a spontaneous jam whilst Ritchie's gear was sorted out (bootlegged on vinyl in Germany, the label gave the jam a made up title of *Mumblin` Thing Blues*). Ritchie asked Ian

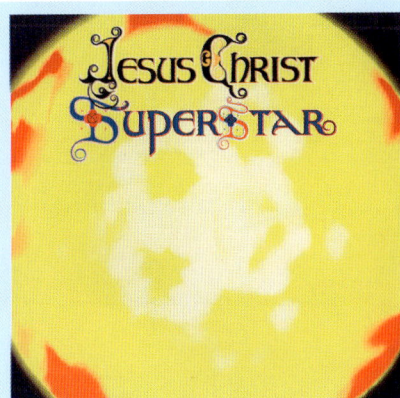 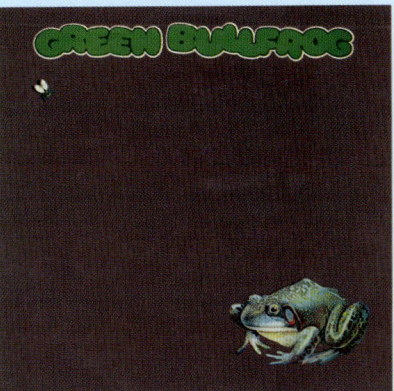 

left : the Jesus Christ Superstar, Green Bullfrog and Lord Sutch albums, all stemming from this period.

"You know what is wonderful is when ... you see somebody standing there with his eyes shining and he says you changed my life. I kinda go yeah, and that's a big responsibility and I think that's one of the great things for anybody that's in any band that's had any kind of impact at all ... because that's what music does to people. It defines a moment in time for them." JL to SC

Three photographs taken on-stage in Kiel, Germany, 1970. One of his photos won a competition prize for the 15 year old photographer Holger Rudel.

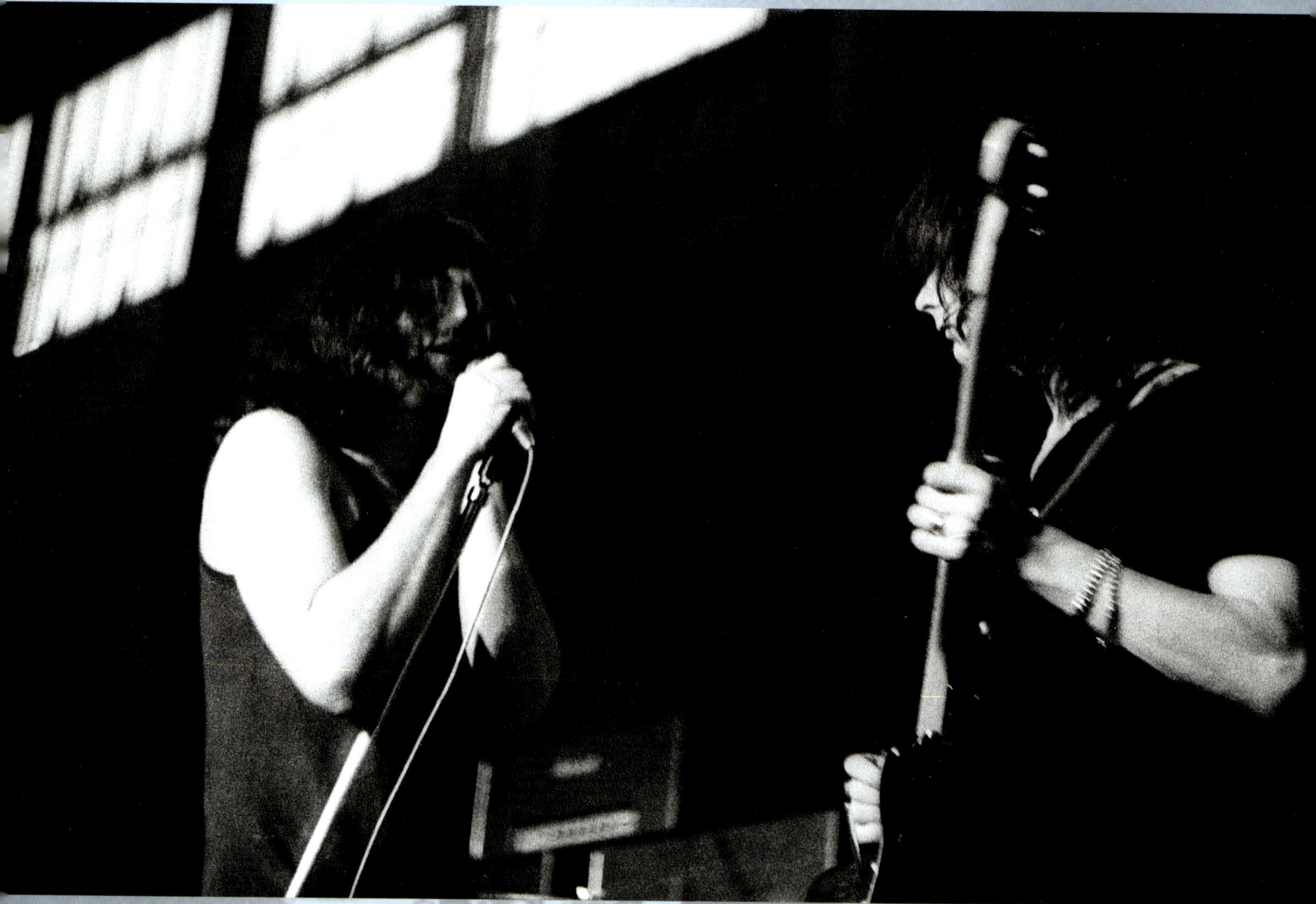

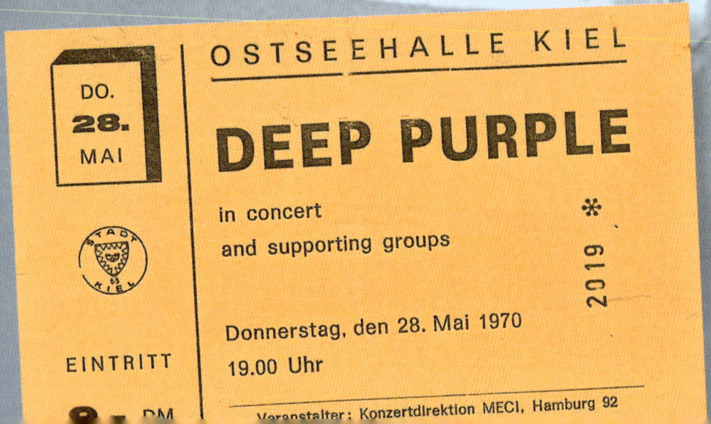
OSTSEEHALLE KIEL
DO.
28.
MAI
DEEP PURPLE
in concert
and supporting groups
2019 *
STADT KIEL
Donnerstag, den 28. Mai 1970
19.00 Uhr
EINTRITT
DM
Veranstalter: Konzertdirektion MECI, Hamburg 92

PURPLE TOUR

Deep Purple begins a tour of Germany today (Friday) which lasts until June 10, then plays Twickenham Eel Pie Island (12), Croydon Fairfield Hall (14), Cambridge Jesus College (16), Manchester John Dalton College (19) and Oxford University College (20).

Gillan to apologise to the audience over the problems and Ian told him to do it himself, which he did! The band even got to appear on the popular Vicky Leandros German TV show, fronted by the former Eurovision singer (albeit probably filmed back in February).

Back in the UK they played the Central Hall, Chatham on the 11th April (supported by Genesis according to the adverts) before recording the final *In Rock* track *Bloodsucker* on the 13th. The recording sessions had been protracted, but the album was finally complete. EMI put it straight into production, and it was mastered on the 20th at Abbey Road (with the studio doing further work on the quarter inch over the next few days, including the preparation of the single b-side on May 15th).

Fans got a preview of the album when the group recorded their fifth BBC session (in Studio 5, Maida Vale) on the 21st April, with just two weeks to go before release. They recorded *Hard Lovin Man*, *Bloodsucker* and *Livin Wreck* (for a second time) for Mike Harding's Sounds Of The Seventies, three new tracks which had not been heard live (and which they seem never to have played live in the 70s). The session survives but only in edited form. It's possible the edits were done when the BBC Transcription department compiled them for sending abroad, the band's sustained attack was perhaps felt to be a little too much for the radio.

Bloodsucker is nearly a minute shorter than on album as the third verse is cut. The whole band sound solid from the outset and the song mirrors the album version but is even more aggressive in tone. *Hard Lovin Man* still sounds stunning despite the loss of a verse and the guitar solo, and is faded out as well. *Livin' Wreck* is also much changed, the song comes straight in on the verse and the second verse is moved to after the solo, with the third verse omitted. Even so all the tracks sounded incredibly raw, full of energy and life. The band certainly did not try and tone down their work for the BBC and tellingly this would be their last regular session for the broadcaster. It is also interesting to ponder what Deep Purple's live show might have sounded like had they brought these titles into their set, possibly at the expense of one of the longer tracks like *Wring That Neck*, but not for the last time they neglected to look to the wider picture.

Incredibly, with a new album on the cusp of release, members of the band also got involved in session projects during April. Ritchie and Ian Paice took some time out for a project initiated by their original Deep Purple producer Derek Lawrence, who still kept in touch. The project was a hard rock blues album, cut over two long sessions at De Lane Lea in April (20th) and May (23rd). The tracks were a mix of old standards, a Derek Lawrence penned slow blues and the Blackmore instrumental *Bullfrog*.

The project came about because Derek Lawrence wanted to put together the ultimate 'house band' to back singer Tony Dangerfield (then Screaming Lord Sutch's bass player). He had produced some Dangerfield tracks while working with producer Joe Meek (with Ritchie on guitar) in the sixties. Lawrence initially brought together Ritchie, Ian Paice and Chas Hodges on bass and they recorded three tracks, *Walk A Mile In My Shoes*, *Who Do You Love* and *Makin' Time*. It didn't quite work with Dangerfield but Lawrence felt musically it was worth persuing, so he drafted in more musicians. *Green Bullfrog* was lauded as a 'guitar' album, but showcased everybody in equal measure and had a great atmosphere. The rapid fire instrumental *Bullfrog* is the highlight of the album with Ritchie, Big Jim Sullivan and Albert Lee trading solos over a recycled Deep Purple riff. Lawrence recalls that Ritchie really pulled out all the stops playing alongside his peers and it does fit right into the *In Rock* era guitar style (and is worth a listen for fans of the period). Work on the album was finished in early January 1971 but hit contractual issues straight away. In the end Lawrence had to resign himself to using nicknames on the sleeve credits, so it disappeared without trace beyond a few Deep Purple fans who heard of it through the musician's monthly Beat Instrumental. News of the session led to some speculation in some music papers that Ritchie was preparing to leave Deep Purple, while so many rumours grew up around *Green Bullfrog* that a dodgy US label reissued it in the 80s, but named people who were not on it. (It was finally reissued properly by Connoisseur records in 1991 with three unissued tracks, *Ain't Nobody Home*, *Louisiana Man* and *Who Do You Love*, though Jim Sullivan had to overdub some new guitar to complete these.)

Ritchie also busked through some rock and roll classics with his former boss Screaming Lord Sutch, which would later surface on a live album, *Hands Of Jack The Ripper*. Even Ian Gillan had cut a session, though his was a little more profitable. Hearing that Andrew Lloyd Webber and Time Rice were planning a rock opera called *Jesus Christ Superstar*, Tony Edwards managed to get Ian a role on the project. Biking round an acetate of *Child In Time*, the writers were impressed and offered Ian Gillan the lead. He sang the role of Jesus on just four tracks (recorded in April), but (at Tony's suggestion) took a small royalty for every album sold rather than a fee. It went on to hit the top of the US charts three times during February and May the following year. He turned down the role in the resulting film to concentrate on Deep Purple.

It was around this time that the band's situation vis-à-vis America

Posters for shows in Germany (March) and UK (April) 1970.

were resolved. Unable to do a separate deal for the four Deep Purple albums, they had to wait and see who would take on the bulk of Tetragrammaton's rather mixed catalogue. Eventually during the first half of 1970 Warner Brothers made an offer, primarily it seems to get their hands on some of the label's property portfolio. When the deal was complete, Deep Purple found themselves with a new American record label and the managers were told to expect some sort of cash payment in lieu of the missing royalties. Tony Edwards recalls that period: *"The assets of Tetragrammaton were purchased by Warners in such a way that they paid an over-ride, as far as Purple were concerned, into the creditors' fund so that a dividend could be made available for sharing out amongst the creditors. In quite a complicated release deal from Tetragrammaton we found ourselves with a new contract with Warner Brothers and we received the sum of $40,000 which I insisted was non-recoupable and went some way towards paying our outstanding royalties, the money we should have got from Tetragrammaton."*

Normally advances such as this are claimed back from royalties due to bands from the sale of records. It's difficult to know whether Warners were actually obliged to cover any royalties from the Tetragrammaton period, but when the offer was made, by negotiating to have it non-recoupable and working closely on the new U.S. record contract with Warner Brothers' President Joe Smith, Edwards made a smart move which helped the bank balance enormously.

Warner's were certainly taking a risk in buying the label. In the end very few

Backstage in Germany, April 1970.

of the acts generated any lasting success apart from Deep Purple. It was largely thanks to their efforts that within a year Warners had recouped their costs and the creditors of Tetragrammaton were paid in full. *"They were very pleasantly surprised"*, says Edwards, *"It was a hard fight. At this stage we didn't detect any enormous enthusiasm on the part of Warner Brothers. They were more concerned with other artists on Tetragrammaton, singer-songwriters who were in vogue at the time. They got Deep Purple almost by default and they didn't know what to do with us once they had us."*

And after acquiring the Deep Purple catalogue and contract, Warners actually did very little with it. Perhaps recognising that the band were now a very different proposition, they left the first three albums alone beyond releasing a double compilation called *Purple Passages* as a way of making some of the old material available again. By not issuing the first three albums in full (and it seems there was still some legal grey area over the rights), Warners ensured that for thirty years poor quality pirate copies were the only source of the Mk 1 albums in America.

May/5th June 1970 • May was hectic. Amongst all the gigs, they had to dash back to the studio to write and record a single in the first week of May 1970, relying on their professionalism to bring something together.

They then returned to the routine of UK one-nighters, including a return booking at the Roundhouse on the 9th and a show at Dunstable Civic Hall with Wishbone Ash as support on the 18th. Ritchie always liked to check out the support bands, and would often sneak out to stand at the back of the venue to catch a few numbers, and get the feel of the crowd. On this occasion, during the sound check Andy Powell , Wishbone's guitarist/singer, was on stage warming up when Ritchie walked on and joined in. He then left the stage without speaking to anyone. However, he had been so impressed with the band that he mentioned them to Derek Lawrence, who got them a deal with MCA and went on to produce them[8] (Ritchie had shown an interest in helping out but couldn't find the time.) Deep Purple's last UK gigs before the release of the album were two shows at the Queen Elizabeth Hall on the 25th May. As if to illustrate their growing status, all the major music papers covered the gig, and all were impressed, with the NME giving them a rave review and, like others before, being amazed by the strobe climax. *"Paice kicked his drums all over the stage and Blackmore physically toppled two six foot speaker columns over the top of his guitar. It took the audience about 30 seconds to recover from their shock before giving Deep Purple a much-deserved standing ovation."*

"Each number achieved a more intense peak of excitement than the previous one. When they started Ring (sic) That Neck you wonderd how far it would all go. Nobody would have been disappointed if they had ended with the instrumental. Both the organist's and the guitarist's solo were outstanding. Both illustrated their skills, their taste, their aggresion and their humour. But it didn't end there. Gillan returned to announce a rude song and invited people to take their clothers off. And two girls did - in the middle of Mandrake Root. It was devatsating, almost wicked, and probably just as well it ended when it did." •
Disc. Roy Shipston.

Melody Maker was a little sniffy, complaining that the *"decibel count is allowed to soar montrously high"* and that the band tended to *"become embroiled in the trend to noise and exhibitionism"*, but seemed to come down on the positive side: *"We had a pre-hear of their new single*

Black Night and they ended with Speed King, both explosively capturing the undeniable excitement of an attacking rock outfit. Lord is a remarkably strong organist whose fusion with the rest of the band is superb. And his timing is especially strong. Blackmore's habit of wiping his guitar strings on the floor and against the amplifier; and Lord's anger as he hurls his seat away and crashed down the organ lid, add to a dynamic, blistering performance. Deep Purple are already riding high in popularity: their new album Deep Purple In Rock should enhance the standing of an invigorating unit." [MM]

A headline in Sounds during that May announced "Deep Purple Taking Over The World."

The final burst of shows before the album came out took place in Germany, now a firm stronghold for the group, which particularly pleased Ritchie who was a big admirer of the place (and had lived there briefly in the late sixties doing sessions and gigging with The Three Musketeers). Starting at the Ostseehalle, Kiel on the 28th May and ending on the 10th June 1970 in Hannover. Cassettes of a couple of these shows give us the set list as *Speed King, Black Night, Child In Time, Wring That Neck, Paint It Black* and *Mandrake Root* (plus encores). The Berlin show on the 29th May is the earliest audio confirmation of Black Night having entered the set and given prominence as the second song in. The band's gear was confiscated after the show in a problem with border guards (forcing postponement of the following concert). The Melody Maker had sent a reporter to cover these shows and was unimpressed by a blasé Berlin crowd. *"Deep Purple ignored the atmosphere and proceeded to tear the crowd apart."* They eventually began to stand up and applaud, only to be silenced again by the climax of the set: "*Lord throwing his Hammond all over the stage and Paice kicking his drums every which way. And Blackmore finally topples his speaker columns over onto his screaming guitar and the band walks off stage. The audience just sits there stunned.*"

The single and album were released while they were away in Europe. From their first gig at the Speakeasy back in July 1969 to the last show before the release of the album in June 1970, Deep Purple had managed well over 100 concerts. To put this in perspective, over the whole period they averaged a gig nearly every 3 days, but towards the end of the period that average rose; between October to December 1969 it was a gig every 2.4 days, while in February and March 1970 it averaged out at a gig every 1.8 to 2 days.

The bulk of these shows had been in Britain, with around two dozen in Europe across eight countries. Noticeably there were no gigs in America prior to the release of the album (a plan for some exploratory shows there in late September 1969 was mentioned in Melody Maker, but came to nothing, possibly scrapped to let them get ready for The Concerto. Another visit in February 1970 was considered but lacked label support.) This intense gigging had helped the band establish a solid fan base right across Europe, and they must have at a conservative estimate reached at least 25,000 people before the release of the album. After the release of the album they would continue to work at the same manic rate for some time.

Shortly before the release of the album, Ian Gillan took the chance to play an advance pressing to his Uncle. The idea backfired a little and his feelings on the possible success of the album were initially dashed: *"I had an acetate and I played it on my radiogram, and my Uncle Ivor was in the room. He ran, screaming, holding his hands over his ears. I felt vaguely let down because I wanted to impress him!"* Thankfully Uncle Ivor's horror was a singular reaction shared by very few people.[9]

1 - Studio paperwork confirms that Dutch TV erased the video, and then taped Black Sabbath over it!

2 - Simon Robinson was chasing down their 1972 In Concert for the band's manager. A memo came back from the BBC to say they also had a show from 1970 'if we were interested'. Amazed that it had survived (many didn't) a double LP set, In Concert, came out on EMI in 1980, one of the very first releases by any band from this BBC show.

3 - Jon Lord returned in 2011 to record the orchestral parts for his definitive version of The Concerto, his final studio work.

4- Bless Liverpool audiences. I remember seeing groups of excited fans steaming out of a Rainbow show in 1977 with rows of seating held aloft, torn from the stalls. It led to a lifetime ban on Ritchie by the venue, who had it must be said done a fair bit of damage to the listed building's ornate plasterwork himself that night. SR.

5 - In recent years Japanese labels in particular have issued many CD bootlegs using audience cassettes of often variable quality, very different to the early vinyl bootlegs scene.

6 - A venue now credited as the band's first ever show in early 1968 (though evidence exists for a hall on the South Coast having that honour).

7 - Later in life Blair was asked if he wasn't PM who would he like to be and answered "Ritchie Blackmore."

8 - Derek also came up with their famous twin guitar sound, when he recorded more guitar without wiping the first take.

9 - I remember a similar reaction, playing the album at home for the first time. As Child In Time ended I was absolutely stunned. My father said he felt it wasn't bad, but spoilt by all that screaming. It was my first experience of the generation gap. SR

the concert chronology continues on page 117

10 • Album Artwork and Release

"I trawled the Fleet Street photographic agencies in search of Mount Rushmore pictures..." Tony Edwards

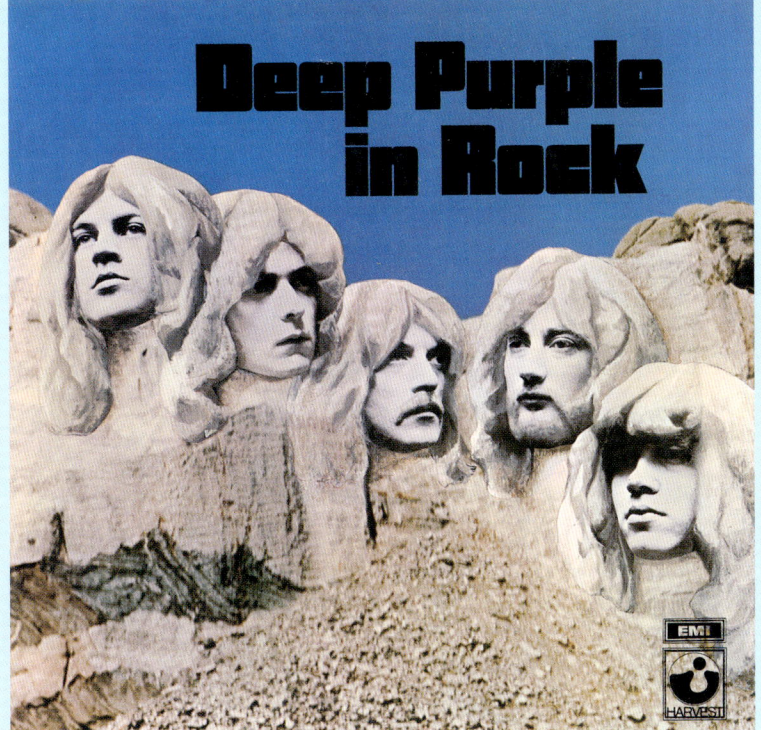

Which brings us to the cover concept and artwork, as well as the actual production and release of the album. *Deep Purple In Rock* was simple and direct as a title, devised (nobody quite remembers by who) to counter their previous album *Deep Purple In Concert*[1]. Once *In Rock* was agreed on, Tony Edwards quickly came up with what Jon later referred to as *"a vexatiuosly smart idea for an album cover."* Tony, who had been involved in a few of the band's previous sleeves, recalled his particular involvement in this one: *"I trawled the Fleet Street photographic agencies in search of Mount Rushmore pictures. It took me some four hours but eventually down the side of Lord Beaverbrook's Express building I sniffed out the four presidents in a dust filled Dickensian cubby-hole of an office presided over by a wing-collared Bob Cratchett. As my eyes met what had become by that time the Holy Grail I nearly caused Bob to jump out of his skin by shouting 'I've got it. I've got it!' And when he learned what for him was a questionable end use to which the transparency was to be put he was far from joining me in my certainty. It took considerable persuasion for him to agree that he was empowered or even wanted to sanction such sacrilege."* • TE to SR 2007[2]

It's easy to forget that sourcing photographs back then was a case of working through the archives of one of the many long standing London picture libraries (or employing a researcher to do so; Tony however was a man who liked to get involved). With the title settled and the Mount Rushmore image found, the London design agency Nesbit, Phipps & Froome were engaged. The agency had a number of designers working for them and Colin Lynch did the artwork[7]. He knew John Coletta from when they both worked at the Central Art Studio (where John was a sales rep). There were only seven weeks from the end of recording to release date so it was a real rush job, although this was often the case in the days before albums had carefully managed production schedules.

An album sized print was made from the Mount Rushmore transparency. Tony's clever idea was that the musicians's heads would replace those of the four American Presidents (L-R; Washington, Jefferson, Roosevelt and Lincoln) carved into Mount Rushmore. The print revealed the limitations of the original, which was quite blurred, but there wasn't time to look for something better.

For their cover images, Deep Purple used a photo shoot done back in early January from which their heads and shoulder images were selected. (Roger appears to have been rephotographed later as he is not sporting the sideburns in the original photos). The heads were printed, cut out and stuck onto the blow-up. Quite how they were greyed to match the background image isn't certain. It was left up to the agency to decide whose head went where.

Once in place, the hair was painted over (using gouache or something similar) and an attempt made to cover over the joins and blend the images together (though even a cursory glance at the LP cover reveals the joins). There were no digital retouching tools available then, but even so it does suggest a rush to get the artwork finished[3].

The title lettering was produced by hand. Unable to find a suitably heavy looking typeface Colin simply decided to invent one. This was not unusual; much album titling was still done by hand as the available type designs then were mostly traditional or old fashioned and designers were keen to come up with something more modern.

With a pale blue background, the resulting sleeve for *In Rock* was certainly a striking and memorable image, and very much of the period. The only surprise was having it repeated on the back. It's unlikely that it was ever going to be a single sleeve as the group's albums on Harvest had all been gatefolds, a trademark feature of the label (giving the releases an air of opulence to justify their higher retail price).

On the front were added the EMI and Harvest logos. On the first pressing run, these have one bold rule box around them; on later editions a thinner outer rule was added to both (see above). The back cover had the local and international catalogue numbers, plus the word 'stereo' (mono releases were fast disappearing at this time - no mono edition of *In Rock* was ever prepared - even though many people still owned mono record players[4]).

1995 Anniversary CD and two early musicassette editions.
Right: G&L's original album sleeve patent application.

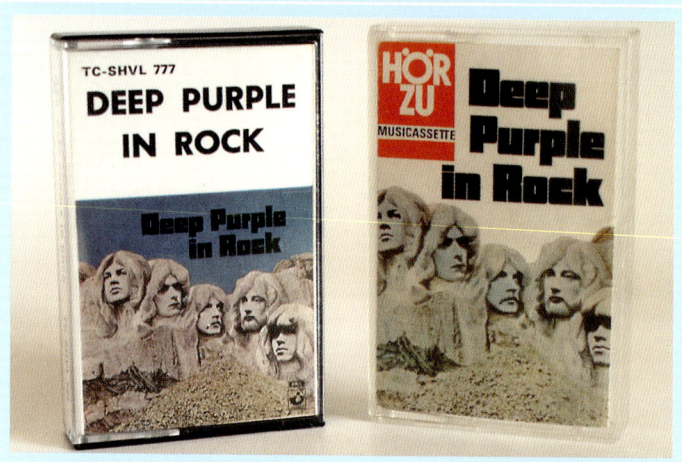

The inside gatefold was largely white text on black with, for the first time on a Deep Purple album, lyrics (which were reasonably correct) and five moody black and white head and shoulder photographs (Ian Gillan said later they had decided they must never smile in photographs) sat beside an extra panel containing details such as the names of the band, songs titles and the studios where they were recorded, along with further production credits. In small print was the helpful 'genre' tag for retailers (file under POPULAR : Pop groups!). There is also the Garrod & Lofthouse factory code 7006 which denotes June 1970 as the first month of printing (in the fifties it was not unusual for sleeve printers to continuously update the code on each reprint, but this useful - for archivists if nothing else - practise had ceased by 1970.)

Using the artwork, a specialist reproduction house prepared the final films from which the printing plates were made. The printers would normally run a few sheets through a 4 colour printing press to provide 'proof' sleeves for approval. The covers were then printed, laminated (outside only) and assembled by Garrod & Lofthouse, one of the two biggest British record sleeve printing companies of the time[5].

The disc was pressed at EMI's massive plant in Hayes, Middlesex, and shipped in a protective (and patented) generic paper polylined record bag showing other Harvest label albums. The regular Roger Dean designed green Harvest label was used. Pressed into the run off grooves (or dead wax as it is known) were the catalogue number Harvest SHVL 777 and matrix numbers SHVL A-2 / B-1 (this seems to indicate that matrix A-1 was rejected before production).

While this was going on, duplicate filmwork and tapes could be sent out to any EMI offices outside the UK releasing the album, leaving them to amend where necessary. The album was issued in over two dozen countries, though not all in 1970 (see discography).

Formats • Vinyl was by far the most popular music format in 1970. *Deep Purple In Rock* would remain available continuously on vinyl for approximately twenty years, only deleted in the early 1990s with the domination of the compact disc. The album has been reissued on a number of vinyl limited editions since (the latest being in the UK in 2012). Over that time a great number of variations (mostly minor) appeared both in the different EMI territories (UK, Europe and many former UK colonies and Commonwealth countries), as well as from other countries. There have even been a few pirate editions.

There were three available tape formats in 1970. The music cassette, launched in 1965, was regarded with derision by most rock fans due to the limited audio quality and poor packaging.

In Rock was also issued as an eight-track cartridge. This format (a quarter inch tape carrying 8 separate pre-recorded audio tracks) had been primarily designed for in-car use but there were decks for the home. The tape played as on a loop, so there was no need to turn it over. To minimise the amount of tape for cost reasons it was common to reorder tracks or even split them in two (so *Hard Lovin' Man* and *Into The Fire* were split on the Warners US cartridge).

The reel to reel format was aimed at the serious hi-fi fan, more popular in America and Japan. *Deep Purple In Rock* was released on this format. Some fans of the format claim because it was on quarter inch tape, it was as close as you could get to the album production master.

Original unique German Hör Zu version of the album

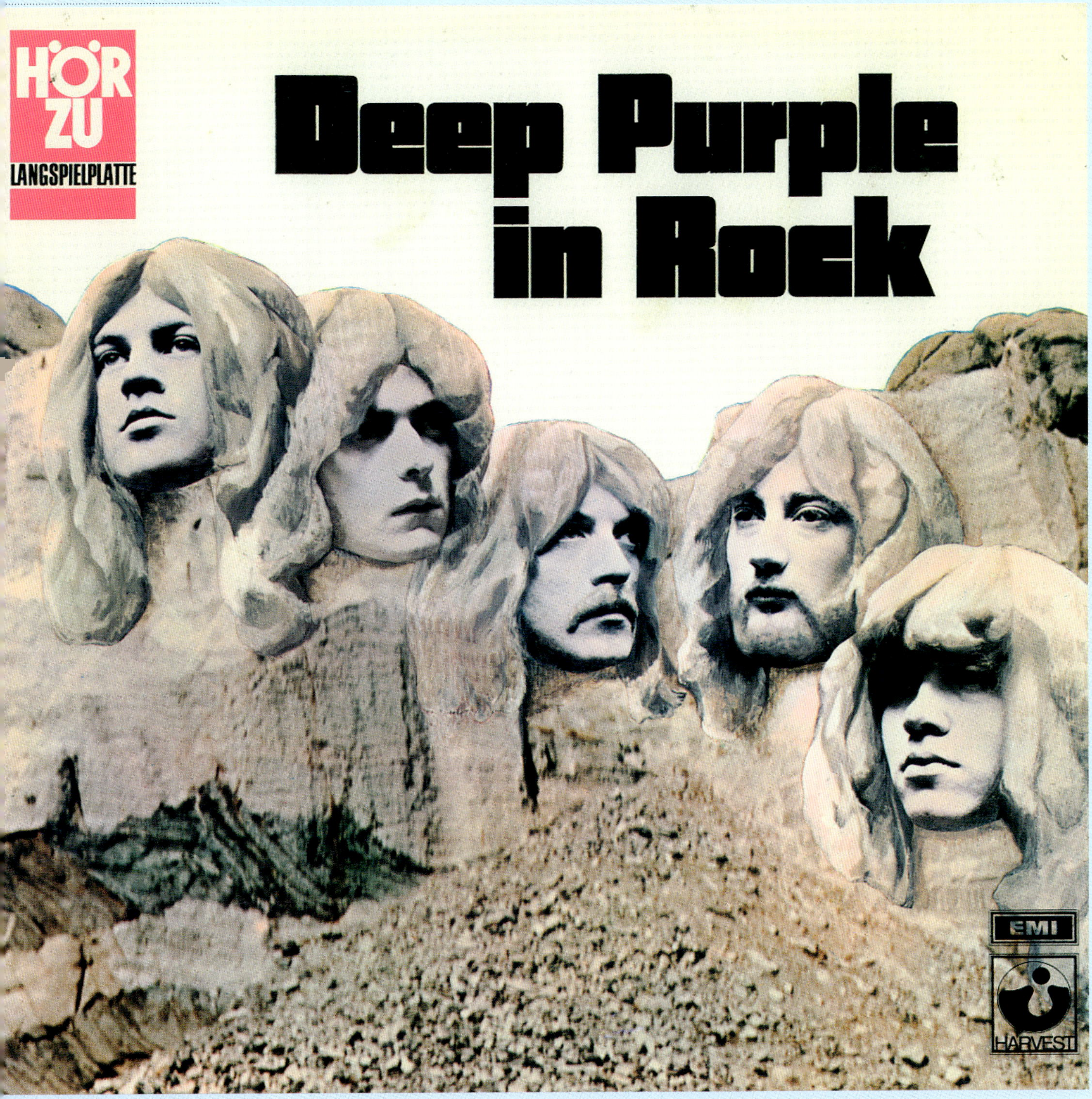

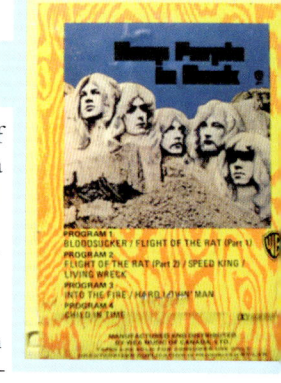

Right, an early Warners Canada 8-Track release. Below, the original 1970 quarter-inch production master tape lid.

Anniversary Edition • The album was first mastered for CD at Abbey Road on May 6th 1986. In June 1995 EMI started a long-running series of remastered Deep Purple titles with *Deep Purple In Rock*, with input from members of the band and manager Tony Edwards, and co-ordinated by Tim Chacksfield and Simon Robinson: *"I'd been a bit of a pest after Deep Purple split, suggesting various idea for archive releases to the managers, some of which were taken up. Many of the early CDs were rushed out and poorly mastered, so when the anniversary of Deep Purple In Rock came around, I put some ideas together for an upgraded CD edition, then worked with the catalogue staff at EMI, primarily Tim Chacksfield, to help co-ordinate this. Digital copies of the 8-track master recordings were sent to Roger Glover in America, and he chose to tackle Flight Of The Rat, Speed King (both as a close match mix and a slightly different mix to bring out one or two new sounds), Cry Free and Black Night (which was left unfaded).*

Remastering of the original album (and a-side) was handled by Peter Mew at Abbey Road, a studio engineer who has been based there since the sixties. Abbey Road remasters of the 'piano' version of Speed King and Jam Stew were also included. We also added six short sections of studio chat between the bonus tracks to give a bit of context. This was quite a pioneering approach to a CD reissue and nobody was sure how well it would sell, and with hindsight we could have gone further, but it was a great sounding release. Although there was commercial pressure on engineers to push volume levels on reissues, Peter Mew managed to resist that."

Simon designed the CD jewel case with the band's signatures overprinted in black[6]. Sadly all this work was rather spoiled when errors on the sound processing hard-disc at the mastering stage caused two jumps in *Living Wreck*, and clipped off the end of *Hard Lovin' Man*, giving EMI a hasty repress and replacement job. A vinyl edition was proposed and sounded out through the EMI sales team. Getting positive feedback EMI did a limited pressing (2,000 copies) as a double album gatefold sleeve (with inner bags) which came out in October 1995 on coloured vinyl. The pressing quickly sold out and this is now a collectable edition. A 12" single (also on colour wax) of *Black Night* with an otherwise unavailable match-mix of *Speed King* was also tied in.

1 - It was actually titled *Concerto For Group & Orchestra* but most listings gave it as *In Concert*.

2 - Tony appended his account by adding: *"I just wonder how much louder I would have yelled and how much more I would have upset him had he and I known then that I would be writing now, some thirty seven years later, about this legend in the making!"*

3 - On the Anniversary CD Simon Robinson spent some time retouching the image to eliminate these paste-up lines.

4 - My only record player at the time was a mono Fidelity machine. SR

5 - G&L were there at the start of the vinyl album in 1952 and took out patents for sleeve manufacture in 1961 and 1963. Although they also handled other work, G&L are estimated to have done around 90% of all EMI's sleeves with E.J.Day & Co. handling the rest. G&L went into liquidation in the mid-nineties.

6 - It looked good, but I hadn't thought through what would happen if the case broke, as my sample copy did! SR

7 - Colin Lynch also worked on the 24 Carat Purple and Burn sleeves through the same agency, though he was never credited. Colin's son Paul remembers his father bringing home a copy of 24 Carat Purple and getting into the band's music himself.

11 • Reviewing The Album

"The whole thing had a very strong purpose, and that was to show that Deep Purple is a rock group." Jon Lord

The sequencing of songs on an album such as this involved weighing up how the tracks worked against one another, the different dynamics, as well as more mundane factors including how much material could fit comfortably on an album side without degrading the audio quality. Certainly on at least one of the later Deep Purple albums the engineer's jottings survive showing him working out how best to equal up the running times of the two sides, which helped at the mastering stage (a chore that became irrelevant once the CD format was the prime music carrier). The songs that made it to the album were recorded in the following order: *Living Wreck, Child In Time, Into The Fire, Hard Lovin' Man, Speed King, Flight Of The Rat* and *Bloodsucker.* It was always important to try and kick off with one of the strongest tracks to draw the listener in, though given that most of the numbers were equally powerful, this can't have been easy. *Speed King* presents the most obvious opener and given its status as such live, may have been ringfenced early on. On rock albums at the time is was also common practise to end sides with the longest tracks, making *Hard Lovin' Man* and *Child In Time's* place in the scheme of things obvious. A more even running time across the sides could have been achieved had they swopped *Bloodsucker* for *Living Wreck*. As this was not done there must have been an artistic decision to arrange side two as it appeared. The final running order was:

1 : Speed King / Blood Sucker / Child In Time (20.13).

2 : Flight Of The Rat / Into The Fire / Living Wreck / Hard Lovin' Man (22.24).

It's difficult to appreciate how fans first reacted to hearing *In Rock*

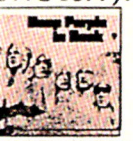

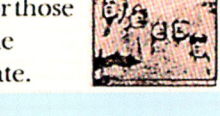

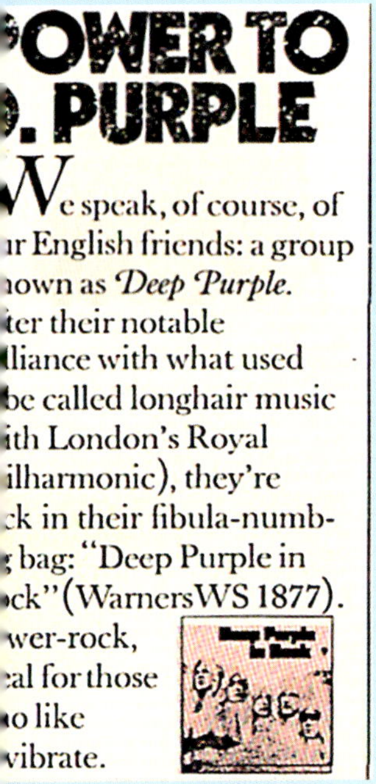
'OWER TO
). PURPLE

We speak, of course, of
ır English friends: a group
ıown as *Deep Purple.*
ter their notable
lliance with what used
be called longhair music
ith London's Royal
ilharmonic), they're
:k in their fibula-numb-
; bag: "Deep Purple in
ock" (Warners WS 1877).
wer-rock,
al for those
ıo like
vibrate.

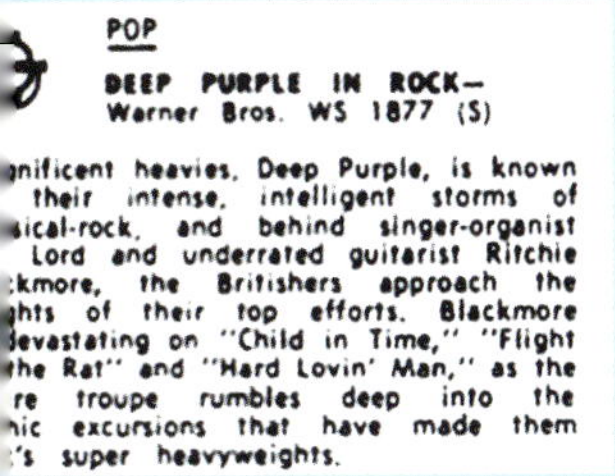
POP

DEEP PURPLE IN ROCK—
Warner Bros. WS 1877 (S)

gnificent heavies, Deep Purple, is known their intense, intelligent storms of sical-rock, and behind singer-organist Lord and underrated guitarist Ritchie :kmore, the Britishers approach the ghts of their top efforts. Blackmore devastating on "Child in Time," "Flight the Rat" and "Hard Lovin' Man," as the re troupe rumbles deep into the nic excursions that have made them :'s super heavyweights.

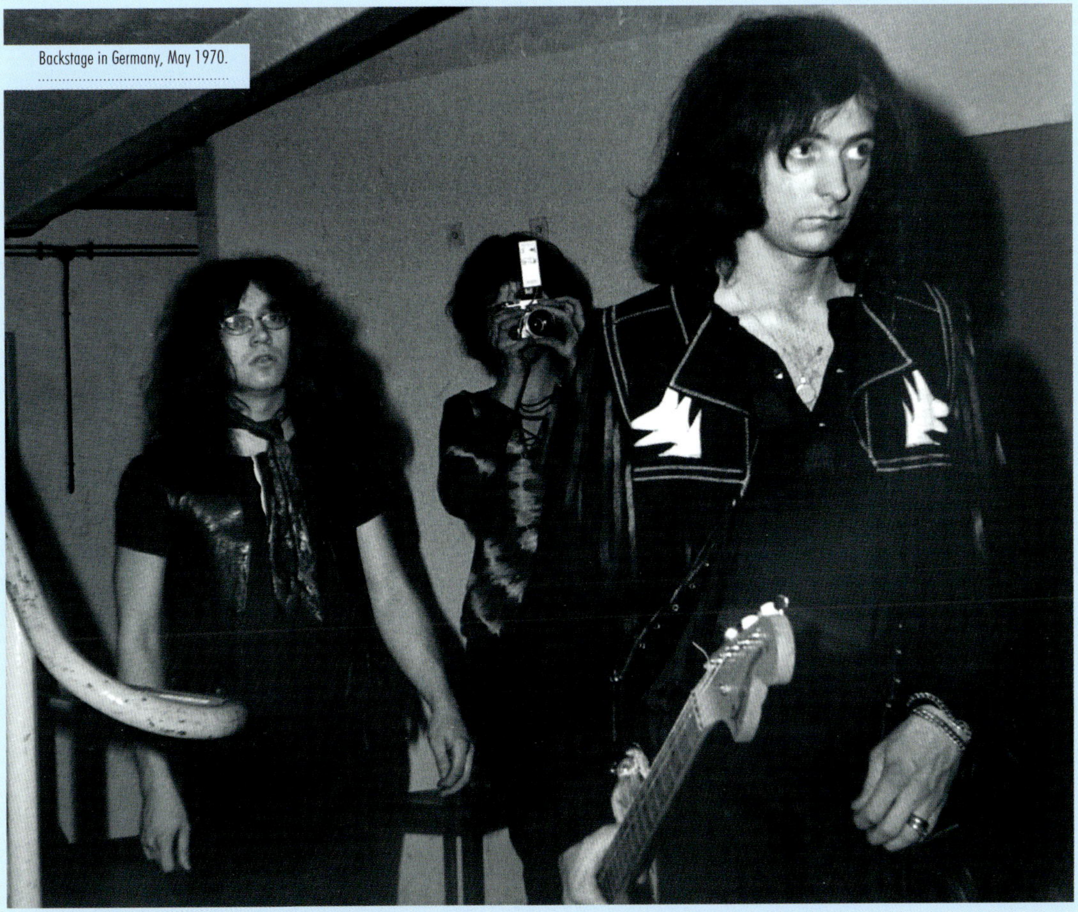
Backstage in Germany, May 1970.

AN EXCITING MONSTER ROCK ALBUM FROM DEEP PURPLE

back in June 1970[1]. Some had been lucky enough to see the band live, others maybe heard them via a BBC session, but the majority of purchases came through word of mouth, peer group recommendation and hearing the single.

However they came to hear the album, listeners were presented with a record which was utterly without compromise, a lasting testament to a band who lived their musical life on a nightly knife edge of technically brilliant but controlled chaos. Arguably with *In Rock* they managed to capture that astonishing experience inside a studio more completely than they were ever to do again.

The band had set out to work single mindedly within the heavy rock genre and succeeded beyond anything they might have imagined. Clearly with hindsight *In Rock* was (and remains) a landmark rock album which ranks amongst the finest examples of the era.

Speed King (just a few roots replanted).

What an album opener. Back in 1970 there were few albums which made such a unique and memorable impact (although Black Sabbath's debut, released in February, came close). The dramatic cacophony jumps out of the speakers at full volume with no warning. Sheer power and extreme volume, Ritchie playing like a man possessed, precise phrases one moment, strangling the life out of the tremelo arm the next. Ian Paice sounds like he is hitting every drum and cymbal he owns (upping him in the mix might have given the opening even more impact). Roger slides up and down the neck building up the tension while Jon gets seemingly impossible noises out of the organ, adding up to one hell of a din, but which still manages to sound controlled, bizarrely melodic and alive.

It all dies down and fades into Jon holding a quiet chord, drifting into what sounds like a piece of church organ music before the track proper comes slamming straight in at full volume. The band hammer the riff home and then for the second half of the verse Jon and Ritchie hold the G chord while Roger injects the tempo. Ian Gillan launches into the lyrics with unbridled passion and conviction and drives the song along just as much as the band, the perfect rock vocal.

Ian Paice, despite still being mixed back a shade too much, avoids the temptation to let adrenalin get the better of him, his fills are tasteful and almost 'set-up' the band for song sections, a real big-band approach (take the two-bar fill at 2.39; it's very simple, but provides a 'set-up' point to bring the band in for the instrumental section that follows).

Jon and Ritchie work the solos so deftly it is almost as if the phrases have been written by one person. Whilst it is a dual, with all the implication of a combative competition, neither party tries to out-do the other. Rather they are working together to produce a solo passage which sounds incredibly unified and just plain right. Jon is effortless in his execution while Ritchie is equally melodic and precise, almost climbing over the end of Jon's phrases but without ever spoiling the overall flow. To bring it to an end, Jon takes a fast rising run out of the soloing and Ritchie double-tracks the well established melody from earlier versions of the track for the end of the solo section.

Many of the lyrics honour classic rock and roll songs of the fifties and sixties, singles all the musicians would have heard growing up as teenagers. The song was a new heavy/progressive rock take on the past and Ian Gillan took rock and roll phrases from his (mis-spent?) youth and threw them together in a new way, as well as delivering them with overwhelming power, feeling and honesty. They were the perfect lyrics for the song's style. He had been rearranging the lines to the song for awhile during concerts before settling on the final order. Trying to pin down exactly where all of the phrases came from is difficult (how many songs mention *New Orleans*?) but some of them are more obvious. *"Good golly miss molly"* and *"the house of blue light"* come from *Good Golly Miss Molly*, while *"Tutti frutti"* and *"to the east... to the west"* are from *Tutti Fruiti*, both tracks recorded by Little Richard.

Richard also supplied *"Lucille"* from the song of the same name, along with the phrase *"when she didn't do her daddy's will"*, Ian Gillan's knowing rework of the line *"won't you do your sisters will"*. Gillan delved into the Richard song *Rip It Up* for the phrase *"Saturday night and I just got paid"* and then rearranged the line *"I'm a fool about money, don't try to save"* into *" gonna fool around ain't gonna save"*.

The lines *"Some people gonna rock, some people gonna roll, Gonna have a party to save my soul"* are inspired by the Elvis song *Party*; *"Some people like to rock some people like to roll, but movin' and a grooving gonna satisfy my soul"*.

Elvis also recorded the Claude Demrtrius song *Hard Headed Woman*, which gave Ian Gillan *"hard headed woman, soft hearted man"*. He rearranged the line *"been the cause of trouble ever since the world began"* to *"they been causing trouble since it all began."*

So whilst the inspiration for the lyrics did draw heavily from a number of earlier classics, the end result was something else altogether. And we shouldn't forget that Ian Gillan was a massive fan of Elvis, Little Richard and others of that era, and covered their material with his early bands such as The Javelins (even going so far as to get the group back together many years later to cut new versions of them.) One thing the song was not about is drugs, as Jon Lord was keen to point out: *"Speed King was not a song about Speed, about drugs, but*

970s the NME front cover was often a paid advert.

New orchestral-rock epic from Purple

a song about playing fast. Just go through the lyrics, 'Good Golly, Miss Molly... Tutti Frutti...' a text we didn't have to write ourselves, because it existed almost entirely of quotes from old rock'n'roll songs. It certainly wasn't about drugs, it was just 'How fast can Gillan sing?!' Speed King is speed metal, no question about it." • JL to Modern Keyboard, Jan 1989

Disagree? Check out the blistering version on the Knebworth reunion show in 1985. Some have even floated the idea that *Speed King* verges on having invented thrash metal. Discuss.

As we've seen, *Speed King* was also the first *In Rock* single release in February 1970 in Holland and Germany (Led Zeppelin's *Whole Lotta Love* was number 1 in Germany that same month.) It's tempting to think that the track might actually have done quite well if they'd saved it until after *Black Night*. Instead it was chosen as the B side to that single just about everywhere else.

A TV performance of *Speed King* was done for the Vicky Leandros Show in early April 1970. It was a time when TV producers were determined to make an imact and 'interpret' rock and pop music, coupled with having a lot of new video effects to play with. But even so, the sight of the band amidst piles of rubbish and 'dead' bodies, with an overlaid blue screen background of irrelevant images remains quite bizarre. Ritchie played a white strat with white scratch plate and not his usual black and white model of the time.

As we know the song opened Deep Purple's set at least as far back as 24th August 1969. It would remain the set opener for nearly two years and was still there on 5th July 1971 at the Stadhalle in Speyer, Germany before being replaced by *Highway Star*. It wasn't dropped, just relegated to an encore number (though they did choose to open their US shows in early 1972 with it.)

Over the months on stage the solo section became longer, Ritchie and Jon would solo for anywhere around a minute each before they eventually dropped into the 'dual' type exchanges. Ritchie would sometimes do a call and response section with Ian Gillan before going in to the ending of the solo.

Bloodsucker (a particularly nasty sort of fellow, there are lots of us).

A track which lacks both a chorus and doesn't use the title in the lyrics. Ian Gillan does a great job of making it all flow easily and getting more words into each line than would seem possible. Ian Paice recalls the song: *"That was not so typical of us. I think it was one which showed the way to a lot of other bands of a really hard nasty sort of playing. A little gem."*

Not just nasty, but also a heavy, dark guitar/bass piece which doesn't revolve around a riff as such, but instead relies on a concise and super tight solid rhythm to give the song its character. Rather than playing a straight half-time 2 and 4 back-beat (perhaps the obvious choice), Ian Paice decides to mirror the guitar line with a syncopated funk-feel.

The first verse is backed by an almost hypnotic rhythm with alternatively a short chromatic scale, harmonised by the organ, or a short phrase that rises then descends the scale to the end of each vocal line. Each verse climaxes with a stuttering drum fill and an ear splitting "Oh, no, no, no..." from Ian Gillan.

The bridge into the second verse is an almost jazzy phrase, again dominated by the guitar and bass. There is a short drum fill which brings everyone to a pause, the organ fills the void with five mean chords, Ian Paice drops in a few tom hits for good measure, then the band come crashing back into the second verse.

Ritchie is first up on the solos and plays a precisely phrased, lyrically fluid break. Jon matches him, before Ritchie is off again, making use of the termelo in a controlled way. There are no particularly fast, flashy runs or manic playing here by either musician; instead they aim to control the flow of the notes in keeping with the song's style and tempo, and pull this off absolutely perfectly.

By the end the lyrics are incomprehensible, Ian Gillan's vocals are layered and put through an echo effect. The effect of this strange blurring and stuttering of the words gives a unique sound as the song fades out, challenged by Jon who pushes up in the mix and joins in.

This song was seemingly never played live, though a BBC version gives us an idea of how good it could have sounded. Strange then that the track resurfaced as *Bludsucker* on the band's 1998 album *Abandon*. Ian Gillan explained how this happened: *"As I recall we didn't choose the song, it chose us. There we were jamming in the studio and it got taped. I think it was Bruce Payne our manager who said it sounded as good today as it did when it was originally recorded, so it kind of sneaked on to the record, with an attitude!"* • IG website

Child in Time (the story of a loser – it could be you)

Whilst it had already become a majestic song live, in the cold environment of a studio *Child In Time* could quite easily have lacked life. Not a bit of it. They produced perhaps the most enduring track on the album, five individual performances of enormous skill which combine to create a masterpiece.

Organ - Jon's opening sound helps set the tone, a clever contrast to everything else on the album. Once Ian Gillan gets into his stride, the organ revolves around the basic chords, harmonising with them and then raising an octave for the second half of the verse. By moving

Although the idea of chopping long rock numbers in half seems anathema today, back in the 1970's it was not unusual. The Knife by Genesis, Oh Well by Fleetwood Mac and as here Child In Time are examples. Child In Time was only issued like this in a few territories and most of the editions shown here are from Holland. The single was a top ten hit there in 1972 (the colour changes came about when the single was repressed.) It was then reissued to mark the occasion of the song topping the top 100 hits of all time and again went to number 10. By the last couple of Dutch 7" editions, they'd given up trying to get a photograph of the right line-up onto the cover. The final row shows two sleeves from Belgium and (the rarest) Denmark.

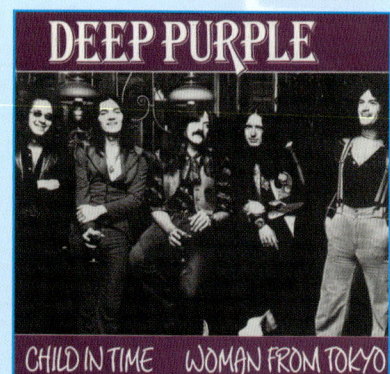

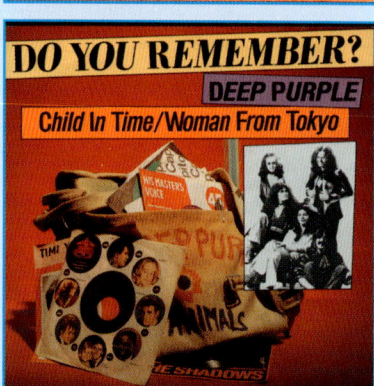

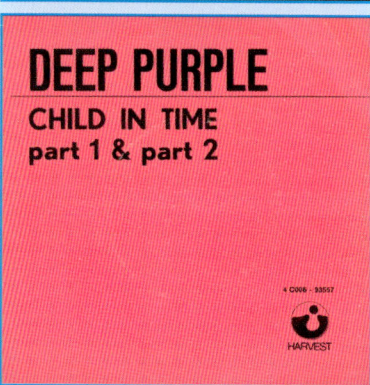

RITCHIE BLACKMORE: 'use your little finger.'

around the chord structure it is the organ which builds up the tension during the abstract vocal section, and also a military grandeur to the bolero chord sequence leading into Ritchie's solo, before slipping quietly into the background to provides colour to the backing.

Rather than repeat the first opening for the second half of the track, Jon instead improvises around the original melody lines and extends them beautifully. He is also more upfront behind Ian Gillan's extemporisations than the first time around, heightening the tension still further, before dropping dramatically down into the E minor mayhem which marks the runout of the song, taking the lead melody line and drawing the whole band into the chromatic build-up to the songs climax.

Vocals - The lyrics and vocal delivery are heartfelt, sung with total commitment and passion. The tape boxes indicate double tracking but if so it sounds like a single track. Ian's work on this track (and the whole album) is very individual, not something that can be said about every rock singer. The oohs and aahs are one of the defining moments of this or any other Purple song. And while any other vocalist might have used the odd scream here and there, Ian Gillan turned it into an art through the octave rising three note phrase delivered after each verse.

Some wondered how he did it. Each week the music paper Melody Maker ran a question and answer column where readers could enquire and the paper contacted musicians for answers. Melanie on the Isle of Wight wrote in about the track: *"How does Ian Gillan produce the very effective screaming effect in Child in Time from the LP Deep Purple in Rock?"*

"Thanks for the compliment (came the reply) *but I haven't the faintest idea how I manage it. Although lots of people regard it as incredible and ask me how it is done. It's simply a vocal effect and I do it every night on stage, considerably endangering my health. I've never had any special training but I think that it helps that I wear tight trousers!"*

In more recent years Ian has offered a perhaps more reasoned explanation of his scream: *"Prior to joining Deep Purple, Roger Glover and myself were in a group called Episode Six, which was a kind of harmony rock band. Quite often, when not singing lead vocals, and with six voices to arrange, I would take the highest harmony, which involved everything from a conventional falsetto voice to what has become known as screaming."*

"Basically I just explored my range and got as high as I could with everything under control. The word screaming implies an uncontrolled yell, but I saw it as a way of broadening the scope of the harmonies. It had to be in tune or it wouldn't work."

"So, when I got into Purple it seemed quite natural to employ this technique for the melody. When I got to the top of my natural range I just slipped into another gear as seamlessly as possible and took it up there. I don't think I invented it; it was just one of those things."

Despite their later differences, Ritchie praised Ian's vocals on this track a few years ago: *"Child In Time is a great song. Ian Gillan was probably the only guy who could sing that. It was done in three stages, sort of like an operatic thing. That's him at his best. Nobody else would have attempted that, going up in octaves."* • RB to Guitar World, December 1996.

We mustn't forget the lyrics either, which are almost universal and can be applied to many of the world events in the subsequent decades. As Ian put it recently: *"Child in Time is not a song against war, it is about stupidity. One is inevitable, the other is not. A missing comma from the title gives a false impression and - as happens so often - rhyme defeats reason."* The missing comma referring to the opening lines: *"Sweet child, in time you'll see the line."*

Guitar - Ritchie, using the Gibson, opts to quietly underpin Jon for the opening, playing the three chord backing and maintaining this simplicity through the vocal verse, rightly leaving the organ to weave around the backing. He gradually begins to make his mark, pounding into the bolero section before exploding into the lead-in melody that runs into the main solo.

The solo itself isn't overlong, 1.45 minutes or so, but he pulls together all the best ideas and memorable phrases he had been trying out live into a structured order to build a classic tour de force. The solo is executed with expert technique, linked together with fluid melodic runs, a perfect structure and pace which leaves you breathless at it's end. Considering the huge progressions in guitar technique that have been made over the years, the solo still delivers a massive impact. Back in 1970 it must have been a jaw dropping listening experience, pretty much in a league of its own. It's a struggle to find anything comparable from any of the big players of the time.

DOES Ritchie Blackmore use plectrum or fingerstyle on his electric guitar runs? Did he hammer the notes in the fast guitar and organ passage in "Child In Time," because it sounds as if each note is plucked individually, which I have found difficult. — Kevin Oliver, Catford.

I use plectrum on my runs. Some notes were hammered and some played straight on "Child In Time." It depends where you mean. A lot of guitarists tend to play just down strokes but you should learn from the beginning to use the up stroke as well. That makes it much easier. In the time it has taken for the hand to come up and do another down stroke you could have done an upstroke of the same note or another note of the run to make it faster. It sounds long-winded, but it's quite simple, really. Also, if you want to play faster, you can use your little finger as well. Hammering the notes is very important when playing fast. A hammer note is a note which is plucked by the right hand, but two notes are obtained by the plucking of the first note and the hammering by the left hand of the second note. — RITCHIE BLACKMORE.

advert from September 1970 which appeared in the South Bank Pops souvenir programme.

In September 1976, Guitar Player magazine were still citing it as one which had to be listened to: *"The solo in Child In Time is exhausting: a tempo that fast gives you no time to pace yourself. You've got to deliver and he does. He sacrifices harmonic intricacy for the sake of sustaining the mad energy. Purple produces, but to keep your wits about you in that situation and pull off a solo that makes sense takes an expert."*

Ritchie spoke about the arpeggio phrasing twenty years later: *"Sometimes on stage I would play it much faster than the record. I'd like it real fast and Paicey would like it really fast. Only problem was, coming into that part at the end of the guitar solo that the band would do in unison. You can only play that so fast, unless you start tapping which I don't do, out of principle. It's just an A minor arpeggio but it's all downstrokes. You try and play that really fast after you've had ten scotches! That's hard to do."* • RB to Guitar World, December 1996.

Ritchie has called his solo *"relatively average"* in the past, but many would disagree. In a poll on the Deep Purple Appreciation Society website to find Ritchie's best guitar solo, *Child In Time* from the studio album was a very clear winner, polling more votes than second (*Highway Star – Made In Japan*) and third place (*Highway Star – Machine Head*) combined.

Drums - After gently tapping out a loose improvisation on the cymbals, Ian Paice quietly slots in the bass drum to accent the chords towards the end of the intro. For the verse he brings in the hi hat to accent a subtle, almost hidden beat, before adding the snare for the high pitched vocal section. Paice's fills in the song are crisp single-strokes with a few ruffs (a drum rudiment) thrown in for good measure, almost Mitch Mitchell style. The 'Bolero' section at 3:20 leaves little room to manoeuvre other than to mirror the theme on his snare drum, before setting up the guitar solo section with a tightly squeezed 32nd note single-stroke roll. Look out for the nice shuffle from 4:00 onwards displaying Paice's natural feel for Blues based music.

As with *Speed King* the drums are perhaps a little too low in the mix for some tastes; it would be interesting to hear this adjusted and how it might add to the power of the recording.

Bass - It is easy to overlook the contribution of the bass in the track. Roger plays exactly what the song needs to give it a rock solid anchor, without trying to fill in the natural gaps in the song or being over busy. He plays the G G A, G G A, F F G in the first verse high up the neck around the twelfth fret area, then drops down a couple of octaves for Ian Gillan's three note vocals to give the song some real bottom end. As this section progresses, he builds up the volume by strumming the notes as simple three note bass chords. He allows himself some freedom to improvise on Ritchie's lead into the guitar solo before settling down to a solid tempo backing. This had to be kept a little bit safe to give Ritchie the flexibility he needed when overdubbing the solo.

He remains prominent throughout the remainder of the song and plays a strong supporting role in the chromatic end. He finishes off the song with an understated short violin style notation at the end.

Not an obvious choice for a single, clocking in at just over 10 minutes long, Harvest released the track in Belgium and several times in Holland, with one verse to each side (se discography.)

Child In Time was generally the third song in the set through the mid 70's, around the time of the album's release, before pushing back a place during April 1971.

On stage whilst the song would later become famous as a guitar solo vehicle (largely because of the version on *Made In Japan*), almost from the outset Ritchie gave way to a keyboard solo in the middle of his own, pushing the song to nearly 20 minutes on some occasions. This remained the case until early 1972. Jon added jazz influences and classical overtones, then he and Ritchie would trade a phrase before the guitarist would come powering back in. The song's structure would be developed to improve the dynamics within, producing a much more powerful performance over time.

After Who Do We Think We Are came out, Child In Time was replaced by Mary Long from that album at the start of January 1973, but reappeared for Mk 2's final shows in Japan. After Ian Gillan left, the band dropped the track altogether. When they reformed with Ian in 1984 it was revived from time to time, with the singer taking the decision on whether he was up to tackling it or not. In later years Jon would provide discreet keyboard backing for the screams, and possibly even vocal samples. Eventually Gillan dropped it, mainly to save his voice but also because there was a feeling in some quarters that the song belonged to a bygone era and didn't mean the same to newer audiences.

Flight Of The Rat (just to remind you there are other ways of turning on)

The most complex lyrical and musical arrangement on the LP, *Flight Of The Rat* blasts open side two of the album, the searing power chords (Ax4, G and D) of the guitar aggressively pounding out the simple riff a couple of times. It's an up-tempo song featuring some blistering triplet fills around the drum kit (and another drum sound that suffers from limiting recording techniques, though still retaining just enough clarity to convey the fire of Ian Paice's performance).

Ian Gillan stretches out some of the vocal phrasing to meld them into the song's key changes, along with some neat double tracking which fits in nicely with the backing. At the end of the first verse, the song drops down to provide a bridge/chorus. The band then hold a chord and the guitar plays a repeated flurry of notes building up the scale to provide a link into the second verse. This follows the same pattern before shifting up a key to B for a few vocal lines. We then have a different link of five chords with a two note pull-up by the guitar over it, before the band drop back to the main key again for the third verse. After this the song shifts up again to B and the keyboard solo comes roaring in, an exercise in deftly thrashing around the keys with repeated and evolving rocking phrases, key drags, a long run down the keys and wild/wailing noises. It is very reminiscent of the heavy solos Jon was playing live. The band play a repeated descending chromatic chord sequence over which Jon provides a strong melody to end his solo spot. A short rising chord sequence then brings us to the guitar solo in E.

Ritchie starts with a simple repeated rhythmic phrase, making effective use of the tremelo before rising up the scale a bit and then reverting back to the earlier phrase. Given the song's tempo, both Ritchie and John could have gone for ultra fast runs; instead the solos are improvised in sync with the song, very difficult given this would have been developed during takes in the studio. A rising note pull-up phrase then brings the song straight into a rhythm section where the guitar plays a dampened double tracked rhythm with straight and wah wah guitar alternating over the funky drum backing.

Ian Paice plays a great mix of Big-Band style fills leading into a tight little funk jam, Jon playing his own version of the rhythm section using the organ in sync with the drums. This rhythmic work had appeared in the live versions of Mandrake Root for a while.

Ian then really jumps on the gas with one of his trademark 32nd note single-stroke snare drum rolls and we are back into the song. It seems to be coming to an end with a plaintiff plea by Ian Gillan to *"Please stay away"*. Instead as Ian's voice dies away the drums start a building beat across the toms, dropping the snare and bass drum in

American trade advert for the album and single, with the Warners promotional pressing of Black Night inset.

The French went their own way on the single cover with a Victorian engraving and psychedelic lettering.

almost at random until a solid, almost double bass drum type wall of sound emerges (an idea developed on stage in *Paint It Black*), which quickens to a pounding peak after nearly 40 seconds. Ian Paice achieved this by building up a hand-foot triplet ostinato, climaxing into the classic, fast snare drum\tom\bass drum riff. It may seem clichéd by today's standards, but back then it had a beauty and innocence that had yet to be bettered. Two final resounding chords by the band, a cymbal splash, and it's all over.

Ian Gillan commented on the idea behind the lyrics: *"This was during my transition from Jack the Lad to whatever it was that I became next on the journey to where I am now. Deep Purple effected a big change in my life and so I had to think about how to deal with it. I had started meditating a year or so before and was just getting the hang of it. Fairly primitive and uneducated stuff to start with but there was a glimmer of hope as I took a little control over my ways; having been fairly sure that I knew it all up to then - ah, the folly of youth. On reflection, most (of my) early songs have an endearing naivety about them and this attempt to expunge my dark side was quite uplifting."*

The track never became part of the live set, which Roger says was down to the drummer: *"Flight Of The Rat, I would love to do that. Paicey hates it. Doesn't hate the song, he just hates the rhythm. We tried it once several years ago, 'Nah, I don't want to do that'."*

Uniquely the track was issued as a single in New Zealand in early 1971 (see previous page, with a Mk 1 track *And The Address* on the flip.) It wasn't a hit.

Into The Fire (out of the frying pan).

Easy to overlook, with the slowest tempo on the LP (*Child In Time* aside) and a straight forward composition, *Into The Fire* packs a huge punch and became one of only three tracks off the album that Deep Purple would regularly play live.

The whole band come straight in on the beat. The riff is simple and the song quickly settles into a thumping, mainly guitar and bass driven backing for the vocals. It has that classic relaxed 70's groove with a big, fat half-open hi-hat sound. Ian Paice follows the riffs and structure closely, accenting passages in unison with the rest of the band (rather than playing free-form over the top of it, a mistake that many less disciplined players of the time would have made), staying tight and funky and keeping the vibe chugging along nicely.

The lyrics give a second clear anti drugs message. *"What a strange and innocent, but incredibly powerful anti-drug song. We all grew up in a drinking (alcohol) environment."* • IG website.

The vocals are delivered with real feeling and conviction and whilst they are double tracked this is kept quite low key in the mix and serves only to reinforce the vocal line without any real harmonisation. The solo is taken by the guitar and playing over the same backing used for the verse. Again the playing is not flash; it is put through an echo/reverb effect and is quite precise, measured and almost lyrically haunting in nature and mirrors the verse in its length (this is the only song on the album that has a guitar solo but no organ solo).

On stage the song structure stayed close to the original format and stayed in the set until the very end of 1970 before it was replaced by *Strange Kind Of Woman* in the new year (only to resurface briefly in May 1971.) The track was used as a B side in the USA and Japan.

Living Wreck (it takes all sorts-support your local groupie).

For a song that came close to being discarded, *Living Wreck* fits very well into the overall album. It slowly fades up with a solid drum beat from the end of *Into The Fire*, a clever touch given the songs were recorded a month apart. There is a sharp break filled with the organ providing something similar to a vocal 'scream' and the whole band come in with the riff which has a stop and start motif. The vocals to the verse is not backed by the riff; instead the band provides a rock steady backing with the guitar prominently strumming a dampened chord and Jon providing highlighting.

It is also another fine example of Ian Paice's funky, syncopated style captured on tape with a crystal clear drum sound. There is some great syncopated bass drum work on show, comparable to John Bonham's style, and the middle-eight is a treat with Paice dropping some great 'linear-funk' hand-foot patterns (before the term was even invented!) Look out for another super-quick single-stroke roll at 3:18 in the last verse, lifted from the Buddy Rich school of drumming.

The vocals tell a sad story of someone whose best days in life appear to have slipped (unrealised) behind them. Ian is not particularly stretched by the melody and he sings it effortlessly.

Hit Talk
by OZ OSBOURNE of Black Sabbath

Aretha Franklin is the greatest; she has such a beautiful voice. A very nice record.

The **Deep Purple** record is really good. It's about time groups like this had a look in the chart. Up to now it's been all Tamla and bubblegum that's made the chart.

I like **Family's** record; they're a good band. Not their best but still all right.

Tremeloes record is really great. It's almost like a poor man's Beatles track but I like it a lot.

Richard Green

DEEP PURPLE IN ROCK (Harvest)

THE album that put Deep Purple back on the right tracks after their brief flirtation with the classics.

All the guts and force of the group come to the boil and erupt in an ear-splitting frenzy. But quality is not sacrificed for volume and, as usual, the music is of a high standard — Richie Blackmore excelling on lead guitar.

Ian Gillan's voice control deserves praise, especially on "Child In Time" with its amazing crescendos and partly on the strength of that track he was chosen for the "Jesus Christ Superstar" album. Good, meaty rock all the way.

AN EXCITING MONSTER ROCK ALBUM FROM DEEP PURPLE

"DEEP PURPLE IN ROCK." Rock being the operative word. Ritchie Blackmore's gutsy guitar tears its way through the album, dominating it, and Jon Lord keeps very much to the role of backing musician. When he does contribute his delicate and thoughtful pieces, he uplifts what is generally a very fine sound.

Their wild "Speed King" is a conglomeration of early rock-n-roll lyrics strung together, and is in line with other groups looking back to their roots. At times the album is "Nice-ish" but on the whole a monster album and very exciting (Harvest). ★★★★

Except for Richard Green's review in NME's round up of the previous year's best albums (published in early 1971), these are all contemporary reviews from the British music press. Steve Peacock's piece appeared in ZigZag. Two reviews of the single Black Night are also shown, including one from Ozzie Osbourne in Hit Talk, a weekly feature where a musician was asked to listen and comment on the week's new releases (the other is from Disc & Music Echo). In the early 1970s album reviews, which might just have been a few lines in the previous decade, began to get longer as the format became taken more seriously. By the end of the seventies, buoyed up by much more advertising, the papers increased their page count dramatically and could devote even more space to new releases. Meanwhile, a photograph of Ian Gillan on the front of Melody Maker that year inspired this vending machine art!

Deep Purple in Rock.... SHVL 777

On the whole, Jon's attempt to mix the group and an orchestra in his Concerto worked pretty well; it was certainly an enjoyable evening and I like listening to the LP when I am in the right mood. The new album "Deep Purple in Rock" is really very good indeed.

This time they have really "got it together, man". They set out to produce a pure rock album, and they certainly succeeded – it is loud, aggressive, thumping, joyous music that takes you along with it. Really exhilarating. Even in the gentler moments, like on "Child in Time", there is a tremendous sense of latent power, as if they are about to explode again any minute. This album is bursting at the seams with ideas but, in contrast to the earlier stuff, it is all worked into context subtly and naturally so that it doesn't sound contrived or "look-at-us-we-can-play-lots-of-different-things". Some people tend to compare them to the dread Zeppelin, but that isn't really fair. I can't honestly find much beneath the knicker-wetting, lemon-squeezing, and plastic climaxes of the Plant/Page cockrock combo, and though part of Deep Purple's more obvious appeal lies in their musical sex-drive, there is a lot more to them than that. Everyone is contributing so much to the music that beneath the excitement there are a lot of interesting things happening. Technically and emotionally, "Deep Purple in Rock" is one of the most exciting, articulate, and enjoyable rock albums I've heard, certainly by a British group.

Steve Peacock

DEEP PURPLE: "Deep Purple In Rock." (Harvest). A stunningly good album from a group that proves several things on it: 1. That rock, given a fresh stab and alert material, is still one of the most rewarding areas of contemporary music. 2. That it need not all be frenzy, but can also reach out and project a message when it's cool and wistful. 3. That Ritchie Blackmore is not merely a fast guitarist, but one with immense style and presence. The recording quality here is so good that, perhaps for the first time, the textures of some fine instrumentalists, and let's not forget a powerful singer, are given the correct emphasis. On " Child In Time," Ian Gillan's blistering vocal, moralising in too-general terms about the State Of Things, is matched only in style by Blackmore's masterly guitar work which is completely in context. His sympathy with the mood of each work throughout this album is quite remarkable. Jon Lord's exciting work at the organ is another strength and as a unit they are perfectly integrated. A magnificent album, which no enthusiast of today's music dare miss. — R.C.

DEEP PURPLE: "In Rock" (Harvest SHVL 777).

Yerse... very 'eavy, just in case you thought the DP5 lads had taken a trip back to the boppin' fifties when Waxie Maxie was a groupie(!). Certainly they take a few well-tried lines from a few of those old twelve bar things on "Speed King", but they never came out like this before. Some nice things emit from Ritchie Blackmore on guitar and Jon Lord on organ but the overall product seems to be over-fussy and *too* heavy. Subtlety can be far more exciting.

Deep Purple's "Black Night" sounds very familiar. Vocals slide around with a backing which chugs along. Deep Purple fans will love it (Harvest).

DEEP PURPLE: Black Night (Harvest). One of those complex, deep-thinking progressive groups who necessarily take a little time to get their musical message across — which is why Purple has fared so well with albums.
 To condense all they have to offer into three minutes is asking a lot. But the boys have well nigh succeeded with this heavy rocker.
 Based on a simple yet penetrating riff, it's outstanding for some mind-blowing lead guitar breaks. And the hand-clapping beat injects a touch of commerciality.

The guitar solo appears at first to be Ritchie's only slide offering on the album and it has a slight echo to it which underlines the melancholic lyric. In fact Ritchie plays it with his fingers. Rather than slide overtly between notes and merge them together in an exaggerated slide style, Ritchie plays the notes he wants precisely, and can move quickly between notes, fretting the notes with his fingers. The playing impressed Roger enormously: *"One of my favourite Ritchie solos; he had an octave box and was experimenting with it, seeing how long he could sustain notes. The solo is one long, barely controlled note, elegant in its simplicity and tense with the fact that it seems on the verge of disintegrating at any moment, but he holds on to it beautifully."*

The octave box was an Arbiter Add-A-Sound unit. The organ plays a more up tempo rock solo for the 48 second run out and fade of the song, with Ian Paice throwing in evolving and ever more complex fills into the fade. It is only Ritchie who, unusually, keeps the songs riff going without adlibbing it.

Hard Lovin' Man (for Martin Birch – catalyst).

Just when you thought you had heard it all on the album, (the aggressiveness of *Speed King*, the majesty of *Child In Time* and the complexity of *Flight Of The Rat*), here to close it out comes the heaviest song on the album, one which took no prisoners. It still remains a stand-out for Roger: *"A monster groove. I loved it. This is my favourite track from the album, there is so much fire in the playing, and Jon's solo is so close to his performances on stage. The song embodies the real character of the band at that time; driving power, oddball writing, experimentation, two great solos, cocksure lyrics, exuberant attitude. I can sense a band that had found itself."*

The opening just leaves you guessing; a short drum fill in to a held chord, then another drum fill into a lower chord with the symbols crashing away and Ritchie pick scraping slowly along the strings. The sound fades leaving him holding the chord on his own. Out of the dying chord Roger's bass builds up and introduces an octave stepping A note phrase (with a couple of variation towards the end) before Ritchie quickly arrives to power it along via a galloping style riff (around the chords of A, G and C). The whole band comes in, Jon lets rip with a slow discordant drag across the keys and then his signature piece, a thunderously crashing wall of sound which he resolves over the 'monster grove' of a backing. A short phrase, then the song drops to G for the verse.

This type of galloping guitar riff would become a staple of many a heavy metal band from the late 70's onwards, but we're hearing it here being laid out as a blueprint. Ian Paice keeps his drumming under tight control, choosing to play a Motown style beat for the entire song, showing extreme discipline and dedication in so doing. A few fills here and there sure, but nothing that would have got him thrown out of Berry Gordy's 'Snake Pit' studio.

Ian's vocals are, as throughout the album, impassioned. The verse is very closely double tracked, Ian using his fast becoming trademark scream at a few well chosen points to great effect, without over-playing the effect (which would have been all too easy given the nature of the track).

Jon takes the first solo and as Roger pointed out managed to deliver the same standard of virtuosity, excitement and showmanship as he was regularly delivering on stage in the wilder sections of *Mandrake Root*. There are no compromises to musically sensibilities. He deliberately plays phrases that are off-key and drags ear splitting noises from the Hammond that no other keyboard player could match quite as effectively as Jon (with the possible exception of Keith Emerson on stage). It is very easy to imagine Jon rocking the Hammond backwards and forwards (as he did live) to wring these sounds out of it for this solo.

We've mentioned the band and Ritchie's 'new direction' delivering this album, but clearly it couldn't have happened without this sort of astonishing work from Jon, which more than matched Ritchie's level of invention. Fittingly for the close of the album, here was Deep Purple's new sound in toto. The world of hard rock would never be quite the same again.

The end of the track seems designed to emulate the finale of a live show (in the same way as *Speed King* aimed to match the opening cacophony of a gig). This was Ritchie making the nosiest, most

LUXEMBOURG PROGRESSIVE

1	3	IN ROCK Deep Purple
2	10	BUMPERS Various Artists
3	8	WOODSTOCK Various Artists
4	14	LIVE AT LEEDS Who
5	6	TOM PAXTON SIX Tom Paxton
6	1	QUATERMASS
7	2	LADIES OF THE CANYON Joni Mitchell
8	4	LIVE CREAM Cream
9	7	IF
10	18	ACCEPT Chicken Shack
11	17	BAND OF GYPSYS Jimi Hendrix
12	5	SOLID BOND Graham Bond Organisation
13	–	PARACHUTE Pretty Things
14	–	THANK CHRIST FOR THE BOMB Groundhogs
15	15	BARCLAY JAMES HARVEST

Another amazing chart. The word 'progressive' describing rock was at least in use by 1968, along with the word 'underground'. Progressive Jazz had been in use before, and so the adjective was just reapplied to rock. It was only later that the term 'Prog Rock' came to be applied to a very specific style of rock music, and the meaning changed.

discordant and brashest possible statement from any guitarist outside Hendrix. 'Here I am. I can play the guitar anyway I want and you are going to listen'. And even Hendrix, without doubt the most important rock guitarist of all time, rarely managed to achieve this level of mayhem inside a studio.

It is interesting to note that this track was laid down only a short while before they recorded the final version of *Speed King*. Whether it was the end result which prompted them have a second bash at *Speed King* we don't know, but that early piano take must have seemed pretty tame alongside this amazing piece of work.

Despite a try out during a BBC session the group never attempted this on stage. Until 2009 that is when much to everyone's surprise (particularly the hard-core fans) Deep Purple finally played it live. Arguably *Hard Lovin Man* (as well as *Flight of the Rat* and *Livin' Wreck*) never became as famous as it could have been because the band had never played it live.

Cry Free / Jam Stew

Two further tracks form part of the *In Rock* legacy. *Cry Free* first appeared on the *Powerhouse* LP in 1977 (from a contemporary quarter inch safety copy) and was then remixed by Roger for the 1995 *In Rock* Anniversary edition.

A short punchy track, the riff appears to come from an old Elvis song, developed through a short riff Ritchie used to play in his solo section during *Mandrake Root*. He would play the riff (heard at the opening of this song), the band would copy it, and then it would be developed between them before falling back into the chaos of Ritchie's solo. It also has similarities to the riff for *Jam Stew*. On another level it sounds more like a Mk 1 piece, vaguely reminiscent of *Bird Has Flown* (from that line-up's last album.)

It is difficult now to imagine it on the *In Rock* album. It's not a bad song, but it was up against a lot of strong competition and the vocals fall below the standard Gillan achieves on the rest of the album. Likewise Ritchie's two solos do not match the level of invention or intensity of his other work and even Jon's organ sound lacks the single minded approach shown elsewhere.

Jam Stew is interesting from a fan perspective but doesn't quite fit the more progressive heavy rock style they had already recorded by then. Ritchie resurrected this riff when he and Ian Paice guested on the Green Bullfrog session album in 1971.

In closing *Grabsplatter*, sometimes referenced as an *In Rock* out take, didn't appear until it was recorded at a BBC session in September 1970, some 4 months after the album was finished. It was really an early idea for the *Fireball* album (the riff would evolve into an album b-side, *I'm Alone*).

Summing up In Rock

Quite how the band reached the point where *In Rock* was possible is a question some have asked, such was the change within their music over a twelve month period. Was it a natural progression, a sheer stroke of good fortune, or an extreme reaction to the orchestral project?

In truth, a mixture of all three. Fans who know the earlier albums can readily point to examples of brilliant individual musicianship and certainly by their third album some of the solo work from Ritchie, Jon and Ian Paice is as interesting and original as that on *In Rock*. Indeed many of the songs there provide the link between the original Mk 1 sound and that which they knew instinctively they were wanting to develop. And it was the same story live where *Wring That Neck* and *Mandrake Root* had already started to become impressive solo vehicles, with jazzy dynamics from Ritchie, and showing the influences of rock, classical (from Jon) and swing (Ian Paice.)

That decision to make line-up changes, and their luck in finding Ian Gillan and Roger Glover at a point when their own careers were moribund (a few years earlier and they might well have stayed put), provided the impetus. The rest was musical chemistry of a sort many classic bands experience at crucial points in their history, but which Deep Purple took full advantage of on *In Rock*. It was a moment which was to sustain them for the rest of their musical lives. There was also the conscious decision to go down the hard rock route come what may. *"We were trying to make a point, the whole thing had a very strong purpose, and that was to show that Deep Purple is a rock group. You either had to love or hate that album and we trod a very fine line as far as attracting fans was concerned."* • JL. Aug 1971.

In Rock showed everyone what could be achieved on a full out rock album, and did so in a manner which was clearly very different to their contemporaries Led Zeppelin and Black Sabbath.

Four decades on, the musicians still get asked about the album, and are perhaps able to get a better perspective on it than they could at the time. Jon : *"The people who put the money up that enabled Ritchie and myself to start Deep Purple, I think they wanted a pop band and they got this kind of two faced thing that they got with Purple at first cause the band didn't know what it was. We had a hit single with a cover of Hush and yet we were doing these weird psychedelic, prog rock intros to other people's songs."*

"Hendrix was an obvious influence on Ritchie. Vanilla Fudge was an obvious influence on the band as a whole. But what made us go where we

went with Deep Purple In Rock, which if you like was our calling card, our statement, this was us, this is where we've arrived at and this is what we want to be. That came from inside. That came from within the band. That's where we were headed from the moment Ritchie and I sat at 14 Gunter Grove in December 1967 and discussed what we were going to do together, that's where we were headed was Deep Purple In Rock.

"I love this album more than any other we've ever made. The energy and invention we summoned up in the back of vans, smelly dressing rooms, in colleges, concert halls and unforgettably and most potently, in that wonderfully shabby and echoing rehearsal room at Hanwell, combined to make In Rock an album which to me defined an era and style. This is the one I'd take to a desert island, along with a bit of Mahler of course. I have to say it was a very enjoyable time, a most wonderful time." • JL to BBC Heavy Metal Britannia programme.

Roger has been similarly upbeat: "To this day Deep Purple In Rock remains my favourite album. I can vividly recall my mental horizon being stretched beyond my wildest imagining. Nothing like it would ever happen again. As a writer I felt the floodgates had been opened. In a way it is too easy to mythologise the album, but it stands as such a potent symbol to me."

Even the normally taciturn guitarist rated it: "The new album is the only one I really want to be associated with; we haven't compromised at all, we've just put down our music and if people don't like it, well we're going to be a bit worried." • RB to Zigzag, Aug 1970.

"(It) is certainly the nearest to what we are like on stage. And it's the first to represent the band as it is now. It's much harder, raucous and exciting. That is what we are trying to get across, rather than musical ability. It's hard and simple." • RB to Disc, June 1970.

"The album was the biggest thing in our lives - it was a make or break album. We were worried about getting what we really were across to the audience. But that album typified exactly what we were at the time - a hard rock band." • RG to Jerry Gilbert, Sounds, Nov 1970.

Ritchie spoke to Steve Rosen in 1974 and was still upbeat. "It was a good LP, everything was about 1,000 miles an hour. A good LP that, objectively speaking, everything on there was good. I don't think there was one track I really hated. This is my favourite LP along with Machine Head."

Perhaps surprisingly even Mk 1's producer Derek Lawrence rates it as their best album. "We had so little time in the early days. In Rock was their best album because they had time to jam and work things out. It was all there before but it came out properly on that record."

And it remains influential. Klaus Meine, the Scorpions' lead singer, was a typical admirer, listing In Rock as his second favourite album of all time in an American interview in 1985.

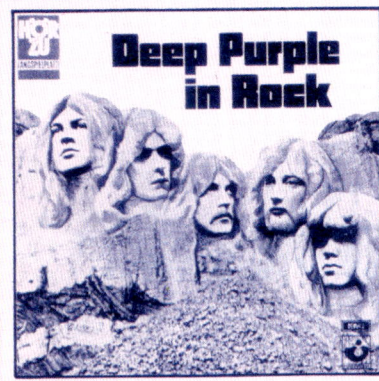

1 - I did buy In Rock during 1970 while still at school, so can provide one perspective on this. Though enjoying many pop singles of the late sixties (The Beatles and The Searchers in particular, Telstar and other strange instrumentals) I was relatively late getting to rock music, largely as a result of not having older siblings to learn off and parents who were not especially interested in pop, though my mother did buy the occasional single, Little Red Rooster by The Stones is one I remember. Black Night was one of the first singles I bought with my own money. It was the utterly absorbing b-side Speed King which really captured my imagination. Clearly even better than the a-side. I played it through three or four times back to back, revelling in the organ introduction, hard edged guitar work and the sheer drive of the piece. With a vague recollection of having heard the band on the radio (a BBC session I imagine), I resolved to buy the album as soon as I could scrape the money together. I'd never owned or heard anything like it and played the record endlessly for a time (while studying the sleeve - a real eye-catching image which looked so grown-up - for any information on the band). Even on a very lo-fi mono player (of which I was still inordinately proud), the power and energy of the tracks sounded incredible. Child In Time in particular defied description, sending shivers down the spine. Side two repeated the trick, culminating in another wall of noise which just sucked the listener in. It absolutely worked for me at the time, and whenever the teenage nobody-understands-me blues came round, this album took them away. There's a recent engaging documentary film, Sound It Out, centred on a second hand vinyl store in Teeside and the people who frequent it. One of two young rock fans interviewed explains that he'd been close to suicide at one point until he got into metal music. Whilst never falling that far, I totally understand the way music can provide a life-line at times, especially to kids who are struggling to fit in (in my case because I was stuck at a highly academic school but was only really interested in art and design).

Spotting other Deep Purple albums shown on the inner bag, I determined to get hold of them. I went from In Rock to Shades and The Concerto (second-hand via mates at school who had bought these but weren't struck), leaving me with the impression of a very schizoid group indeed. But while both were a long way off In Rock, they still had enough about them to further my interest.

Most of the kids at school were into the more predictable rock gods; Floyd, Zeppelin, Zappa, Hendrix, etc. Many of them tended to look down on Deep Purple a bit, a snobbishness which only changed when the band hit town in 1971 and converted most of them overnight. SR.

Flyer for the band's show at Eel Pie Island in June 1970. Roadie Ian Hansford recalls Ian Hunter from Mott The Hoople coming backstage to congratulate the band, but voicing criticism of their guitarist (who had to be phyiscally restrained until Hunter had disappeared!). Right: Ritchie, Berlin 1970. Below: another shot of Deep Purple on the film shoot for the Black Night promo.

12 • Touring The Album

"It's got to the stage where Ian Paice collapses after gigs, I have to carry him off." John Coletta

Deep Purple Mk 1 had only made any significant chart impact (unless we count a Swiss top ten) in America, their debut album *Shades Of Deep Purple* for example reaching No. 19 in Canada and No. 24 in America. Much of the chart action there was centred on the single *Hush* which peaked at No. 2 and 4 in the same territories respectively. However each successive release faired progressively worse. In Europe (Switzerland aside) they'd never had hits. *Hush* was released twice in 1968 and still failed to click. By 1970 they had largely been written off in America as well. It was on the back of this low level of chart interest that *Deep Purple In Rock* would be released.

Many bands (and managers) would have called it a day but there was enough of a momentum at Mk 2's live shows (with audiences and fees rising) to indicate that the new line-up were on to something, as well as a considerable financial investment to recoup. Contemporary remarks about how the group regarded the ongoing progress of *In Rock* are scant, but there must have been enough of a vibe to sustain them through to 1970 in the hope that enough fans out there would appreciate the new album. With the tapes at EMI, press releases were starting to appear as their managers organised a better flow of news to the music press.

"DEEP PURPLE are to release a single and an album simultaneously on June 5th. Both the A and B sides are group composed and produced, and are on the Harvest label. Their seven track album 'Deep Purple In Rock' is fully representative of their current act and is again all their own material self-composed. At the time of release, the group will be on a major concert hall tour of Germany..." ran the first of many from the Tony Barrow International press firm. And now the papers were starting to pick up on these, a sure sign that their profile was growing.

EMI had been busy following the completion of the album on April 13th, with only seven weeks between then and release. Given how long it had taken to record, everyone was keen to see it out as soon as possible. But then with few other musi-

SHVL 777
(1E 062 • 91442)
stereo

Deep Purple in Rock
10th week high in the charts

DEEP PURPLE'S GREAT SINGLE BLACK NIGHT harvest HAR 5020 is now in the charts

EMI / Harvest

Advert repromoting the album on the back of growing single sales in August 1970

E.M.I Records (The Gramophone Co. Ltd.) E.M.I House, 20 Manchester Square, London W1A 1ES

DEEP PURPLE: MOVIE SCORE, TV SPECIAL, EIGHT-WEEK U.S. TOUR

cians on their books the managers could devote most of their time to pushing it through; chasing tape deliveries, biking round acetates, checking artwork, sorting press releases and the rest. And the major record labels had huge capacity back then, most of it on their doorstep. EMI's plant at Hayes in Middlesex, to the west of London, was one of the busiest. They were more than capable of turning round a single in a matter of a few days, and a new album could also be pressed quickly.

Deep Purple In Rock was released in the UK on Friday, June 5th 1970. Friday was a regular day for issuing new albums, making sure they were in stores for Saturday, the busiest day of the week for record buying[13]. The album was also released in locally manufactured pressings across Europe and eventually in many more countries round the world that year (see discography), which meant organising copy tapes and duplicating artwork film.

John Colleta spoke about the excitement of the moment: *"We came out with Deep Purple in Rock which was fantastic for us to promote. Of course, between the Concerto album and the Deep Purple in Rock album was nearly a year, but in that year from being £125 a night we got up to £350 to £400 a night, purely on the Concerto and their stage performance which had really improved a hell of a lot, and also the change in the group at that stage. And I think this made a lot of difference to the act on the stage."* • JC to Voxpop.

Black Night was released on the same day as the album. *Speed King* was the default b-side, but some countries opted for a different album track (notably Holland and Germany who had already issued *Speed King* ahead of the LP). Having had one of the pre-release promotional copies of the single, the New Musical Express was able to run a (typically brief) review the same week: *"To condense all they have to offer into three minutes is asking a lot. But the boys have well nigh succeeded with this heavy rocker. Based on a simple but penetrating riff, it's outstanding for some mind blowing lead guitar breaks. And the hand clapping beat injects a touch of commerciality."* Record Mirror were less enthused: *"this particular track seems to lack something musically."*

June 6th/July 1970 • There could be no let up in the touring. Finances were still tight and the album's destiny was by no means a forgone conclusion. So on release day in Britain, Deep Purple were half way through a ten day tour of Germany. Many histories of the group refer to this period of gigs as the *In Rock Tour*, running from June 1970 to October 1971. It wasn't really seen like that at the time. The concerts, one nighters and short bursts in different countries, were simply a continuation of what they'd been doing since July 1969, touring hard. A few tour posters used the new album art but many more did not, and there was certainly no advertising of an *In Rock Tour*. And while the *In Rock* tracks were obviously prevalent when the album came out, more than half the evening was given over to earlier material, and this would remain the case well into 1971. Perhaps a more appropriate title then would be the *In Rock Set*, and we will see how this developed once the album came out.

A tape survives[1] from the one Swiss date on this tour in Basel on June 8th and with *Speed King, Black Night, Child In Time, Paint It Black, Wring That Neck* and *Mandrake Root* on the list, it confirms that the group made no special changes at all to the set which had been in place for some time, beyond adding the new single. But then why change overmuch? There were still lots of people who had not seen the band live, and even if they had the bulk of the show was about improvisation.

From Germany it was back for seven UK shows starting at Eel Pie on the 12th June and the band would shuttle between here and Germany until the end of July. Even the managers realised the pressure the group were under. *"It's got to the stage where Ian Paice collapses after gigs and I have to carry him off stage."* John Coletta to Disc July 1970.

Being in the UK at least enabled the band to be around for press interviews and promotion duties. The advertising budget was limited but the NME did take adverts across their front page, and so this was booked for June 13th issue. The idea was to give the band a fortnight's break at the end of the month, which the two Ians and Roger used to hire the Lady Roberta (a canal narrow boat) and relax on the waterways of the Thames, or get into scrapes. *"We went into a pub near Pangbourne for two nights running, and spent a lot of money. Then on the third night a skinhead behind the bar told us to leave, and suggested we went into the public bar. He explained that it was suits only in the saloon."* • IG to MM, July 1970. Ian Gillan decided to 'write to the brewers' about the pub incident. A Radio Onederful DJ told listeners the band were holidaying on the river. *"Everytime we went through a lock someone would say 'hey are you Dick Pimple, the pop group. It was quite funny to see forty-year olds craning their necks to get a glimpse!"* • IP to MM, July 1970.

The Croydon Advertiser reviewed the Fairfield Hall concert on the 14th: *"...and when the end came the whole placed stamped for more. Deep Purple had won, England had lost".* The weekly UK charts were announced on Sundays and on the day of this show, *Deep Purple In Rock* went straight in at the No. 24 spot. Disc and Music Echo interviewed the group: *"Really, they should be bigger than they are. And that is why their new album and single are so important to them. The album is the* first one that really features Ian Gillan and bass-player Roger Glover, although the two former members of Episode Six have been with Deep Purple since last July. It is also the nearest album to what they are like."

In Rock emerged into what we've already noted was a very busy year for what are now regarded as all-time classic albums. *Bridge Over Troubled Waters* by Simon & Garfunkel was the years most dominant album, at No. 1 when *In Rock* entered the charts. The Beatles *Let It Be* was No. 2 and The Who *Live At Leeds* was No. 3 that week. Ignoring MOR offerings lower down, amongst what you might argue as Deep Purple's contemporaries were Ten Years After's *Cricklewood Green* (10), The Groundhogs' *Thank Christ For The Bomb* (11), King Crimson's *In The Wake Of Poseidon* (12), Black Sabbath *Black Sabbath* (13) and Led Zeppelin *II* (18 - it had been No. 1 in February 1970 for 1 week)[2]. Black Sabbath's *Paranoid*, one of the few rock rivals to *Black Night*, made the No. 1 spot on 4th October 1970.

And although *In Rock* did not reach the chart heights that Zeppelin or Sabbath achieved that year, it sold steadily from day one. In the end the album spent a remarkable 68 weeks in the UK top 50, albeit moving up and down. Zeppelin II did better, 125 weeks in the chart, but Black Sabbath managed 'only' 42 weeks.

The album charts were newly organised. In 1969 Record Retailer magazine got together with the BBC to establish a reliable official chart and used polling company BMRB to collect the figures, which they did from around 500 UK retailers a week (Monday to Saturday). The figures were released on a Tuesday

Deep Purple for big Hollywood Bowl date

and printed in Record Retailer (later retitled Music Week), Record Mirror and aired on BBC Radio 1 on the Thursday, dated for the following Saturday as next week's official album chart.

New albums came out on a Friday. BRMB compiled the singles chart first, and were a week behind on albums. So when *In Rock* entered the album chart on June 20th 1970 at 24 this was based on just two days of sales during the week of May 31 to June 6 inclusive. On June 27 *In Rock* was No. 4 based on sales for week June 7 to June 13.

Promoters of a big rock and pop show at the Eyrie, Bedford Town football club's ground, on Saturday 4th July must have felt they'd struck it lucky having booked such a happening band. They were talking of 10,000 music fans filling the place but as a local newspaper reported on the following Tuesday, only 1,250 turned up. It's never easy running a big event like this for the first time and they'd overestimated the drawing power of many bands on the bill and rival events that summer.

Local residents had been against the concert from the outset and reporters spoke of them vowing to leave the area or lock themselves in their house and refuse to answer the door to anyone! *"That noise could never be described as music,"* one deafened local told the newspaper. The concert ran late due to the delayed arrival of one of the bands, so Purple did not finish their set until 11.30 p.m. (an hour and a half later than scheduled).

The last of the UK shows for the moment was a return visit to The Lyceum on the 5th July, with *In Rock* reaching No. 9 in the charts that very day. The Lyceum was a major London gig which it was important to get right as all the music journalists covered the gigs there. The New Musical Express's Roy Carr went along: *"Deep Purple have now found the first level of acceptance in England, it's now up to the pubic to enjoy, enjoy, enjoy."*

With the album high in the charts, would fans get to hear some of the other tracks that had not been in the set before? The answer was no. *Bloodsucker, Livin Wreck, Hard Lovin Man* and *Flight Of The Rat*, over half the album in fact, were not played. As three of them had been done for the BBC and sounded stunning, it's a great shame. Arguably it also means these tracks are not as well known today as they ought to be. Clearly it was a band decision and as we've seen the general rule of thumb was if one of the group really didn't want to play a track, then it was left out. Maybe they were simply enjoying the freedom for improvisation that the long Mk 1 tracks gave them and were happy to bookend these with a few shorter tracks.[3]

The band now left for two festivals in Germany. It seems these (which both ran over two or three days) were set up by the same organisation, who switched the bands around between the sites. The first was the Aachen festival at the Reiterstadion in Soers, which they played on the 10th July, the second of the three-day event. The bill also included headliners Pink Floyd (on the final night), Traffic (on the opening night), with Free, Caravan, Golden Earring, The Edgar Broughton Band, Taste, Fat Mattress, If, Quintessence, Tyrannosaurus Rex, Hardin And York, Keef Hartley, Champion Jack Dupree and Kevin Ayres And The Whole World billed. One hell of an attraction to any unreconstructed '70s rock fan, with a couple of local "kraut rock" bands thrown in for good measure (see poster opposite.)

Cult musician Holgar Czukay was at the festival. Trying to find his own musical direction at the time he told the NME years many later: *"I was very unsure. Then I saw Deep Purple. They were unbelievable. This was in front of 8,000 people at a festival with Tyrannosaurus Rex. T Rex were complaining that nobody was listening, then come Deep Purple who rolled over the audience. I thought, that's it! One is not to reason, shout or condemn the people – one has to overpower them! I had never before seen this kind of total victory over an audience!"*

Happily for some fans, enterprising bootleggers were able to record many of the acts. Compared to most tapes from the time which (due to the often imperfect PA systems and primitive recorders) are of poor quality, the tape of Aachen is in a different league and provided one of the best Deep Purple bootlegs of the era.

Bootlegging was a relatively new phenomenon in rock music and was in part inspired by the anarchy movements in Europe. The high price of vinyl was just another example of how kids were being ripped off by capitalist record companies, according to the agitators. Bootlegs were designed to sell for considerably less than regular albums. Pressings were fairly crude, covers printed or silk-screened as cheaply as possible. The discs were sold across Europe via the network of small record shops which then existed.

This era of the cheap bootleg lasted probably six months before less idealistic individuals realised they could make a lot of money exploiting the idea. This, coupled with bootlegs going underground after legal action was taken against shops which stocked them, pushed prices up.

History has it that the Aachen recordings were done direct from a feed off the stage using a basic stereo tape machine hidden inside a Volkswagen Camper van. We've no way of knowing if this is true but the sound does exhibit some expertise, and they may even have mixed it live. Pink Floyd's performance turned up soon after and Free's set also circulated.

The bootleggers found themselves with a good recording of a top ten album band. The first pressing was *Space*, available in late 1970.

FÜNF ROCKER SCHWEIGEN – UND KASSIEREN

Deep Purple ist Englands verschwiegenste Gruppe. Ihr Erfolgsmotto: Psst! Dieses Wort jagt ihren Managern und Reportern Schrecken ein, denn keiner weiß, was die Deep Purple gerade aushecken. Ihr größter Coup: Ein Konzert in der ehrwürdigen Royal Albert Hall, bei dem sie ihre erste Rock'n'Roll-Sinfonie aus der Taufe hoben. Damit begann der Siegeszug der Deep Purple auf der ganzen Welt

Sänger Ian Gillan (24), Organist Jon Lord (29), Schlagzeuger Ian Paice (22), Baßgitarrist Roger Glover (24) und Sologitarrist Ritchie Blackmore (25) — von links — lieben Tempo und Rhythmus. Und das nicht nur in der Musik . . .

The discs had the word 'Italy' etched into the deadwax, which may or may not indicate where they were made (Italy fast became a centre for the pirate record business). They were relatively cheap to buy too. [4]

From there the tape spread. The second pressing was more commercial. Titled *H-Bomb*, this dropped *Mandrake Root* (and also edited Ian's between song patter) to get the remaining numbers onto single album. On the Kustom Rekords label, this was pressed in bigger quantities and distributed widely across Europe and the UK during early 1971[5]. Melody Maker even carried a bootleg top ten in their news pages before a test case was brought against Virgin Records which effectively outlawed the albums. Deep Purple's management were one of the organisations pushing for the law to change. Other shops took the hint and the discs quickly went underground.

Ritchie was quizzed about *H-Bomb* by Melody Maker in April 1971. "I think we all were pretty flattered but it was a shame that the technique of recording was so bad. You see it was done at a concert in Aachen and that night the stage caught fire. So for like about twenty minutes of the album there's just the sound of burning wood, no music at all. If we were bootlegged again then I think I'd be just as flattered. I look on bootlegs as being collectors' items. If I was really into an artist and I wanted to hear how he performed live, then I'd buy one. If it was bad and the recording was bad, it would be my fault for buying it and I would be lucky that it wasn't on general sale."

Ritchie's comments about the fire were puzzling but explained later: *"If you ask me what was the best date we played recently I'd say the Aachen festival in Germany, my amplifier caught fire and the whole stage went up in smoke."*

He also had a go at the people who knocked his stage presence. *"I like to think Deep Purple are an exciting band musically, but what gets the audience reaction is the shwomanship that goes with it. There are hundreds of good guitarists in Britain, but most of them are so boring to watch! I love to jump about on stage, I'd far rather get the reasction 'what a great show' than play musically for the heads. But we try not to let the music suffer as a result."* • RB to Disc and Music Echo, October 1970.

By May 1971, helped by the press reports, shops in London reported that *H-Bomb* was their fastest selling bootleg. In June a Melody Maker journalist returned to the subject: *"With the dexterity of a member of the magic circle I transformed my vodka and lemonade into a copy of H-Bomb, the Purple bootleg which is selling strongly both here and on the continent."* He showed the album to his interviewee Roger Glover: *"I view bootlegs with mild amusement. It's nice to be considered of the calibre where people will take the trouble to do it and I like to find out how much they make out of it and how it's turned out, I don't mind that. If you're going to be part of society you have to play by its rules, that's just not what's happening and the reason I'm against it. I bought a Deep Purple bootleg in Germany and it cost me a fiver so they're making money out of me. You can stop the big time operators because they have to have huge pressing plants and distributors and you can get an injunction, but you can't stop the small operators."*

Roger was quite impressed by the end result though: *"It's a bit fast; on stage you tend to do things a bit faster than for a record. (Black Night) is the old arrangement, we don't do it anymore. Actually for a bootleg it's not bad quality, there's reasonable balance."*

Jon was also quizzed about the album: *"They were a cunning lot whoever did that one. Apparently they recorded it in Aachen and had an eight track in a Volkswagen right under, the stage. Everything was mixed up to the machine so they were getting a beautiful sound, I play an amazing organ solo an it, best thing I've ever heard me doing and miles ahead of my studio work so I reckon we must get into putting down some stage work on tape. The only complaint I have about the album is that Ian Gillan was suffering from a bad throat that night so he doesn't come off too well."* • JL to Disc, August 1971.

The last version of the album in Europe was *Back To The Rock* which had a glossy live cover shot of the band. From there the tape spread over to America in the mid-seventies (where the bootleg record industry overtook that of Europe and dominated the market for the rest of the decade). The albums were then copied for CD bootlegs in the late eighties[6]. The source material was finally cleaned up for an official release on the Sonic Zoom series.

The recording remains a fascinating example of the band in their early prime. Jon tends to dominate *Wring That Neck* and is (as he himself later remarked - see above) on great form, while the band's almost jazzy improvisational music allowed deft touches far removed from the "heavy metal" name tag they would later be saddled with.

Ian Gillan, who was offstage more than he was on at this time, sounds well out of it on *Black Night*, but the energy level remains high despite the vocal overload which the bootleggers were unable to prevent.

Paint It Black clocks in at over ten minutes, Ian Paice making it an entertaining tour de force and an object lesson for would be drummers. The

● Latest bootleg LP to hit the British market is a triple-album set recorded at last summer's Rotterdam Festival. Acts featured include the Byrds, Jefferson Airplane, Pink Floyd, Country Joe, Santana, Hot Tuna and Dr. John. It is selling at £5.50. Best-selling bootleg set in Britain at the moment is reported to be Deep Purple's "H Bomb," which includes only three long tracks — "Paint It Black," "Black Night" and "Wring That Neck."

The first Deep Purple vinyl bootleg from a 1970 concert, this copy signed by all the band at the time.

excitement generated on *Mandrake Root* is tangible. It is also one of the longest versions recorded and once more showcases Jon's incredible Hammond playing, with some remarkable effects wrung from a machine which was clearly not intended to sound like this. The band bounce ideas off one another as Glover and Paice keep the beat going (with some exuberant conga work from an otherwise unoccupied Ian Gillan) and the track builds until around 25 minutes in when all hell breaks loose. For the next eight minutes a wall of white noise assaults the senses as Ritchie puts his equipment through the wringer.

Despite the loss of income and the obvious demand, neither group nor management made any serious effort to release a live album. It would not be until late 1972 that they tackled the issue, and even then the idea had to come from outside the organisation. But *Made In Japan* is another story.

From Aachen the group were shuttled over to Munich for another festival slot, before making two pre-recorded live UK TV broadcasts, the first on the 14th July for Granada's Doing Their Thing (aired in the North West on Friday the 21st August, 6.10 – 6.40 p.m.). The show focussed on a mesmerising *Child In Time* alongside edits of other three other tracks (including Speed King). A typically well produced Granada show (they covered popular music better than any other ITV region, or the BBC) it remains an aborbing viewing experience,

ROCK ALBUM SOLVED DEEP PURPLE RIFT

and if you look closely, you can spot an impressed George Best in the audience.

Their second was on the 28th July, at the South Bank Pops, filmed at the Queen Elizabeth II Hall in London (and directed by Brin Izzard). Made and broadcast by London Weekend Television to celebrate their move to the The South Bank, it would not be broadcast until September. They played two tracks, *Child In Time* and *Mandrake Root*. Ian Gillan was asked about the show: *"We haven't wanted to do television before, with all the hassles and three-minute spots playing to back(ing) tracks. But the Southbank thing was great, we got top billing above Blue Mink and The Settlers. The other groups played to back tracks but we took all our gear and played live. Of course, as usual, the audience was made up of a lot of older people. Anyway we played Child In Time which is a pretty quiet one for us. It was funny - when we finished we said we were going to do a loud one and half the audience walked out."* • IG to Melody Maker, 1970[7].

At the end of the show, following Ritchie's guitar trashing, he and Ian Paice sent their gear flying across the stage, with Jon rocking the Hammond back and forth and Roger scraping his bass across the top of the Hammond. By screening the clip out of context, the show did produce some negative comment in one of the music papers from John Peel about them copying The Who. The Daily Telegraph noted (in their own special way) the next day that *"Deep Purple, a rock Group as classic in their own way as the Benny Goodman Five once were, performed last night with all the splendor and animal power which their reputation has always boasted."*

One still unanswered question has to be when did Ritchie first actually smash one of his guitars on stage? It does seem as if a lot of reviewers describe the breaking of guitars when they were only in fact being mistreated. Even the Gibson 335 is described in one review as being broken up even though it clearly wasn't. It looks as if this maltreatment was always there, an expression of on-stage aggression by the guitarist (and somewhat unfairly dismissed by some as a copy of Pete Townsend's act - an accusation never levelled at Jimi Hendrix, Nirvana or others), but seems only to have reached the point at where guitars got broken beyond repair sometime in 1970. A combination of the increasing number of shows there were playing and not having to worry quite so much about being able to afford to get kit repaired may have been factors. A review of the Koln show in April 1970 mentions two guitars 'destroyed' and a wrecked amplifier, and holes in the fabric covering the speakers where guitar necks have been shoved can often be seen. The gear smashing prompted one of the music papers in 1970 to run a Deep Purple Destruction Stakes, which put the odds of various bits of gear ending the night in one piece as follows: Guitar 2-7, Speaker and amp evens, Drums 3-1, Bass 5-1 and organ at 100-1.

Through July *In Rock* remained a top ten UK album and their achievement began to sink in. Ian Paice: *"I think it really became obvious to me after the first two months it had been in the charts. We realised we'd done something rather good for ourselves."* It was doing even better in Germany. There, released through EMI as a regular edition as well as through a promotion in the country's big selling TV guide Hör Zu (who added their logo to the cover and sold it via mail-order), it entered the German charts (compiled monthly) at No. 7 on 15th July and would sell more there than any other country over the next 16 months. The album also entered the Norwegian charts at the end of July at No. 15.

Although *Black Night* had entered Deep Purple's live set before it was released, it had not charted anywhere so far. Maybe without much radio play and little other promotion people had missed out on it. By the end of July the group had virtually given up on it.

August/September 1970 • Festival time loomed again. They were booked for two in France, but made it to neither. Instead their last European show for a while was as headliners of the 10th National Jazz Pop Ballads & Blues Festival at Plumpton Racecourse on the 9th August. How things had changed. Two years before they'd been well down the bill in the afternoon. Now they were due to go on stage between 9.00 and 10.15pm. The NME's Richard Green ad Roy Carr reviewed the event and noted that *"Deep Purple proved good show closers with an exciting act that threatened to get out of hand. Ritchie Blackmore poured petrol over a stack speaker and set fire to it. It was all a bit silly and the group didn't need to resort to things like that. The extrovert number Speed King and the slow and sombre Child In Time had done the trick and when the latter number developed into a rave-up with Ian Gillan literally screaming into the mike, the crowd was with them all the way. During Mandrake Root Ian fell off the stage in the midst of the excitement. It's not hard to see why Deep Purple are so popular, I only hope the fire incident didn't upset too many people."* • NME.

Melody Maker wrote of the gig: *"Deep Purple proved the ultimate in show-stopping acts. Throughout the entire weekend, no group created the excitement and atmosphere that this quintet brought with them. One Ritchie Blackmore solo included a passage from the national anthem - shades of Hendrix and Star Spangled Banner- but it was their final number, Mandrake Root, which capped the lot. Blackmore set upon his stack with the rage of an executioner. It caught fire, only to be put out by a*

Munich, Germany, June 1970. Blackmore puts the Strat through the wringer.

The smashing-up bit is valid!

Deep Purple's Ritchie Blackmore answers those complaints...

WHEN DEEP PURPLE smashed up their equipment on a TV show recently, there were howls of protest throughout the land.

A flood of complaints hit MM's Mailbag, and there were rumbles of discontent from Caithness to Beccles.

How do Deep Purple react to this outburst and why do they indulge in tactics, once the perogative of the Who?

In the main they are unrepentant, although they point out they only do it on rare occasions, and are likely to calm down soon anyway.

Chief among the targets for abuse is Purple guitarist, Ritchie Blackmore, a mild-mannered, dark-haired chap who occasionally sets fire to his amplifier.

What did he think of all his controversy?

"Well, it's better than nothing," he smiled slightly, sipping tea. The TV show from the South Bank just didn't go off as well as we expected. It was a tele-recording, and they cut out some of our numbers and just showed the climax, which was annoying. Apparently the sound was bad and everything was cut to pieces. We just did our usual stage act and it didn't come off. But so what? If we want to do it — we will. We'll be changing our stage act completely soon. A lot of people have seen it now — especially reporters."

"I think the smashing-up bit is valid. It's how you feel at the time. I like to jump around. People will have a go at you whatever you do. I remember Jimmy Page saying once that an American writer thought Led Zeppelin 'were a terrible band because Jimmy Page wears snake skin boots.'

"Lots of people prefer a guitarist to use a tiny amplifier, wear worn-out jeans and be ever so humble. Well I like flashy musicians. It's taken us two years of hard work to get any recognition. We had a long struggle. Now people write in and say — 'ooerr, look at him smashing up his guitar.' Well, I've been playing for 13 years, and if I feel like smashing it up sometimes, I will.

"I don't go on stage and say to myself: 'Right, tonight it happens.' It's often when I'm feeling fed-up and I can't get anything in tune. There is so much to worry about when you get on stage and have to play. Maybe the amplifiers won't work, or some fool turns all the lights on — or off, and there is the audience reaction to think about."

Underneath the showmanship, he is a highly rated player among the musicians, but it is often the age-old way of any kind of music business, jazz or rock, that sheer musicianship, does not always score the bread, or win the audience.

Ritchie talked about his early influences: "I used to idolise Les Paul and Wes Montgomery. But it's more of a challenge for me to play rock than jazz, and control a 200 watt amplifier. Sure rock is harder to play than jazz. You see rock is so limited. In jazz you can play anything. I don't think there is a single guitarist who has MASTERED rock guitar playing.

"You could say Segovia has mastered classical music, but nobody has yet mastered rock and roll. I like Jimi Hendrix and Jeff Beck as guitarists, but they are not brilliant. They just play gutsy, screaming music.

"Deep Purple's main thing is excitement. Sometimes we get too much out of hand on stage, and people say 'how disgusting.' But four years ago I used to play very technically and other musicians would say: 'Oh brilliant.' But I wasn't getting anywhere. I'm not being big-headed but if I wanted to be a straight guitarist — I could. Those days are over. Albert Lee is brilliant — but he's not exciting. Big Jim Sullivan, to my mind, is the best in the country and earns thousands, but he is unknown to the public, as he is a session player.

"A few years ago it got to the point where I didn't want to play anymore, not just play the guitar in a corner. I wanted to ACT and play the guitar. When I was a kid, my whole thing was to be the fastest guitar-anywhere.

"I'm 25 now and I got my first guitar when I was about 11 years old. At first I wanted to be a jazz player, and my big influence then was Django Reinhardt. It's funny, I hear the latest thing among guitarists now is speed. But I don't want to know about that now."

The Deep Purple story is a strange one. They had a hit in the States, although not as big as first reports suggested, before they were known in Britain.

"I remember our debut here at the Kempton Park festival. We went on and our amps blew up, then a train went by. There was a complete lack of interest all round. We started off in a REALLY great way! Nobody knew who we were, so we said, 'right, that's finished us with England.' We were going to chuck it in and go back to America. After all, we were superstars there — we had a record (Hush) in the top 100!',

"But I don't think the music business has ever been better than it is now. Really. Bands like the Cream and Jimi Hendrix Experience made it possible for musicians to be rated, not just on their looks alone.

"And Britain has the best groups in the world."

"There are a lot of things that can build you up or bring you down in this business," said Ritchie. "You read in the 'papers one day — 'Great Group.' Next day, it's 'Silly group.', CHRIS WELCH.

Deep purple appear on tonight's Top of The Pops

fireman, and was then hurled across the stage into the crowd. Guitars were flung around stage in wild abandon, Jon Lord's organ rocked like a boat in a storm as the strobe lighting flashed. 'Actually, we meant to set the whole stage alight,' Ritchie said afterwards. 'I couldn't get in tune so I just threw the guitar wildly out, I guess the Gibson won't be much good anymore', he added looking at the red wreck!"

Which unless he'd broken all his other guitars sounds a bit strange, as he never normally played the track on his Gibson. Either way, they'd gone down very well and left a lasting impression[8].

Having made clear headway in Europe, thoughts turned to America. It had been over a year since their last tour there and it was obvious that Mk 2 needed to try and re-establish the Deep Purple name. The short tour consisted of around seven gigs across sixteen days, covering close on 4,000 miles, ending on the 30th at the Civic Centre in Pasadena. One story of the tour suggests that they were advised not to move around too much on stage as the American audiences 'did not like that sort of display'. You can imagine how much notice they took of this advice.

Warners were helping with promotion, with adverts for *In Rock* and *Black Night*. The music trade magazine Billboard reviewed the album, heaping praise on it and the band: *"Magnificent heavies, Deep Purple, are known for their intense, intelligent storms of classical-rock. Blackmore is devastating on Child In Time, Flight of the Rat and Hard Lovin Man, as the entire troupe rumbles deep in to the gothic excursions that have made them rock's super heavy weights."* • Billboard 29th August.

The dates were hung around another performance of *The Concerto*, staged at the Hollywood Bowl on the 25th. *"It wasn't as easy with the American musicians when we performed the Concerto with the Los Angeles Philharmonic, there's a much stronger feeling over there about rock music and long hair and those musicians didn't like us at all."* • RG to John Halsall, 1970.

The band got the news of *Black Night* making the UK charts while sat backstage at the Hollywood Bowl concert. Roger recalls the experience: *"It took awhile before the public noticed it. We received news of its entry into the charts as we sat in the dressing room, waiting to go on and perform the Concerto. It cured us of looking down our noses at hit singles because the change in our public profile was dramatic. Black Night more or less rounded off our first year together, and what a change we'd been through. Barely a year before Ian Gillan and I had been scuffing around, scrounging cigarettes, sharing one good pair of trouser tramping up and down the M1 in the back of a van. Now here we were flying back from America to mime to our hit record on Top Of The Pops."*

Amazingly Ritchie was persuaded to write a short diary about the trip for Beat Instrumental magazine, though he pointedly left out any mention of the Concerto. *"Our first gig in Denver was fun, when we started off someone, presumably the local promoter, set off a smoke-bomb on stage, and then had all kinds of coloured lights shining through the smoke. I suppose it was his idea of a freak-out! The kids were calling out for Mandrake Root and Wring That Neck, even calling out for some numbers off Deep Purple In Rock."* (it had been getting some advance air-play in parts of the country.) With a fairly relaxed schedule they got to do some rock an roll socialising, seeing Fleetwood Mac at the Whiskey A Go Go, and Little Richard at the same venue. Jon and Ian Gillan were invited up to visit Graham Nash and have a bit of an acoustic jam. Roger Glover even supplied a couple of cartoons to illustrate the piece.

On the 28th August they were booked to play two sold out sets at the Jam Factory in San Antonio. Unfortunately Ritchie collapsed after the first one due to a reaction to a flu vaccine. Anxious not to have to cancel, promoter Joe Miller suggested they try Christopher Cross (19 at that time, he would go on to be known for songs such as *Sailing* and *Ride Like The Wind*). Ian Gillan didn't much like the idea, but Jon made the call and the gig went ahead. Cross was thrilled to be playing with Purple, but did feel a bit uneasy about standing in for Ritchie. They did a few Deep Purple numbers that Cross knew and jammed on some blues tunes.

This handful of shows wasn't going to make much impact and Warners (a huge label at the time with many acts to focus on) were relatively slow to really get behind the band. There was a vague and poorly documented attempt to lay down a couple of backing tracks in a Hollywood studio, nobody seems to remember why, and the LP didn't actually come out until after the group had flown home. Because of the inertia, *In Rock* only entered the US charts in the second week in September at No. 198 (it didn't reach it's best position, 143, until nearly a year later in November 1971). *Black Night* reached No. 66 at the end of December 1970.

Back in Europe however, as Roger had noted, things were really happening. *In Rock* stayed inside the UK top ten for most of August and in Germany it went No. 3 on the 15th (it climbed to No. 2 the following month). *Black Night* had proved to be what DJs love to call a slow-burner. It made the New Zealand charts in mid-July (though quite what was driving sales there remains a mystery) and was moving up the UK charts in August, from No. 50 on the 9th, then 48, 46 and 32 during the same month. It entered the German chart at No. 33 in mid August. The NME ran a promotion in its 25th August issue highlighting the success of the album and pushing the single.

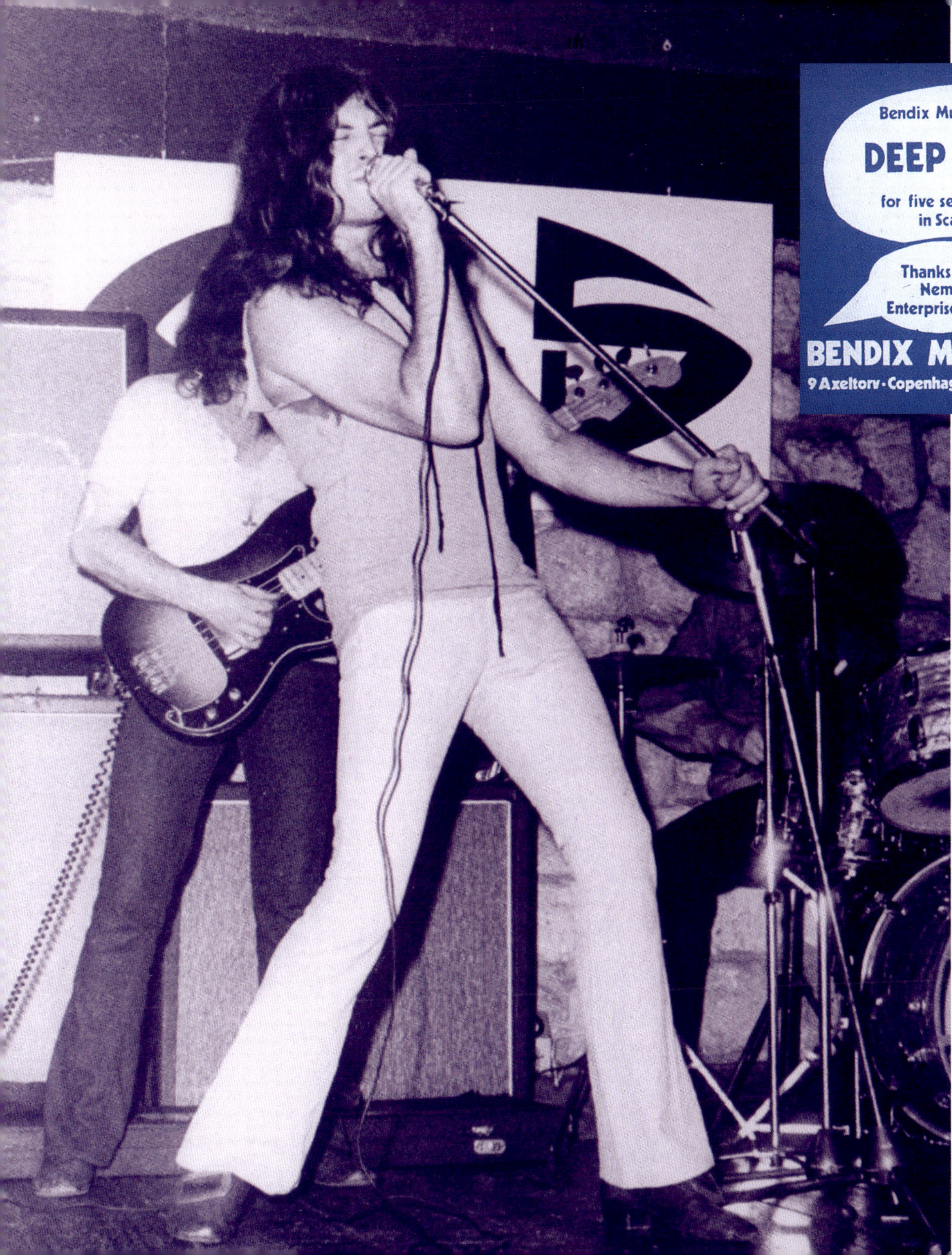

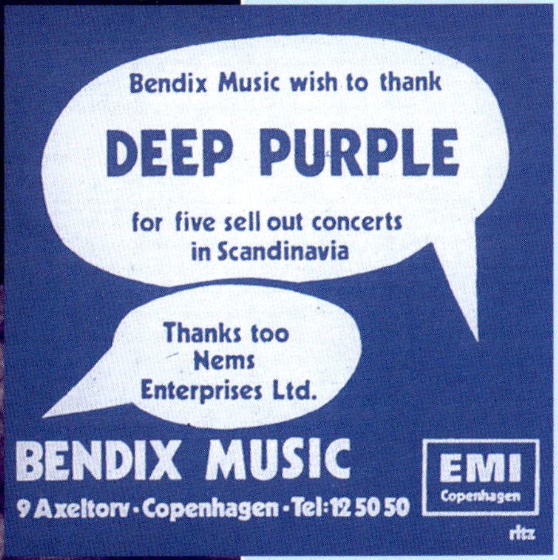

Bendix Music wish to thank
DEEP PURPLE
for five sell out concerts in Scandinavia
Thanks too Nems Enterprises Ltd.
BENDIX MUSIC
9 Axeltorv · Copenhagen · Tel: 12 50 50
EMI Copenhagen
ritz

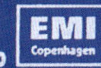

Ian Gillan fronts the stage for an after-hours set at the Gibus Club in Paris in November 1970.

'People began saying we had no direction'

Apart from a gig in France on the 6th September, the band had a few days off at the start of the month. *In Rock* continued to bob up and down the UK charts but the single was helped by the band's first appearance on Top Of The Pops on the 10th. *Black Night* reached No. 20 on the 13th.

On September 17th the group honored their commitment to play Jon's second orchestral/rock piece at the Royal Festival Hall, London. *The Gemini Suite* was again conducted by Malcolm Arnold, this time with The Orchestra of the Light Music Society. *The Suite* was in three movements, organ/guitar, voice/bass and drums. Jon wrote a section for each member of the group in which he tried to reflect their personality and style of playing. Jon had to write most of it while they were on tour, putting it together it in small sections, revising each bit at a time.

It was broadcast live on BBC radio, and lasted around 35 minutes. In some ways it was a far more reflective piece, with Jon really providing a clever background for the soloists. Ritchie's movement was first. It is quite simply stunning. The orchestral part is well written and fits in superbly with Ritchie's playing. He was using the Gibson again, and the whole movement is full of atmosphere and emotion; quiet runs, lovely out of tune jangling playing and bending notes. Ritchie was one of the people who had been against the idea of doing these projects, but he didn't let that prejudice him on the night. He later said he did it out of loyalty to Jon.

The other member of the band who voiced his discontent over the idea was Ian Gillan, yet he too turns out a brilliant performance. He builds up near the end with a soaring screaming passage over some dramatic orchestral work which is spine-tingling. It is always to be regretted that Jon could never persuade them all to take part in further work, as this remains a highlight of all their careers. Questioned about the possibility of a record of *The Gemini Suite*, Jon said diplomatically that he would like to do it "sometime", but would rather concentrate on the group for the time being[9].

Deep Purple's manager had also been approached to see if the band wanted to record some soundtrack music for a Western, *The Last Rebel*. They declined but Jon Lord took on the project, working with Tony Ashton, and fitting the late September recording sessions in between UK dates with Deep Purple. The side project is an important one for Jon Lord afficianados. He played on much of it, wrote (or co-wrote) all the tracks, oversaw the studio recordings, and conducted the orchestra (the album was completed in October).

Deep Purple record sales were still confounding everyone. *Black Night* broke into the top 10 at No. 9 on the 20th September. The TOTP appearance had really got them noticed (and pushed concert ticket sales as well). The same week the album suddenly climbed back up from the No. 38 spot the week before to No. 7. In Germany the album did even better, holding the No. 2 spot throughout the whole of September. *Black Night* also did well in Ireland, achieving its highest position of No. 4 and peaked in New Zealand at No. 13.

On the 23rd Mk 2 also did their final BBC session. The DJ fronting the transcription special was Brian Mathews, who interviewed Jon on air: *"You've also got an album that's doing pretty well it seems." "Um yeah, Deep Purple In Rock it's called." "Any idea how many it's done?". "In this Country it's over 75,000, it's doing stupid things in Germany, and it's doing well in America". "Nice to know". "Yeah, lovely to know".*

Jon was able to expand more in the papers. *"We spent six months in England playing up and down the country at every reasonable gig we could find to get across to people what we were doing. If we were good we thought the word would spread, and that's the way it seems to have worked."* • JL to record Mirror, Oct 1970. Roger, talking a year later, made the same point: *"We expected it to sell well because we'd been touring up and down the country, going over like a bomb every night, drawing huge crowds and getting quite a fee for a group that hadn't had a hit record. We knew we had lots of fans. Every track was treated with equal care. I know this might sound terribly big-headed for us but I really do think we set out to give quality and we achieved it."* • RG, Oct 1971.

Another burst of British shows followed, starting on the 25th September, an all nighter kicking off at 11.30pm at the Odeon, Romford. This seemed to help the album and single sales still further. In Rock went back to equal it's best chart place at No. 4 on the 27th. There was even a belated sales surge for *The Concerto*, which popped back into the charts for a week at No. 69 after an absence of seven months.

At the end of the month, the group returned to De Lane Lea to begin work on their next studio album. There had even been talk of getting it finished before the end of the year.

The group had also decided that it was time to ease back on the British concerts, partly as the job they had set out to do here was largely done according to Ian Gillan. *"It is very easy to become over-exposed. A year ago we decided to concentrate on this country and the continent. In fact we cut out two tours of America for that purpose."* Ritchie agreed; *"We feel that we have accomplished what we set out to do. So now I think it's time we cut down in this country and concentrated on other countries a bit more."* • IG and RB to MM, Aug 1970.

October/November/December 1970 • The final quarter of 1970 was one of the busiest periods Deep Purple ever went through, trying to balance the enormous success of the record with the demands of touring and trying to plan ahead for a new album and averaging a show every two days across six countries. Both the album and single achieved their highest chart positions across the world during the last quarter of the year, with *In Rock* making that No. 1 slot in Germany on the 15th October where it would stay for three consecutive months (and *Black Night* getting into the top 10 in eleven countries).

The band continued to draw good press. Disc and Music Echo tried to sum the situation up in October, talking to Jon: *"Deep Purple have suddenly reached the highest point of their three-year history, with an album and a single high in their respective charts. They now have the success and recognition they deserve. They're a complete group; fine musicians who don't forget that as well as being 'in music' they are also part of show business. Though some of their recent antics have met with heated criticism, it's worth noting that there has been a lot more dissent from fans recently about the groups who 'just stand there'.*

Jon: *"We were searching for a group identity. Our previous LP's had been a mess of different styles, and it was also the first one with Roger and Ian on. It's the only one we've made with a strong direction."*

"It's the first time we've gone into a studio to make a single[14]*. The ones before have all been off albums. We thought it would be nice to do one that wasn't on the album. I suppose we wanted a hit. It's difficult to work out. I just thought that it wouldn't matter if it wasn't a hit and if it was it would be nice. But I must say, having got it, it's a great feeling, especially to be in both charts at once."* • JL to D&ME, 3rd October.

Black Night just kept on selling, still battling for honours with Black Sabbath's *Paranoid*. [10] When it hit the No. 3 spot on the 4th October, *Paranoid* was at No. 4. Purple moved up a place the following week, enough to merit another reshowing of their Top Of The Pops slot on the 15th. The only thing which stood between *Black Night* and the coveted No. 1 spot was Freda Payne's *Band of Gold*, which could not be shifted. Even so, for a single which they had all but written off a few months before, it was amazing success (the NME incidentally compiled their own chart; on their figures it reached No. 1 in the NME chart on the 31st October. The MM also had it at No. 1 the same day.)

It also brought a more rowdy element to some shows, something the band noticed. *"The single has attracted the screaming element. We dont mind as long as they have a good time and don't annoy others. The atmosphere changes after a hit single - the people seem a lot more willing to enjoy themselves. It seems to have sparked something off. Things always go a bit beserk during Black Night but we don't mind that and they usually hold back till the numbers are finished. I heard Black Sabbath say they got the wrong kind of audiences with their hitsingle, but what do they really expect?"* • IP to Lon Goddards, Record Mirror, Nov 1970.

A clutch of very successful British University shows took place in October, covering Cardiff, Southampton, Leeds and Sheffield. Higher education venues were an important alternative touring circuit back then and quite lucrative, the band's fee having climbed to the £600 mark for a one off show. Deep Purple's awesome form on stage was captured by French TV when the group flew over for a show at La Taverne de L'Olympia in Paris on October 8th. When Pop Deux

Deep Purple recorded an edition of the rock show Doing Their Thing for Granada TV in Manchester on July 14th 1970. They were one of the biggest bands to appear on the show and their edition was shown in the ITV region the following month. Such was the buzz about the recording that footballer George Best was in the audience. This photograph was taken during the performance, and you can also see roadie Ian Hansford stood beside Ritchie's Marshalls. 25 minutes from the performance (including Child In Time and clips from Speed King) was edited down for the show which was issued on VHS many years later.

(which would be aired the following month) finally surfaced amongst collectors it proved to be the most absorbing footage of the band from this time, both in terms of performance and direction, the event captured in typically French style - gritty and up close, with no tricky effects (apart from Jon playing the insides of the Hammond with a drum stick at one point) or cutaways. The packed audience are seated on tiers as well as on the studio floor around the band, and the atmosphere is electric. Yet again the programme editor focused on the long improv sections, and the rest ended up on the cutting room floor.

It is perhaps the eventful four dates in Scotland which immediately followed that best illustrate the frenzy surrounding the band at this time, as Ian Gillan later recalled: *"I remember a night in Glasgow it was just fantastic - just before the end of the concert somebody rushed in and gave us the first edition of the Daily Record and there were pictures of us all over the front page and I thought 'here we go, it's looking alright' and I'll never forget that"*.

The Daily Record were actually covering the near riot which had occured in Glasgow on the 13th. The group had been booked to appear at the Electric Garden Ballroom which holds just over 600, but the demand for tickets was so great that the concert was switched to Tiffanys which could accomodate nearer 1400. But even this wasn't enough and double that number turned up for the show as the paper reported:

"More than 50 policemen, some with dogs, were rushed to Tiffany's in Glasgow's Sauchiehall Street last night, as 3,000 pop fans fought to get in. The club was full, but the street was still packed with youngsters who had travelled from all over Central Scotland, to hear the Deep Purple pop group. An SOS from the staff at Tiffanys, formerly the Locarno, brought 17 police cars and vans to the scene as the frenzied fans blocked the street and hammered at the hall doors."

The venue had been forced to post 'House Full' notices on the doors, and fans without tickets then began trying to force their way past security men. There were similar scenes in Aberdeen, with youths climbing onto the roof to listen to the show through the air vents (apparently the caretaker's wife later chased them off). The Daily Record published a moody group photo, the band posed around the rubble of a demolished building in a slum clearance area, which gave an almost battle zone air to their report. Incidentally the ticket prices back in 1970 for these gigs was 15 shillings at the Edinburgh and Glasgow gigs, and 10, 12, 14 or 16 shillings in Aberdeen and Dundee. We know the band were paid £2000 for the four shows, which means that with their fee of £500 for Glasgow, and ticket income of £700, the promoter had a budget of £200 to cover all other expenses (hire of venue, fee for support band - in this case Tear Gas - etc.).

The Record Mirror ran with the events under the front page headline *"Deep Purple Fans Fever"*, reporting one police source as saying *"We've seen nothing like this since the heyday of The Beatles,"* and a story that fans were removed from the roof of Tiffanys trying to get into the hall by lifting the slates!

On the 16th October Deep Purple co-headlined with Free at Sunderland's Top Rank Suite, together with three other bands for a night billed as the Indoor Festival Of Music (the word festival perhaps being stretched a point here). Deep Purple were delayed travelling down from Scotland so Free took the stage early. Purple's gear van arrived at the venue but the promoter, Geoff Docherty, got a message that the band were not going to appear as it was too late. Geoff was both concerned and suspicious (he was right to be so, a knackered Deep Purple were holed up at a nearby hotel). Geoff got twenty fans to haul the band's gear inside in exchange for free admission, then got on the phone to Purple, telling them there were 3,000 people waiting, desperate to see them. The group relented and soon arrived at the venue to face more pandemonium, as Roger told the Melody Maker (under the dramatic headline *"Now its Purple mania"*): *"I think either of us could have sold the place out, but we went on last and my guitar was stolen. I got it back during the second number. Girls were flinging themselves at Ian and we played Black Night to the backs of bouncers. Girls were fainting, crying and screaming and they were laying them at our feet on the stage. Managed to get out all right thanks to the promoter, but they were screaming for the wrong reasons. It wasn't the music that we played it was just what we looked like that counted because they were all very young. I suppose it's something we will have to face after appearing on Top of the Pops."*[11] Geoff also remembers the band originally weren't even going to play *Black Night*, clearly something had got the band in a bad mood.)

Purplemania • From riots in the UK, the band left for France for a planned eight date, 1,200 mile tour, starting in Lyon on the 25th October. Manager John Coletta travelled with them, something he often did in these early days. The set list had been swopped around a bit, with *Into The Fire* returning as second track in, moving *Black Night* to the encore. This was possibly because a lot of the audience were coming on the strength of the hit single, to play it too early risked compromising the performance.

But as in Scotland the trip was marred by many fans turning up to learn that gigs sold out. The group found themselves in unsuitable venues, way too small for the number of people being allowed in. Everyone was really concerned that something serious might happen. When the group heard the shock news that the packed Cinq-Sept

Club at St Laurent Du Pont, near Grenoble, had caught fire, with well over 100 people killed, they called it a day. As far as the group were concerned, while they'd not been booked to play there, all the venues they were at carried a similar risk. They told Allan McDougall of the NME that just before playing Paris they been booked into a club in Dourges which would hold 800 people comfortably. The promoter had packed 2,000 in and people were fainting and had to be passed out over the heads of the crowd. They cut the tour short after a show at Paris Olympia on November 1st. The Melody Maker's Chris Charlesworth was following the tour: *"Deep Purple cut short their French tour this week after the disaster at St Laurent Du Pont, where 144 people died in a blaze at a dancing club. The group, who have been touring France for the past ten days, have been playing in similar venues. Purple organist Jon Lord told me at his Paris hotel at the weekend 'It could have been us. The other night we played in a small hall where the promoter packed 2,000 kids into the hall. They were packed like sardines and fainting all around us.'"*

Deep Purple decided to go ahead with the Paris show which was at a proper hall, then return home. The NME reporter was at the side of the stage, and was joined by Ian Gillan during the solo spots who gave him a running commentary: *"Just listen to how fast Ritchie's playing these days- much faster than Alvin Lee, yet every note is as clear as a bell. Oh, listen to how they play this next part..." "That's probably the reason that Deep Purple's stature has grown so hugely in recent months. People keep going back to see them knowing approximately what they're going to get - loud, hard, showmanship rock. But never played exactly the same way as the last time."* • IG and Allan McDougall, NME.

Charlesworth also reviewed the gig: *"The climax was the strobes being turned on, giving the old movie effect. It's at this point that Ritchie usually ended up smashing one of his Stratocasters, but on Sunday he was unusually restrained. He did scrape it along his stack, fling it around wildly and play it with his feet, but at least it was in one piece at the end. As the number ends, the strobes flash slow and noises from organ and feedback jerk to an ear shattering climax. The house lights came on to reveal the group totally exhausted, but the cheers brought them on again for Black Night, the hit they didn't really want. Backstage, wiping each other down, the group were besieged by local club owners inviting them to blow in their clubs for a free meal."*

The band on this occasion relented, and did a second short set at the Gibus Club. Gillan spotted someone taping the set and had words.

Back in England there was more press waiting. Ian Paice responded to a reader's letter which had accused the group of 'musical inadequacy and sham histrionics' when smashing their gear on stage: *"Sure, we do get worked up once in a while, but it's only happened two or three times and the equipment is built very well, so nothing has really been damaged. It wasn't just sham histrionics - whether it was frustration or sheer exuberance, we felt all of it - it isn't just for display."* He also commented on the French dates: *"It was terrible. I'll never go back, except for Paris. Of course I hate France anyway. We had van breakdowns and nervous breakdowns, especially Ritchie, who really suffered from exhaustion."* • IP to Lon Goddard, Record Mirror, Nov 1970.

Roger Glover was similarly hacked off: *"After we played the Olympia we went straight off to Calais and then home. I believe we're now being sued for cutting the tour but the morale was so low and everthing about France seemed so wrong that it would probably have broken the band up if we'd stayed another two days."*

Come back Purple

THANK YOU Deep Purple for such a beautiful album. Give it a listen. Come back to Glasgow, Deep Purple. We need you. — Purple Freak, Calderwood, East Kilbride, Glasgow.

He was happy to be back home for a few days. *"It was so nice to play in England again last weekend, we did Margate and the Winter Gardens at Bournemouth where everything was just right."* • RG to Jerry Gilbert, Sounds, Nov 1970.

Margate was hosting an indoor two day festival and Deep Purple headlined day one, with what was described as *"yet another ear-splitting performance"* by writer Michael Benton in the Melody Maker.

The musician's monthly Beat Instrumental talked to Jon: *'At the moment we're trying to keep what we've learnt. Because we learnt a terrific amount with Deep Purple In Rock, it took six months to make*

record mirror

October 24, 1970 — 1s./5NP

New York? Forget it, say Mungo Jerry

MUNGO Jerry calling this week from New York — "This place is a city of freaks!"

Mungo's Colin Earle was quick to give his impression of the smog-ridden metropolis that houses one of America's biggest pop cultures.

"I just wanted to get out of New York as soon as possible", he exclaimed, "the tension here is awful. All the people look absolutely sickly and there is no air at all. Even the television programmes are riddled with nervous tension — it's full of commercials about drug addiction and pollution.

"It's the picture of a country spoiling what could have been a Utopia almost to the point where it's anti-life. And a lot of Americans I meet totally agree. They reckon in 20 years, this city's atmosphere won't be breathable."

Apart from the torture of New York living, Mungo's first stateside tour is rolling along smoothly.

"The gigs we've played here are some of the best we've done — the response is great", continued Colin. "We're cutting a record here, but it isn't finished yet. Playing the rest of the country is great and there is some scenery here, but New York is such a heavy place."

The group return to Britain on November 8.

DEEP PURPLE FANS FEVER

POLICE authorities in Scotland were this week still counting the cost of Deep Purple's flying visit to Glasgow, Aberdeen and other centres. And they said: "We've seen nothing like this since the heyday of the Beatles".

In Glasgow, the group, currently high in the singles' charts with 'Black Night', were originally booked into the Electric Garden, which holds about 600. The gig was switched to Tiffanys, which can hold more than 1400.

And even then there were 3,000 fans from all over Scotland locked out in Sauciehall Street. Five were arrested and later appeared in court. Several more were removed from the roof of the hall where they were trying to dig through the slates.

The group more than consolidated on their success in Scotland earlier this year. And left a trail of damage caused by irate fans who couldn't gain admission.

Meanwhile the tour goes on. This weekend (October 25) Deep Purple go to France for 10 days — and their date at the Olympia Theatre in Paris was sold out within hours of the box office opening.

They then go Scandinavia and back to Britain for a short series of dates: November 18, St George's Hall, Liverpool; 19, Belle Vue, Manchester; 20, Hull University; 21, University College, London; 22, Fairfield Hall, Croydon. And then to Germany for two weeks, with stablemates Ashton, Gardner and Dyke.

German police are making special plans. On the last Deep Purple visit to Dusseldorf, shut-out fans tried to burn their way into the auditorium with petrol blazers.

Though work has started on the group's sixth album, it is unlikely to be on sale before Christmas due to touring pressures. It is more likely to coincide with their 14-day, 14-venue tour of Britain in January — which includes one appearance at London's Royal Albert Hall.

But meanwhile, organist Jon Lord is collaborating with Tony Ashton on the score for the movie 'The Last Rebel'.

A new single? Say Deep Purple: "We just can't say. Really it is a matter of luck whether we come up with something both good enough and short enough to release in single form. In any case, 'Black Night' was something of an accident — just something that happened in the throes of recording studio haze helped along by the odd drop of alcohol!"

THE DEEP PURPLE LINE-UP

INSIDE: TONY BENNETT

that album. I can honestly say it's the first album we've been 100% satisfied with; it gave us a hell of a lot of confidence. During that long time we learnt a lot about ourselves and our music and our sense of direction. I suppose it's our basis now for our whole way of working."

Jon had also made plans to purchase a Fender Electric Piano, though it would be a while before it appeared on stage. *"I won't be using it immediately, work it in gradually. But I feel the need for another sound within the group."* He was also easing off on the Leslies as well. *"I found that I was using it, rather than playing it. It's very exciting to hold one note down and switch in, very exciting, but it's not playing."* • JL to Beat Instrumental, Sept 1970 issue.

There was no let up. The group now left for another territory where they would develop a huge and loyal following, Scandinavia. Six consecutive dates covering Norway, Sweden and Denmark, from the 11th November (Njardhallen, Oslo) to the 16th, another 1,300 miles in total. The show at the Konserthuset in Stockholm, Sweden was recorded by Swedish National Radio for a radio show called Tonkraft. Amazingly it wasn't bootlegged for several years until someone found the tapes again, and it first appeared as *Murky Waters*, then a delux coloured vinyl pressing titled *A Live Tribute To Wally* (the tapes were recovered and released officially in 1988 as *Scandinavian Nights*, then later in a remastered edition on the Sonic Zoom label).

The set is remarkable, with *Mandrake Root* at 28 minutes plus, *Wring That Neck* at over half an hour, and even *Child In Time* passing the 17 minutes mark. If you were into long instrumental passages then there simply wasn't another band to touch Mk 2 for their musicianship and inventiveness at this point, despite the set list remaining as before.

The Dagens Nyheter newspaper reported on a press conference, to which only Ian

The band photographed before the Hamburg show.

Gillan and Ritchie turned up (Roger had lost his luggage, Ian Paice was feeling ropey and Jon had gone for a walk in Stockholm to have a look at the sea. Ian Hansford their roadie was in charge of getting the musicians ready for gigs on time, sorting out the hotels, and handing them 'pocket money' whenever they needed ready cash, but even he couldn't always round them up on time). They were asked about instrument trashing: *"It can be that we get angry with a bad audience, or as a natural climax of a good concert. Sometimes nothing like that happens."* One journalist asked about their next album, and were told it had the provisional title *A Tribute To Wally*. Somebody was having somebody on here, "Wally" was an almost universal audience cry at rock gigs, supposedly originating at one of the big festivals where someone had lost their friend Wally and kept shouting their name to try to find them again.

Ian Gillan introduces *Speed King* as a song about *'somebody who can sing at a hundred miles an hour'*. *Into The Fire* he describes as *'rock and roll with its trousers down, rock and roll back to front, inside out'*. The recording remains one of the best examples of Deep Purple on stage in their early prime and shows just why the band became such a huge live draw across Europe. It's astonishingly intense in places. The balance takes a little while to settle down at the start of *Speed King* but once they're over that hurdle, the band members just seem to be pushing all the time. Instrumentally *Child In Time* pulls the listener in as the performance get harder and heavier, possibly one of the best live version ever heard on disc.[12] At Gothenberg three days later, Pete York (from support band Hardin & York) came out during Ian's drum solo with a snare drum, and jammed with him. As the support group's van had broken down, he'd borrowed Ian's kit for their own set.

More headline shows back in the UK were planned for late November, however gigs at Hull, Wolverhampton and Bradford had to be cancelled when Jon Lord injured his back. Adverts subsequently appeared promising that the group would return to Bradford. It would take them 27 years (the main reason being that Leeds Town Hall was the main West Yorkshire venue, and as it's close to Bradford, agencies didn't often risk

'Deep Purple' at the Festival

booking the two halls in case they couldn't sell them both out.) With Jon just about recovered, they were able to play a big gig at Fairfield Hall, Croydon on the 22nd November boasting a version of *Wring That Neck* which lasted an incredible 34 minutes. Not everyone was impressed though. *"They have taken over as firm favourites of the teenybops. As an example of self indulgence and ignoring what the audience wanted, they excelled. Were it not for the saving grace of Richie Blackmore, this reviewer might well have disappeared into the black night..."* • Bill Kellow, Disc.

The band were still using their second-hand Daimler to travel around in, with their gear, now estimated to be around £8,000 worth of equipment, travelling in a van, along with three roadies. In recognition of their remarkable standing in Germany, the country now claimed the group for their longest series of back to back dates since the band had formed; 15 gigs in 15 days. This tour was also the last to include the *In Rock* opening section of *Speed King*, *Into The Fire* and *Child In Time*. They were bigger shows too, playing to 2,000 people or so at many of the halls. Roger wasn't sure what to expect: *"We had a lot of trouble before, so heaven knows what it'll be like this time. I do feel that it's wrong to (out) down crowd hysteria. If the public dig what you're doing then that's great, even if they show it in different ways."* • RG to Jerry Gilbert, Sounds, Nov 1970. Ashton, Gardner, Dyke & Lieber were the principle support for this tour: now handled by Deep Purple's managers, they were on the verge of having their own hit single. The tour was handled by the new Mama concert agency but it was a frankly ludicrous workload, and poorly organised as well, crisscrossing Germany in a seemingly random manner, passing towns they were to play a day or two later on their way to another gig. 3,700km were clocked up [*2,300 miles], kicking off on the 27th November at Stadthalle, Offenbach and ending on the 12th December at Messehalle, Stuttgart.

The strain was beginning to tell. Jon still wasn't fully fighting fit, then Ian Gillan collapsed after one of the shows. He picked up but before the show in Ludenscheid on the 8th, Ritchie became ill. Ashton Gardner & Dyke did their support slot, but it was not until they'd gone off that an announcement was made explaining that Ritchie was ill, and the Deep Purple set would be done as a four piece. People were disappointed but gave the band a chance. They did four tracks or so, before Ian Gillan left the stage, unable to carry on. The other three tried an instrumental then they also left the stage. Fans thought that the band was taking a break, but it became clear that the concert was over. Trouble began to break out, with bottles being hurled at the stage and equipment. Some fans then climbed on the stage and laid into anything they could. Reports afterwards spoke of 45,000 DM worth of damage along with around half a dozen injured people. Some of the gear was wrecked. Ritchie was flown back home and rather than risk further trouble the following gigs were cancelled.

There was a small but growing anarchist movement in Germany at the time, and these political agitators were stirring up trouble outside some venues on the pretext that all concerts should be free. Water cannons were needed to break demonstrations up at one venue. There were attempts to break in to gigs and even burn one venue down. Ian Gillan was interviewed for the Wochenschau cinema newsreel in Hamburg about the turmoil: *"The packed audiences, inside the concert halls and everything like that are fantastic. But every night, particularly in southern Germany, there's a lot of people outside causing a lot of trouble who reckon that music ought to be free and all that sort of stuff. I am sure all musicians are just gonna stop playing in the end if this sort of thing carries on. (You) have to employ security, dogs, all that kinda stuff and instead of the price being 5 or 6 Mks, the price has to be 10 Mks to cover the cost of all the damage."*

The protesters even printed out some protest leaflets, which singled out Deep Purple and their promoters in particular. New Musical Express's Richard Green had joined the band in Hamburg and spoke to Ian Paice about the trouble and a 'mysterious Fraulein X'. *"They had battering rams in Heidelberg and they were trying to get at the band. I was really frightened. They had us cornered in the dressing room. If they had got to us I hate to think what would have happened. We saw a girl driving round in a car with a loudspeaker on top organising the riots. She was telling them what to do and where to go. She was in Heidelberg and again in Hanover. At Hanover we were about four storeys up and they were throwing lumps of rock up at the windows."*

"The only objection I have to playing free are the obvious ones in as much as we are professionals who have a right to be paid for our work. I'm against the excessive fees which some artists seem to collect and equally against the excessive charges made to some audiences for admission, this is primarily responsible for the movement towards free music." • JL to Record Mirror, Oct 1970. Back in Britain everyone got a short break while Ritchie recouperated. The vague idea was to begin to prepare themselves for the next album sessions, but few of the group were in the mood. And there must have also been a feeling of 'what is the hurry?'. In Rock was still settled in the upper reaches of the UK top twenty (and still at No. 1 in Germany). Even *Black Night* managed to hang on in the top fifty until the 27th December. In Germany *Black Night* was still breaking records, it was only kept off the top slot by *Paranoid*. If only some promoter had been able to tour the two bands together...

The British Market Research Bureau (BMRB) Top 50 singles list

DEEP PURPLE : le 30 octobre au Havre (Maison de la Culture) - le 31 octobre à Dourges - le 1er novembre à Paris (Olympia Musicorama à 17 h 30) - le 2 novembre à Elbeuf - le 3 novembre à Brest.

of 1970 came out in December and of the major rock acts listed (the bulk of the entries were more pop oriented) Black Night was placed at a very creditable 18th place. All Right Now by Free was at 7, but Paranoid by Black Sabbath was well down at number 37.

1971 • The New Year saw them focused almost totally on the next album, with most of January spent either writing, rehearsing or recording. While *In Rock* continued to sell steadily for much of the year, priorities were shifting. At all costs they wanted to try and avoid the drawn-out stop start nature of the previous recording sessions.

The 1970 live routine was last featured over two Dutch shows at the top of the month, after which the band's set went into a period of flux. A big British tour began at the end of January, and saw them replace *Into The Fire* with a new track, *Strange Kind Of Woman* (the *In Rock* stalwart would return for some shows that year, but its days were numbered). In an attempt to bring the set length under control, they also dropped one of the two long improv vehicles, but seemed unable to make their minds up which, so *Mandrake Root* went for a time, with *Wring That Neck* kept - they then reversed this. It was done partly to open up the show a little, but also because they realised it had simply been wearing them out trying to keep two really long tracks going end to end.

Paint It Black was also on the way out. A stalwart ever since the band's first live shows, it was now replaced by another new track, *The Mule*. Drum solo fans didn't have to fret however, as it was designed as a new vehicle for Ian Paice. Ritchie seemed really taken by the riff,

> **BULLEN SCHÜTZEN MAMMAS ARSCH!**
> (Deep Purple mit großem Polizeiaufgebot)
>
> ○ Trotz unserer Proteste, die Horror-preise gehen weiter!
>
> ○ Die Schweine von MAMMA + Hör Zu Springer bescheißen uns weiter! Lassen wir uns nicht länger vom ehemaligen Teppichhändler Marcel Hiram (MAMMA Management) ausbeuten!
>
> ○ Diese Kapitalisten im Hippie Look wollen mit Deep Purple nichts anderes als Moos machen!
>
> ○ Die Musik von Deep Purple ist dufte — aber diese Wucher-preise _Scheiße!_ Schluß damit!
>
> ○ Verschaffen wir uns freien Eintritt!
>
> ○ Stürmen wir rein und sprengen den sterilen Rahmen!
>
> verant. Totalkom eigendruck

which he kept dropping into other tracks as well, but the words still hadn't been finalised. It took them a while to perfect and they brought back *Paint It Black* later for a few months before it went for good.

Speed King still opened proceedings, but was now prefaced by a bizzare routine called *The Yodelling Song* or *Swiss Made* which had appeared in the set late the previous year. Pop singer Eddie Grant had been fairly disparaging about the band in an interview, suggesting they'd stolen their show from him. It was demonstrably untrue, so Ian Gillan devised this as a way of getting back at him - not that the audience quite understood what it was all about. It seems to have kicked off at the Fairfields Hall show in November 1970. *"We're going to do an Equals number..."* But the sight (and sound) of Deep Purple coming on stage and then blasting into a short piece of heavy rock yodelling is something few will ever forget. Ian Gillan later admitted it had been a bit silly, but was clearly annoyed about the way some

Come off it Deep Purple

SOONER or later, someone will see through all the instrument-smashing that Deep Purple perpetrate on stage. They're not the first to indulge in all this sham histrionics, but for my money they're the worst.

I'm not going to talk about starving children in Biafra or that kind of thing, but these displays of devastation are a complete waste of money. That is, Deep Purple's money and my money when I go to see them. Simple fact is that they talk about themselves in a stupid way just to cover up their musical inadequacies. I suppose this'll draw a lot of criticism. But would people fans just stop and think before writing me a load of abuse? — JOHN HARDIMAN, Nelson Street, Glasgow E.1.

CLAPTON NO, BUT RITCHIE YES..!

DEEP PURPLE'S JON LORD

CLAPTON was good, now a new god raises his head, his name— Richie Blackmore. He's left Clapton standing in both guitar and stage performances. On "Doing their own thing" he was too good for words. People pay to watch as well as listen. As Mick Jagger said, "If you are not going to move about on stage, you might as well be behind the curtains." Clapton is the page boy— Blackmore is king.—**Phil Rainford, Lancaster Avenue, Liverpool 17.**

people were now knocking rock bands for having had a bit of success. *"A lot of people are knocking Zeppelin and they are a really great band. Black Sabbath also seem to have suffered lately. I'm just sick to death of all the snobbery that's going on. It seems you are only underground if you are completely ignored. Of course there are people of 14 and 15 who come and see us and I'm sure they would hate to be thought of as 'teeny-boppers.'"* • IG to Roy Shipston, Disc Dec 1970. He returned to the theme in another interview: *"We play for whoever wants to hear us. If the hall is full of heads smoking their joints that's okay and if the next night it's all schoolkids dancing about yelling 'Black Night' that's okay as well."* • IG to Richard Green, Dec 1970.

Along with *Child In Time* (which again got longer to take up some of the slack, a twenty minute take featured on some of the American shows later that year) and *Black Night* (at first the set closer, and then the opening encore when they were shortening the set), this is all that remained from the album sessions.

In March Jon chatted about *In Rock*: *"We made a conscious effort to stop and think about writing material we all understood. And the result was Deep Purple In Rock, which was really our stage act. That was the turning point. And the point is - we do believe in what we are doing together."*

Ian Gillan talked to the NME in April 1971 about the set list: *"We could have been doing new numbers three or four months ago but on the British tour we decided to give In Rock a last fling. We'll probably retain some of the numbers we're doing now; some seem to follow on more naturally than others."*

Jon spoke of the dangers of getting stale and referred to *Speed King* in particular. *"(Sometimes) you know that you didn't play (it) as well as you were playing it six months before. I might do better things in it, but they've become my own cliches. The longer you play a number the more you fall into that trap. Unless you can take a number back into rehearsal and put some new blood into it - we did that with Speed King three times."* • JL to Sounds, 1971.

To Ian Gillan, *Mandrake Root* and *Paint it Black* were as much a part of the *In Rock* era as the album tracks themselves. But from the album, *Child In Time* was the only song which kept a firm place in the band's set, right through until the Mk 2 line-up split in 1973 (and even that was rested in early 1973). *Black Night* would remain only as an encore track. Even as Ian was speaking, the album was still selling, albeit going up and down the charts (hitting No. 10, 43, 21 and 12 spots that month). The album then slowly moved down through the top thirty and forty during June and August. Despite their best efforts, Deep Purple struggled to bring their next album in on time. *Strange Kind Of Woman* had been released as the new single in February 1971 to bridge the long gap but it was to take the band exactly a year from releasing *In Rock* to finishing the follow-up in June 1971. In early May the band did a couple of shows in Australia which gave *In Rock* another boost there. It had been in their top twenty three times already, but this first visit to the country saw it reach No. 1 on the 26th June (with *Black Night* also a hit.)

In early September 1971 in Berlin, at Der Internationalen Funkausstellung, the members of Deep Purple were all presented with gold discs for *In Rock* sales. A German gold disc certified sales of 250,000 copies, so this was a significant milestone. This was quite possibly their first ever presentation disc too (although *Hush* had sold enough copies to qualify in America, Tetragrammaton had got into financial difficulties before organising gold discs. When producer Derek Lawrence complained, they organised a one-off gold record for him.)

It was confirmation that everything the musicians had put in to the band and the album was right. They were also starting to see significant income coming through from these sales. Record royalties always lagged behind sales, the labels would normally account quarterly. Some of the band treated themselves to new cars, others bought houses. Ian Paice began investing.

While in Berlin Deep Purple also appeared as one of the international guests at the Gala-abend der Schallplatte Pop, and played a short set for TV's Music Today. They stormed through *Into The Fire* amongst others, which seems to be the last time it was performed live. *Speed King* also opened their show for the last time early that month at two festivals in Germany.

This really was the last hurrah for a set which had taken them through the best part of two years. By the time Deep Purple hit Britain in September 1971, new songs abounded (including some as yet unreleased), and for a brief time they found themselves with

two top thirty albums (the new one, *Fireball*, entered at No. 5 on the 12th September 1971, with *In Rock* still there at No. 28 that week; it made one last re-entry to the UK charts on the 9th January 1972 at 31). *"I'm very proud of In Rock. We knew it was going to sell because we'd done six months of concerts, but no one expected it to last this long."* • RG to MM, June 1971. As Roger was chatting, sales in Britain were nudging 150,000 copies. *"We thought it would be a big album but no-one envisaged it being up there for nearly a year. I think that every time we do a concert we must pick up new converts."* • IP to Sounds, May 1971.

And while some fans today passionately believe *Fireball* contained material which was even more progressive and unique, as an album the negative reaction from a few reviewers (and the guitar player) did cause the band to reflect and look back at *In Rock* to see what had marked it out. As a result, the next album *Machine Head*, much of which was thought out in advance and then put together rapidly and in very different surroundings, was far more direct and focused. It was also massively commercial and cemented the band's international success, and remains a very contemporary album. *In Rock* on the other hand arguably belongs to it's time, the product of a unique combination of circumstances which could never be replicated. And while subsequent Mk 2 albums are excellent in their own way, *In Rock* remains the band's real tour de force.

1 - Unless we mention otherwise, *tape* means a cassette recorded by someone in the audience with all the attendant problems: noise, tape hiss, echo, missing tracks, overload, etc. For hard core fans really.

2 - What a time to be a rock fan, I scraped the pocket money together for four of those! SR

3 - With hindsight, Deep Purple Mk 2 always erred on the conservative side of things with their live shows. It wasn't until later line-ups that they went for wholesale change in the sets in 1973 and 1975.

4 - I found my copy for as little as £2 in one of the many head shops which lined Hull's Princess Avenue. That they could be found easily in a city which had regular ferry services to Europe hints at the distribution techniques involved. SR.

5 - Curtiss Records in Sheffield had a stand filled with bootleg albums, including H-Bomb, all retailing at £4, twice the price of a normal album. You could save money by sending a postal order to an address in London, who advertised titles in the music papers for 60/-(£3) each.

6 - It was released as an official bootleg, Space Vol 1 & 2, in 2001 on the Purple records offshoot Sonic Zoom, licensed through Deep Purple (Overseas) Ltd.

7 - Only the TV edit of Mandrake Root survives, now available on DVD.

8 - Ritchie clearly remembered the experience and repeated it four years later at the California Jam concert in America. This would be the last event at Plumpton. A high court settlement in December 1970 brought in a ban on festivals at the site and the NJF were forced to move

9 - The studio version came out in October 1971. Roger and Ian Paice helped on it, the others passed.

10 - Many rock fans had of course bought them both.

11 - Geoff Docherty's autobiography A Promoters Tale is highly recommended for anyone wanting to get a flavour of the highs and lows of concert promotion at the time. His repeated attempts to force Led Zeppelin into honouring a cancelled show alone make it worth reading.

12 - Simon Robinson in the band's fanclub magazine commented on the tapes reissue; "It's always been one of my very favourite tapes, ever since the first bootlegs turned up, but the new studio work gives it an added clarity and power which in places made it seem like listening to a new show. Were I to try and decide between this and 'Made In Japan', well - I just hope I never have to."

13 - Monday is now release day, with albums shipped the week before but embargoed until the day of release.

14 - Jon had obviously already forgotten about Hallelujah. And Emmaretta.

July 1969

10 7 69	Speakeasy London	UK
18 7 69	Coatham Hotel 'Jazz Club' Redcar	UK
20 7 69	Mothers Club Birmingham	UK
25 7 69	*Lyceum London* cancelled	*UK*

August 1969

11 8 69	BBC Radio recording session	UK
13 8 69	*Revolution Club London* cancelled rescheduled [20th]	*UK*
15 8 69	*Mayfair Ballroom Newcastle* cancelled rescheduled [?]	*UK*
16 8 69	*Rebeccas Birmingham* cancelled rescheduled [?]	*UK*
20 8 69	Revolution Club London	UK
22 8 69	Jazz Bilzen Festival, Bilzen	BEL
23 8 69	Paradiso Amsterdam	HOL
24 8 69	Paradiso Amsterdam	HOL
25 8 69	Beat Club Bremen TV filming	GER
26 8 69	Railway Hotel 'Klooks Kleek' West Hampstead	UK
29 8 69	BBC Radio recording session (afternoon)	UK
	'Midnight Court' Lyceum, Strand, London (evening)	UK
30 8 69	Kent Pop Festival Gravesend	UK

September 1969

5 9 69	Cue Club Gothenburg	SWE
6 9 69	Store Salen, Lund (8.00pm 45 min set)	SWE
	Hotel Stevns 'Club Dynamite - Midnight Show' Store Heddinge	DEN
7 9 69	Fjordvilla, Roskilde [early show]	DEN
7 9 69	Club Six, Copenhagen [late show]	DEN
9 9 69	*Marquee London* cancelled	*UK*
12 9 69	Queens Hall, Barnstaple	UK
13 9 69	Queens Hall, Narberth, Wales	UK
20 9 69	Winter Gardens Malvern	UK
21 9 69	Coatham Hotel 'Jazz Club' Redcar	UK
24 9 69	Royal Albert Hall London - Concerto	UK
26 9 69	Recording David Frost Show	
27 9 69	Nottingham College of Education 'Coming up Ball' Nottingham	UK
28 9 69	Roundhouse 'Implosion' Camden London	UK

October 1969

4 10 69	Kurhaus / Casino Lido 'Le Sabalier' Montreux	SWI
6-8 10 69	Stuttgart TV filming P2 show	GER
9 10 69	unknown Augsburg	GER
10 10 69	Stuttgart TV filming	GER
11 10 69	*Imperial College London* cancelled	*UK*
11 10 69	'Inernationales Essener Pop & Blues Festival' Grugahalle, Essen	GER
12 10 69	Concertgebouw Amsterdam	HOL
14 10 69	Star Club, Hamburg	GER

GREYHOUND PARK LANE CROYDON
Sunday, December 28th, 7.45 p.m.

DEEP PURPLE
+ FOREVER MORE
3 Licensed Bars — Lights and Sounds — S.U. Cards

Next Sunday: JUICY LUCY

Date	Venue	Country
18.10.69	studio	
22 10 69	St Matthews Baths Hall Ipswich	UK
24 10 69	Lyceum 'Midnight Rave Again!' Strand, London	UK
25 10 69	Winter Gardens Weston Super Mare	UK
30 10 69	University Leeds	UK
31 10 69	BBC Radio recording session	UK

November 1969

1 11 69	New Bristol Centre, Mayfair Suite 'Teenpage Ball'	UK
2 11 69	Lyceum 'The Sunday Lyceum', Strand, London	UK
4 11 69	studio	
7 11 69	Kings Head Romford	UK
8 11 69	Leas Cliff Hall Folkestone	UK
10 11 69	Art College Bath	UK
13 11 69	Regency Theatre Newport	UK
14 11 69	Aston View Birmingham	UK
15 11 69	University Refectory Hall, Leeds	UK
16 11 69	Kinema Dunfermline	UK
17 11 69	Electric Gardens Glasgow	UK
18 11 69	Edinburgh, unknown venue	UK
21 11 69	Avery Hill College, Eltham, London	UK
22 11 69	University Bradford	UK
23 11 69	Wake Arms 'Groovesville' Epping	UK
24 11 69	Bennett Concert Hall Birmingham	UK
24 – 28 11 69	studio	
28 11 69	Guildford Civic Hall	UK
29 11 69	Imperial College London	UK
30 11 69	Roundhouse 'Polytechnic Arts Festival' Camden, London	UK

December 1969

Date	Venue	Country
4 12 69	Assembly Hall Worthing	UK
5 12 69	Polytechnic Sunderland	UK
6 12 69	UMIST, Manchester	UK
7 12 69	St. Georges Hall Bradford	UK
9 12 69	Keele University Stafford	UK
10 12 69	University College London	UK
11 12 69	Rye Royal Ballroom Bournemouth	UK
12 12 69	The Flamingo Hereford	UK
15 12 69	The Cosmopolitan Carlisle	UK
18 12 69	The Flamingo Redruth	UK
19 12 69	Van Dike Club Plymouth	UK
20 12 69	Roundhouse 'The Village' Dagenham	UK
21 12 69	Mothers Birmingham	UK
28 12 69	Greyhound Croydon	UK

January 1970

1 1 70	studio	
5 1 70	Les Anciennes Halles de Paris Pavilion 8, Paris (festival)	FRA
6 1 70	Pavilion Ballroom, Worthing	UK
10 1 70	University 'Coming up Dance' Reading	UK
13 1 70	studio	
15 / 16 1 70	Studio Bellevue Amsterdam, TV filming	HOL
19 1 70	Civic Hall Dunstable	UK
21 1 70	Big Apple Club Munich	GER
23 1 70	University of Lancaster Central Hall	UK
24 1 70	Curzon Cinema Hatfield	UK
29 1 70	studio	
30 1 70	Royal Albert Hall London [support]	UK
31 1 70	Lawns Centre Cottenham	UK

February 1970

3 2 70	Bremen TV filming	GER
6 2 70	Technical College Waltham Forest	UK

IMPERIAL COLLEGE presents
IN CONCERT

Tues., Feb. 24th **DEEP PURPLE**
PRINCIPAL EDWARDS MAGIC THEATRE
Tickets 12/-
Limited number of tickets at door

Tues., Mar. 3rd **LOVE**
BLODWYN PIG
Tickets £1

Fri., Mar. 6th **PINK FLOYD**
JUICY LUCY
Tickets 25/-

Send s.a.e. with P.O. to Social Secretary, Imperial College, 7 Prince Consort Road, S.W.7

at GREYHOUND Park Lane CROYDON
Sunday, February 22nd, 7.30 p.m.
DEEP PURPLE
JEFF DEXTER — Next week: LIVERPOOL SCENE
Licensed Bars — Lights and Sounds — S.U. Cards

Date	Venue	Country
7 2 70	Union Hall, University Leicester	UK
8 2 70	Mothers Club Birmingham	UK
13 2 70	University 'St Valentine's Day Massacre' Cardiff	UK
14 2 70	Free Trade Hall Manchester	UK
15 2 70	Boat Club Nottingham	UK
16 2 70	Kings Head Romford	UK
19 2 70	Paris Theatre, London. BBC Radio rec. In Concert	UK
20 2 70	Harris College, Public Hall Preston	UK
21 2 70	St Mary's College Twickenham	UK
22 2 70	Greyhound 'Croydon Blues Club' Croydon	UK
24 2 70	Imperial College London	UK
25 2 70	Anson Rooms Bristol University Bristol	UK
27 2 70	Tech Faculty Hall, Leeds Polytechnic Union Leeds	UK
28 2 70	Royal Philharmonic Hall Liverpool	UK

March 1970

4 3 70	Volkshaus Zurich	SWI
6 3 70	Berne, Tanzdiele Matte	SWI
7 3 70	Verkehrshaus der Schweiz Luzern	SWI
11 3 70	studio	
13 3 70	Empress Ballroom, Winter Gardens, Blackpool	UK
14 3 70	Winter Gardens Weston Super Mare	UK
15 3 70	Wake Arms 'Groovesville' Epping	UK
17 3 70	University Great Hall / Devonshire House Exeter	UK
20 3 70	Odeon Theatre Edinburgh	UK
21 3 70	Caird Hall Dundee	UK
22 3 70	Kinema Ballroom Dunfermline	UK
23 3 70	Music Hall Aberdeen	UK
24 3 70	Electric Garden Glasgow	UK
25 3 70	Town Hall Hamilton	UK
28 3 70	Roundhouse 'The Village' Dagenham	UK
30 3 70	Sportpalast 'Pop Progressive Peace Konzert' festival Berlin	GER

April 1970

4 4 70	Sporthalle 'Mulheim Progressive Pop Festival' Cologne	GER
6 4 70	Konzerthaus Vienna/Wien	AUS
11 4 70	Central Hall Chatham	UK
13 4 70	studio	
18 4 70	Technical College 'Rag Week' Ewell	UK
21 4 70	BBC recording session	
24 4 70	Kings Hall North Staffs Poly Stoke-on-Trent	UK
25 4 70	Bath, venue unknown	UK

May 1970

1 5 70	College of Art Brighton	UK
4 5 70	studio	
9 5 70	Roundhouse 'The Village' Dagenham	UK
11 5 70	De Montfort Hall Leicester	UK
15 5 70	Chelmsford venue unknown	UK
16 5 70	Town Hall Birmingham	UK
17 5 70	Colston Hall Bristol	UK
18 5 70	Civic Hall Dunstable	UK
22 5 70	Dome Brighton	UK
25 5 70	Queen Elizabeth Hall 'Festival of Progressive Music' London (2 shows)	UK
28 5 70	Ostseehalle 'Das kleinste Superfestival der Welt' Kiel	GER
29 5 70	Neue Welt Berlin	GER
30 5 70	*Circus Krone Munchen cancelled*	*GER*
31 5 70	Rosengarten, Mannheim [? date not confirmed]	GER

customs delays led to dates being moved around

June 1970

1 6 70	Rheinhalle Dusseldorf	GER
2 6 70	Musikhalle Grober Saal Hamburg (2 shows)	GER
5 6 70	**In Rock and Black Night released UK**	
6 6 70	Grosser Sartory Saal Koln (2 shows)	GER
7 6 70	Cirkus Krone Bau Munchen	GER
8 6 70	St Jakob Sportalle Basel	SWI
9 6 70	Stadhalle Offenbach	GER
10 6 70	Niedesachsenhalle, Kuppelsaal Hannover	GER
12 6 70	Eel Pie Island 'Colonel Barefoot's Rock Garden' Twickenham	UK
14 6 70	Fairfield Hall Croydon	UK
16 6 70	Jesus College Cambridge	UK
17 6 70	Grampian TV filming	UK
19 6 70	John Dalton College Manchester	UK
20 6 70	University College Oxford	UK
21 6 70	Waldstadion, Radrennbahn 'Open Air Rock Circus'	

	Frankfurt	GER
	July 1970	
4 7 70	Bedford Town Football Ground, Blues at the Eyrie Festival Bedford	UK
5 7 70	Lyceum 'Summer Sunday Scene', London	UK
10 7 70	Reiterstadion Soers Europop Open Air Pop Festival Aachen	GER
11 7 70	Eissportstadion Grosse Halle 'Euro-Pop 70' Munchen	GER
14 7 70	Manchester Granada TV filming Doing Their Thing	UK
28 7 70	South Bank, Queen Elizabeth Hall 'South Bank Summer' London TV	UK
31 7 70	Mayfair Ballroom Newcastle	UK
	August 1970	
1 8 70	*Chateau De Saint-Pons Progressive Music Festival* (Deep Purple cancelled)	FRA
8 8 70	*Stade Municipal Saint Raphael Pop Festival* cancelled	FRA
9 8 70	10th National Jazz & Blues Festival, Plumpton Racecourse	UK
15 8 70	Rodeo Arena Island Grove Park Greeley Colorado	USA
16 8 70	*Bulfrog Lake Trailer Park '2nd Bullfrog Music Festival' Estacada, Oregon,* cancelled	USA
22 8 70	The Terrace Salt Lake City, Utah	USA
- 8 70	Pepperland San Raphael California [date unknown]	USA
25 8 70	Hollywood Bowl, Los Angeles. Concerto	USA
28 8 70	Jam Factory San Antonio (2 shows) Texas [no RB on 2nd show]	USA
29 8 70	Civic Auditorium 'Summertime 70 Unifest' Albuquerque, New Mexico	USA
30 8 70	Civic Centre/Auditorium Pasadena	USA
	September 1970	
6 9 70	Arras festival venue unknown	FRA
9 9 70	BBC TV filming	UK
17 9 70	Royal Festival Hall, London. Gemini Suite	UK
23 9 70	BBC Radio UK recording session	
25 9 70	Odeon Theatre Romford	UK
26 9 70	St George's Hall, Main Hall Liverpool	UK
28 9 70	studio	
	October 1970	
2 10 70	UWIST Cardiff	UK
3 10 70	University Southampton	UK
2-4 10 70	*Pop Festival Symbad, Lausanne,* cancelled	SWI
6 10 70	University 'Freshers Hop' Leeds	UK
8 10 70	La Taverne d'Olympia, Paris TV filming 'Musicorama'	FRA
10 10 70	University Sheffield	UK
12 10 70	*Eldorado* Tiffanys Edinburgh change of venue	UK
13 10 70	*Electric Garden* Tiffanys Glasgow change of venue	UK
14 10 70	Music Hall Aberdeen	UK
15 10 70	Caird Hall Dundee	UK
16 10 70	Top Rank Sunderland	UK
17 10 70	University Manchester	UK
21 10 70	Top Rank Swansea	UK
	date unknown : filming of Black Night promo	
25 10 70	Theatre Du Huitieme Lyons	FRA
26 10 70	Maison De La Culture Chambery	FRA
27 10 70	Maison Des Arts Sochaux	FRA
28 10 70	*Maison de la Culture Mulhouse* (DP cancelled)	FRA
30 10 70	Maison De La Culture Le Havre	FRA

31 10 70	Club Piblokto Dourges	FRA
November 1970		
1 11 70	Olympia Paris	FRA
1 11 70	Gibus Club Paris (after hours show)	FRA
2 11 70	*Cinema Theatre Elbeuf* cancelled	*FRA*
3 11 70	*Cinema le Celtic Brest* cancelled	*FRA*
6 11 70	Winter Gardens Bournemouth	UK
7 11 70	Dreamland Ballroom Margate	UK
11 11 70	Njårdhallen, Oslo	NOR
12 11 70	Konserthus Stora Salen Stockholm	SWE
13 11 70	[unknown]	DEN
14 11 70	KB Hallen Copenhagen	DEN
15 11 70	Konserthuset Gothenburg	SWE
16 11 70	Fyens Forum Odense	DEN
18 11 70	*St George's Hall, Liverpool* [as 4 piece no JL] cancelled	UK
19 11 70	Belle Vue Manchester [as 4 piece no JL]	UK
20 11 70	*City Hall Hull* cancelled	UK
21 11 70	University College London	UK
22 11 70	Fairfield Hall Croydon	UK
23 11 70	*Civic Hall Wolverhampton* cancelled	*UK*
24 11 70	*St George's Hall Bradford* cancelled	*UK*
27 11 70	Stadthalle Offenbach	GER
28 11 70	Neue Universitat Aula Heidelberg	GER
29 11 70	Rheinhalle Dusseldorf	GER
30 11 70	Mercatorhalle Duisburg	GER
December 1970		
1 12 70	Niedersachsenhalle Hannover	GER
2 - 3 12 70	Ausstellungspark Planten Un Blomen, Halle B Hamburg	GER
4 12 70	Munsterland Halle Munster	GER
5 12 70	Circus Krone-Bau Munchen	GER
6 12 70	Saarlandhalle Saarbrucken	GER
7 12 70	Meistersingerhalle Nurnburg	GER
8 12 70	Schutzenhalle Ludenscheid [as 4 piece no RB]	GER
9 12 70	*Stadthalle Wuppertal* cancelled	*GER*
11 12 70	Huttenhalle Wurzburg	GER
12 12 70	Messehalle Killesberg Stuttgart Stuttgart	GER
17 12 70	*Dome Brighton* cancelled	*UK*
19 12 70	*Roundhouse 'The Village' Dagenham* cancelled	*UK*
January 1971		
1 1 71	De Doelen Rotterdam	HOL
2 1 71	Concertgebouw Amsterdam	HOL

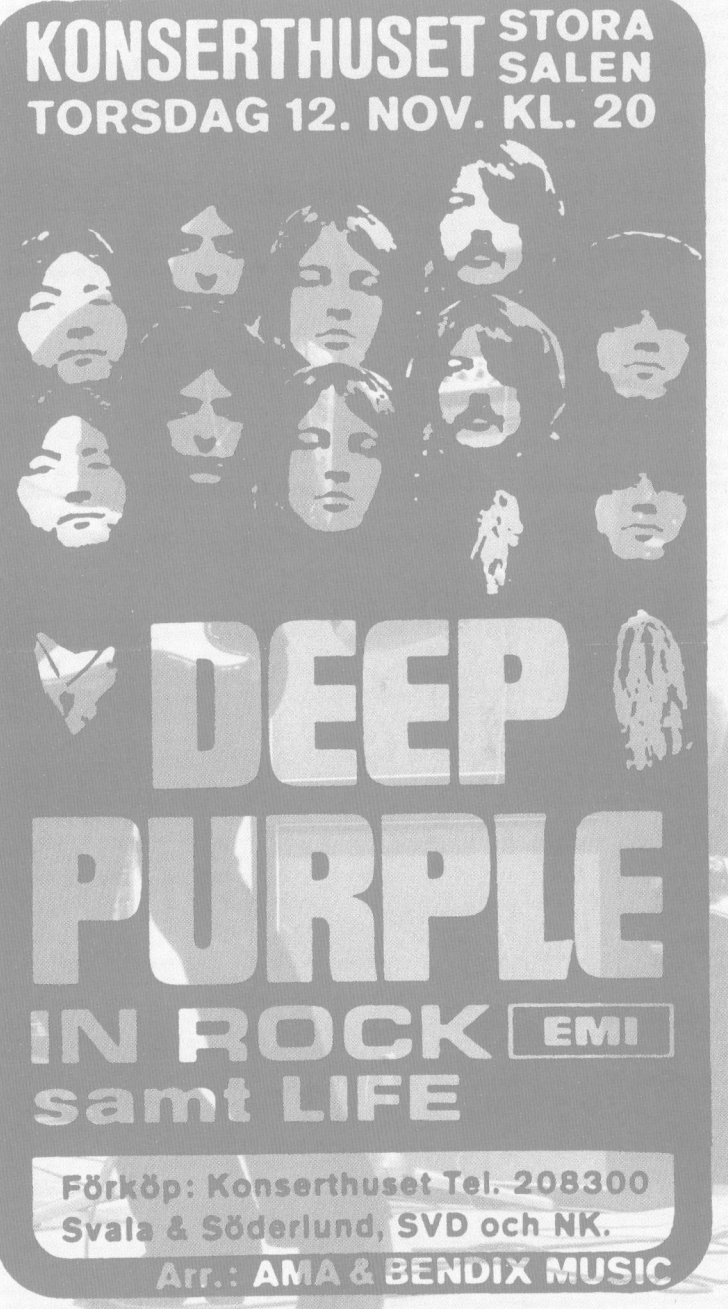

Appendix B • Album Discography

Album sleeves (page 164) : L-R top row first ; Greece, Korea, France purple vinyl, Russia, South Africa, Israel back, UK picture disc, Holland green vinyl, Mexico.
Single sleeves (page 161) : L-R top row first ; Asia, Belgium, Denmark, Mexico, Italy Israel, Spain, Sweden, Yugoslavia.

DEEP PURPLE IN ROCK • VINYL

1 : Speed King / Bloodsucker / Child In Time
2 : Flight Of The Rat / Into The Fire / Living Wreck / Hard Lovin' Man

GREAT BRITAIN V1 : Harvest SHVL 777 : June 1970
Bands heads montaged onto photo of Mount Rushmore; blue sky, black lettering, Harvest logo. Back same but no logo. Inner gatefold has lyrics left, five b/w photo's plus text on right. Record bag had other Harvest sleeve on. Earliest copies have one line round EMI logo on front (later copies two) and no EMI logo on label (see photo below). Printer Garrod & Lofthouse, outer is laminated. One curiosity is a misprint with Sides 1 & 2 switched, plus tracks on side 1 in reverse order. No details about this.
GREAT BRITAIN V2 : EMI Fame FA 3011 : May 1982 SS
As V1, sleeve notes from V1 added to back. Fame logo. Budget reissue.
GREAT BRITAIN V3 : EMI EJ 26 03430 : February 1985 PD
Limited edition picture disc with V1 cover art. Issued with free poster.

AMERICA : Warner Brothers WS 1877 : 1970 DS
As GBV1, track listing added on back. Cover matt. Organ intro to Speed King edited off (SKe). Label subjected to normal Warner Bros. changes over the years.

CANADA : Warner Brothers WS 1877 : 1970 DS as USA SKe

JAPAN V1 : Toshiba BP 80094 : 1970 DS
Short lived edition pressed for Warner Bros by Toshiba Musical Industries. Green Warners label. Promo copies in red vinyl (ultra rare), regular in black vinyl. SKe.
JAPAN V2 : Warner Brothers P 8020W : Feb 1st 1971
As V1 but pressed by Warners.
JAPAN V3 : Warner Brothers P 10108W : 1975 as above

BELGIUM : Harvest Sounds Superb 4M 036 91442 : 1982 SS
Back as right hand half of GBV1 inner gatefold. Sounds Superb logo on front.

FRANCE V1 : Harvest SHVL 777W 2C 064 91442 : 1970 DS. As GBV1
FRANCE V2 : Harvest DC 11 : 1978. DS CV
As V1. Limited edition in purple vinyl with "Disque en couleur" sticker on front.
FRANCE V3 : Harvest 2C 964 91442 : 1978 DS
As V1 but darker colours and poorer quality image. Pale blue spine. Reedition.
FRANCE V4 : Fame EMI Pathe Marconi 1914421 PM 311 : 1983 SS

GERMANY V1 : Harvest HOR ZU SHZE 288 : 1970 DS
Front as GBV1 but white sky. Pink Hor Zo logo top left (later copies had Hor Zu "headphones" logo. Still available 1976.

GERMANY V2 : Harvest SHVL 777 1C 062 91442 : 1970 DS
As GBV1 with Electrola logo below Harvest logo.
GERMANY V3 : Harvest SHVL 777 1C 072 91442 : 197- DS as above
GERMANY V4 : Fame 1A0 38 157051 : 1983 SS

GREECE : Harvest 14C 062 91442 : 1970 - 1982 SS
Front as GBV1 except poor copy. Faces coloured pink. Back as right hand half of GBV1 inner gatefold. White spine.

HOLLAND V1 : Harvest 5C 062 91442 : 1970 DS as GBV1
HOLLAND V2 : Harvest 5C 062 91442 : 1978 DS CV
Sleeve as V1, Limited edition in green vinyl.
HOLLAND V3 : Harvest 1A 062 91442 : 19— DS
As V1 but halves of inner gatefold swopped over.
HOLLAND V4 : Fame 1A 039 1575051 : SS as GBV2

ITALY V1 : Harvest 3C 062 91442 : 1970 DS as GBV1
ITALY V2 : Harvest 3C 062 91442 : 1970 SS
Front as GBV1. Back as right hand half of V1 inner gatefold.
ITALY V3 : Harvest 3C 054 1914421 : 19-- SS as above

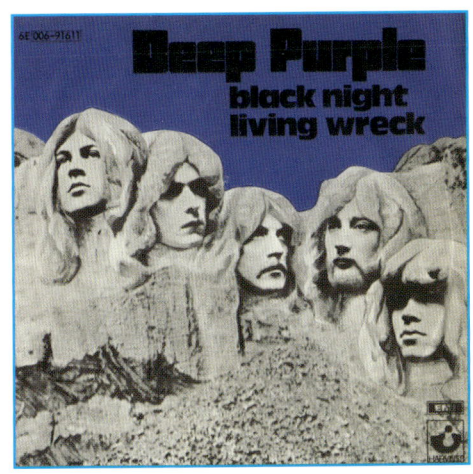
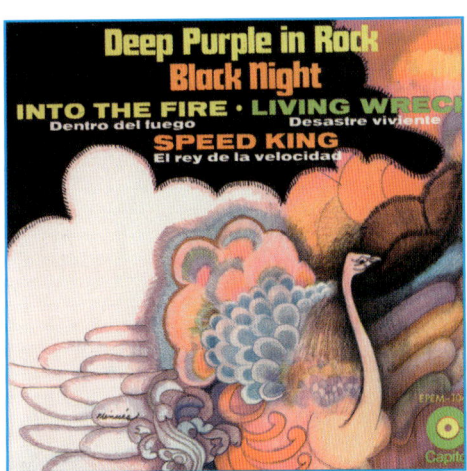

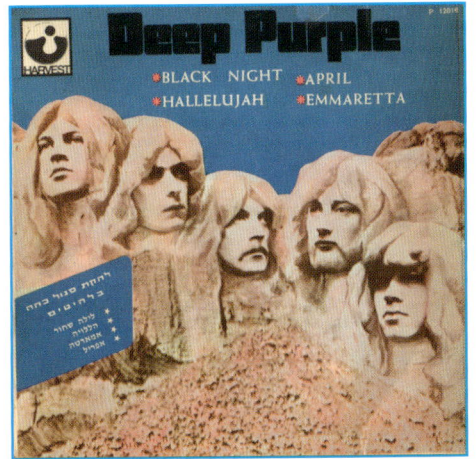
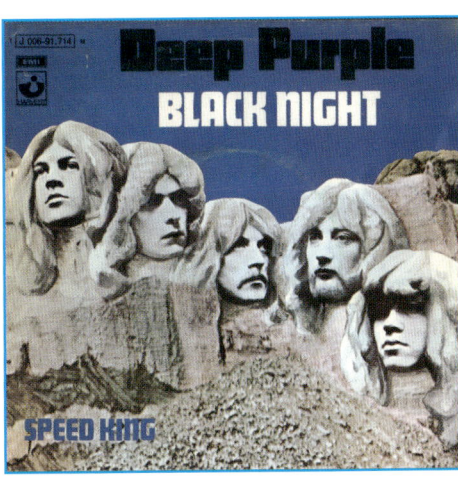
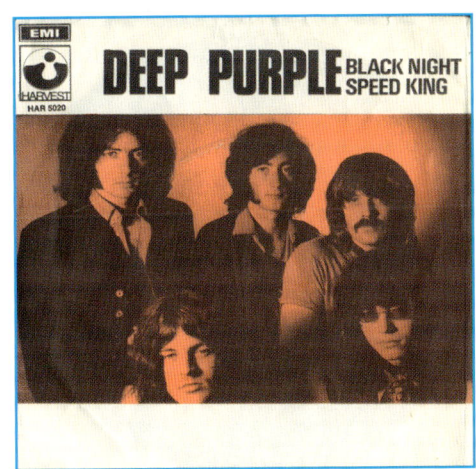

Taiwan edition; there is now a theory that these were done from official Warners US stampers, shipped and pressed locally for sale to US troops in Vietnam.

SPAIN : Harvest 1J 062 91442 : 1970 DS as GBV1
SPAIN : Harvest 1J 062 91442 : 1970 SS
Front as GBV1. Back has photo's plus, titles in English and Spanish.
SPAIN V3 : Harvest 10C 046 091442 : 1982 SS
As GBV2 with Music For Pleasure logo. Back notes in Spanish.

SWEDEN : Harvest SHVL 777 : 1970 DS as GBV1

YUGOSLAVIA : Jugoton LPSHAR 70470 : 197- SS
Front as GBV1 but much darker. Jugoton logo on front. Back as right half of GBV1 inner gatefold. Printed on flimsy dull card.

POLAND : LP 00186 : 1990 SS (pirate)
No record company mentioned. Poor artwork, copied off a CD front. 5,000 copies made.

CZECHOSLOVAKIA : Vydal Globus Int. 21 0096-2 311 : 1991 PD
Picture disc with GBV1 art both sides.
CZECHOSLOVAKIA : Vydal Globus Int. GEO187 : 1991 CV
Green vinyl. Unclear if officially licensed or not.

RUSSIA : Antorn 00221 : 1993 SS (pirate)
Grainy copy of GBV1 art, titles in English & Russian. Pressed in St. Petersburg.

TURKEY : Stateside TLS6 SHVL777 : 197-

AUSTRALIA Harvest SHVL 777 : 197- SS
Front as GBV1. Lyrics on back, black on white.

NEW ZEALAND V1 : Harvest SHVL 777 : 1970 SS
Front as GBV1. Back as left hand half of inner gatefold.
NEW ZEALAND V2 : Harvest SHVL 777 WRCE 1069 : 197- SS
As V1. Issued by World Record Club, two labels exist.

MEXICO : Capitol SLEM 242 : 197- DS
As GBV1. Black Night added at start of side one. Speed King USA edit.

PERU : Odeon ELD 2057 : 197- SS Front as GBV1
Odeon logo and "Linea Economica". Back as GBV1 inner right.
ARGENTINA V1 : Harvest 6175 SHVL 777 : 1971 SS
ARGENTINA V2 : EMI 5019 SHVL 777 : 1971 SS as Belgium
ARGENTINA V3 : EMI FAME 5019 : 198- SS
As Belgium plus large red Fame logo. Back b/w.

BRAZIL : Harvest 31C 064 91442D : 1973 DS As GBV1 but very brown.

NICARAGUA : Odeon 01.SHVL 777 : 19— SS
Front as GBV1 but image reversed. Back as GBV1 inner right. Some of the stereo channel missing so half the guitar is inaudible.

VENEZUELA EMI SOLP 7141 SS

ISRAEL : Portrait SHV 777 : 19-- SS. As GBV1 back as inner right, white on blue.

SOUTH AFRICA : Harvest SHVLJ (D) 777 : 197- DS
As GBV1. On inner gatefold, the credits panel is centred on the right hand side, and the five b/w photo's placed diagonally across the left hand side. No lyrics.
SOUTH AFRICA : Music For Pleasure SRSJ 8115 (FD) : 19— SS
Front as GBV1 + MFP logo + "original artists". Credits etc on back in b/w.
SOUTH AFRICA : FAME (P) 5 : 19— SS
As above + Fame logo top right.

SOUTH EAST ASIA/MALAYSIA/HONG KONG : Harvest SHVL 777 : 1970
SS as Belgium

KOREA V1 : Harvest OLE 459 : 19— SS
As GBV1 front. CHILD IN TIME and HARD LOVIN' MAN left off for cultural reasons.
KOREA V2 EMI EKPC 0020 FA 3011 : 19— SS
GBV1 front reduced with black surround. "Deep Purple" across top, "In Rock"

down side. Lyric sheet inside. No missing tracks.

TAIWAN : Union TD-1762 : 19— SS (pirate)
As GBV1 but poor colours printed on thin paper.
TAIWAN : CSJ 1016 : 19— SS (pirate)
Front as USA but in pale blue. Back same but brick red. Lyrics from GBV1 inner gatefold across in white.

UNKNOWN : Hero Records : 19— SS
Front and back as USA with W.Bros logo blacked off. No details.

COMPACT DISC

JAPAN : Warner Pioneer 20PZ 2603 : 1989 Speed King still edited.
GREAT BRITAIN : EMI CDP 7.46.2392 : 1986
AMERICA : Warner Brothers 1877.2 : 1986 Issued in long card box. Speed King edited.
AMERICA : Audio Fidelity AFZ051 : July 2009 Remastered in USA, 7 tracks.

REMASTERED COMPACT DISC 25th Anniversary Edition.
Album newly remastered at Abbey Road plus bonus tracks: Speed King (piano vsn), Cry Free, Jam Stew (inst), Flight Of The Rat (remix), Speed King (remix), Black Night (remix) + three minutes of between song studio chat.

GREAT BRITAIN : EMI DEEPP1 : June 1995
24 page booklet. CD front has autographs overprinted in black.
First pressing (marked Swindon on CD inner edge) had digital errors, repress (marked EMI Uden in centre) was quickly issued.

REMASTERED VINYL

GREAT BRITAIN : EMI : October 1995 2LP
Limited edition based on the 25th Anniversary CD (see below). Gatefold sleeve, inner bags had CD booklet art, colour purple vinyl. 2,000 pressed.

AMERICA : Friday Music FRM1877 : 2011

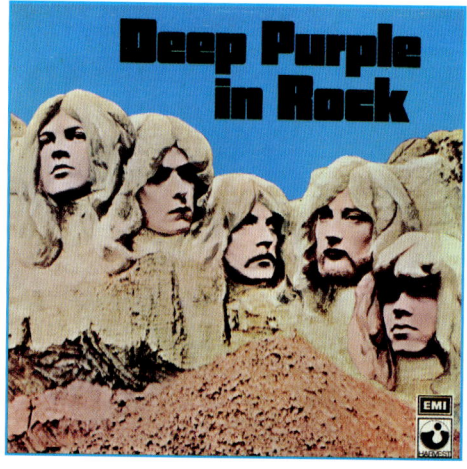
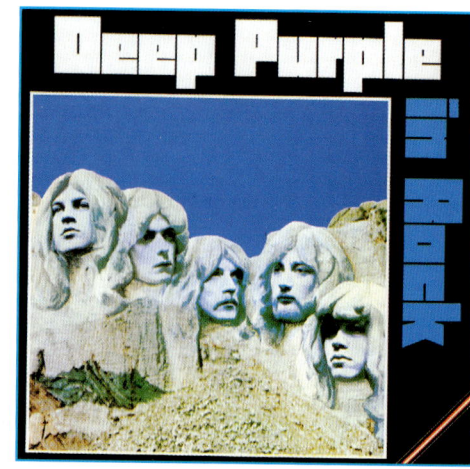

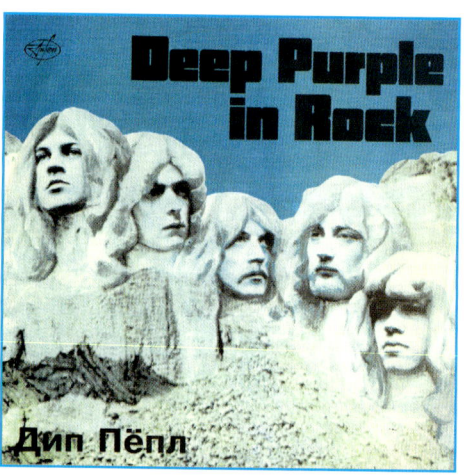
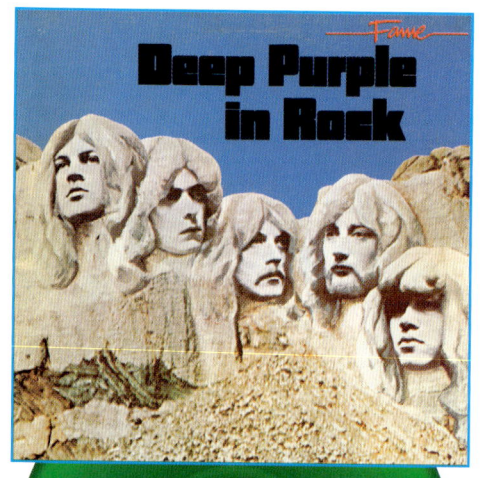

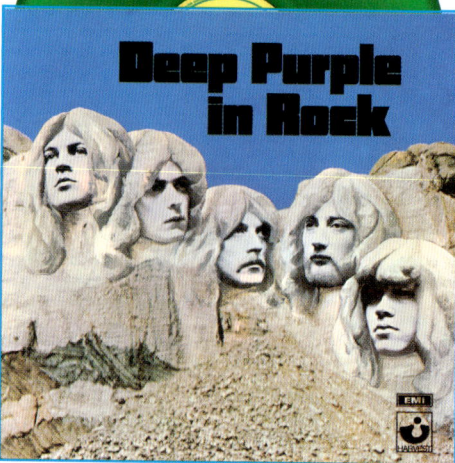
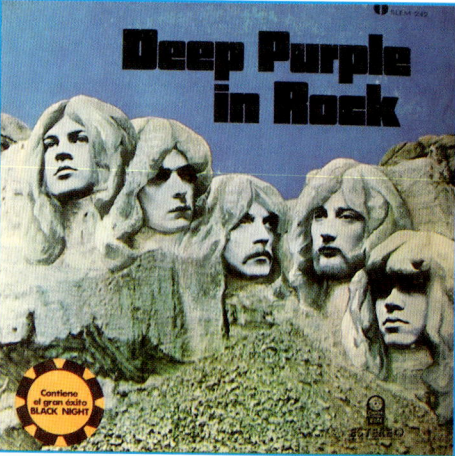

Appendix C • In Rock Chart positions
June 1970 - January 1971

Week ending	UK weekly	Germany monthly	Norway weekly	Australia weekly	USA weekly	Italy monthly	Sweden weekly	Austria monthly	France monthly	Japan weekly
14 / 06 / 70	24									
21 / 06 / 70	**4**									
28 / 06 / 70	8									
05 / 07 / 70	9									
12 / 07 / 70	9									
19 / 07 / 70	10	7								
26 / 07 / 70	7		15							
02 / 08 / 70	8		?							
09 / 08 / 70	15		12							
16 / 08 / 70	8	3	16							
23 / 08 / 70	7		14							
30 / 08 / 70	6		16							
06 / 09 / 70	8		9				15			
13 / 09 / 70	38		13		198		15			
20 / 09 / 70	7	2	12		198		14			
27 / 09 / 70	**4**		12		164		13	9		
04 / 10 / 70	6		9		164		15	9		
11 / 10 / 70	10	**1**	11	17	160		15	9		
18 / 10 / 70	14		13	20	160		20	9		
25 / 10 / 70	5		11		158	**19**	17	9		
01 / 11 / 70	6		11		151		12	9		
08 / 11 / 70	6	1	9		**143**		11	9	**10**	
15 / 11 / 70	5		**5**		160		14	9		
22 / 11 / 70	6		6		155		12	9		68
29 / 11 / 70	13		5		165		16	4		
06 / 12 / 70	8		6		161		?	4		
13 / 12 / 70	16	1	6		171			4		
20 / 12 / 70	14		5		167			4		
27 / 12 / 70	14		5		165			4		
03 / 01 / 71	10		5		162			4		
10 / 01 / 71	8		5		181			4	21	
17 / 01 / 71	14	2	6		180			4		
24 / 01 / 71	7		7	17	180			4		
31 / 01 / 71	9		10	**11**	178			**1**		

Chart details are not available for every country, but this grid gives a good indication of the album's world wide success. The highest position for each is in bold. The first entry shown is when the album was registered in the charts in that country. UK album charts aare compiled from a week's sales data, then published the following Thursday. Some countries only issued charts on a monthly basis. In Rock later reached number one in Australia. It reached 8 in Denmark, 9 in Finland and 21 in Holland, date unknown.

In 1972 the NME did a ten year album chart survey, which placed Deep Purple In Rock as the 18th best selling album of the decade, with a total of 54 weeks in their charts. Of the albums above it, six were soundtracks or musicals, and four were easy listening. The only other hard rock album above them was Led Zeppelin 2 at number 5. And you had to go down to 54 to find another, Led Zeppelin 3.

The single Black Night made No. 1 in Switzerland for four weeks, 2 in the UK for two weeks, 2 in Norway and Germany, 3 in France, 4 in Austria and Ireland, 6 in Sweden, South Africa and Belgium, 8 in Holland, Denmark and Italy, 13 in Australia, 15 in Spain, 35 in Japan, 66 in America and 67 in Canada.

The interior of this Sheffield record shop Cann's was taken in 1970 (seven staff on duty!), Deep Purple In Rock is racked out under D. I did buy albums there. That might be my copy. SR

Wait For The Ricochet CREDITS

This early gold presentation disc was awarded in September 1973. It marked UK sales of £150,000 for Deep Purple In Rock. (around £1.5 million in today's money)

I MENTIONED UNCERTAIN TIMES in the credits to the first edition, they are even more uncertain as this second edition finally goes to press! Easy On The Eye Books print in Europe and the U.K., so rising costs coupled with the currency devaluing delayed plans for the update.

SECOND EDITION CREDITS • We would like to thank John Tucker, Mark Craig, Tonny Steenhagen and Aleksey Kononov for their work on this.

SECOND EDITION INFORMATION • this second edition remains basically the same but corrects typographical, grammatical, stylistic inconsistencies and punctuation errors from the first edition.

ORIGINAL CREDITS • *Our thanks for their help in the production of this book go to the following for the interviews*: Jon Lord, Tarquin Gotch, Roger Glover, Kat Rallis, Ian Gillan, Tony Edwards, Sally Day, Ian Paice. Andy Knight, Denis Blackham (Skye Mastering), Nick Lauro (who also helped with chapter 11).

And for help in other ways big and small: Derek Lawrence, Cary Anning, Nigel Reeve, Abbey Road, Kevin Vanbergen, Simon Glinn, Dave Swallow (Bedford Town FC), Andrew Cornwall, Dirk Kahlar, Barry McKay, Brian Smith, Tonny Steenhagen, Ken Flegg, Martin Ashberry, Marc Brans, Matt Ford (Chartstats RIP), Christian Meyer zu Natrup, Lars Olsson, Jerry Bloom, Aleksey Kononov, David Browne, Sheila Carter, Wasabi, Ian Hansford, Jim Watters, Brent Dehn, Bernt Küpper, Klaus Tiedge, Audie Philips, The Daily Mail, Alistair Young (The Ealing Club), Emma Groundwater (Hanwell Community Centre), Ann Warburton *and on Ritchie's amps to:* Konrad Stief, Matt Love, Nick Robinson, Tim Campbell, Chris Parsons, Richard Groothuizen.

PHOTOGRAPHS : Holger Rudel, Nigel Abbott, Retna, Manfred Rinderspacher, Jean Jieme, Getty Images, Melody Maker, Wolfgang Heilemann, Tony Barrow International, Deutsche Presse-Agentur GmbH, SKR Pictures, SBS, Okej Magazine, Derek 'Blue' Weaver, Rex Features, Russell Berger. All attempts have been made to trace the copyright holders of photographs. We will be happy to correct any omissions in future editions. Additional photographs and memorabilia courtesy: Darker Than Blue Archives, Simon Robinson, Tonny Steenhagen.

CONCERT LIST : Chris Charlesworth (original listing from Illustrated Biography), Martin Ashberry (online gig list). Tonny Steenhagen (Deep Purple ticketmuseum). Simon Robinson (Darker Than Blue archives). Mike Richards (Deep Purple live cassette analysis). Dirk Kahler.

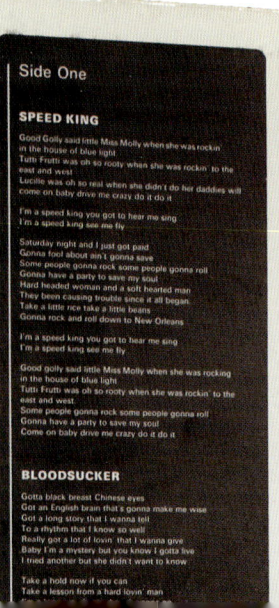
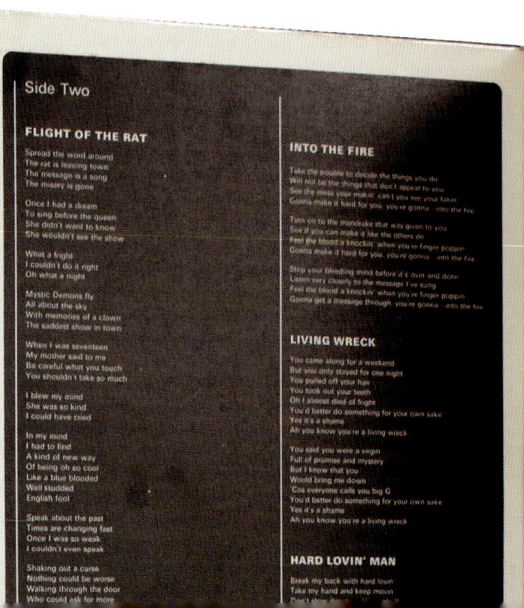

EASY ON THE EYE BOOKS / ST33BOOKS

The "In Rock" COVER PARODIES

COVERED!
Classic Sleeves And Their Imitators
ISBN: 978-0-9561439-2-1   [OUT NOW]

The samples on page 168 explain all. 1,000 different sleeves shown and annotated.

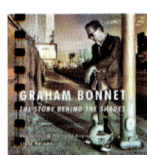

GRAHAM BONNET - The Story Behind The Shades
The Authorised Illustrated Biography. Steve Wright
ISBN: 978-0-9561439-3-8   [IN PRODUCTION]

The first biography of one of rock's most memorable voices, from his days in Skegness clubs to fronting Rainbow at the first Donington Monsters of Rock festival and beyond, right up to the Graham Bonnet Band's new album in 2017. This book brings to print much even hardened fans will not have read about Bonnet's career, with plenty of rare photographs and memorabilia spread throughout the book.

FIRE IN THE SKY - DEEP PURPLE
The Story of MACHINE HEAD and SMOKE ON THE WATER
ISBN: 978-0-9561439-9-0   [IN PRODUCTION]

The follow up to Wait For The Ricochet, this in depth history tells the history of the group's most famous album; the run up to the sessions, the Casino fire, the Grand Hotel sessions and the subsequent touring of the material. Not forgetting the release of what was to become one of the biggest rock records of all time, Smoke On The Water. Lots of rare photographs, memorabilia and much more.

DEEP PURPLE - 1971 - 1974
The Barry Plummer Archives
ISBN: 978-0-9955236-3-0   [IN PRODUCTION]

This large format title comes from Easy On The Eye's sister imprint, ST33Books. It brings together for the first time the best of former Melody Maker photographer Barry Plummer's Deep Purple images, many taken on stage during their early Seventies UK tours. This is a limited edition, and should be pre-ordered to avoid disappointment.

YES - DIALOGUE
The Jon Kirkman Interviews
ISBN: 978-0-9955236-1-6   [OUT NOW]

Another much praised title from ST33Books, telling the incredible story of Yes through a series of unpublished interviews with just about every musician in the group. Lavishly illustrated with rare photographs, memorabilia and images. Special cover designed by Roger Dean. This is a limited edition, and can be ordered now.

More details at www.easyontheeyebooks.wordpress.com and https://stereo33books.com. We would much prefer customers to order from their local bookshop or direct from our official online suppliers http://www.ekmpowershop28.com/ekmps/shops/easyontheeye/. The big online retailers demand massive discounts which are especially damaging to small independent publishers, bookshops and specialist retailers.

One way of judging the success or influence of a classic album or sleeve is by the number of times it has been copied and parodied. Over 200 variations of The Beatles' Abbey Road cover are known for example. Deep Purple In Rock, while not in the same league, has seen a number of copies, paying tribute, taking the rise or just lifting the idea. Some of these are shown overleaf, from top left:

The Hard-Ons, a 1991 single on Waterfront Records (artwork by the Dickcheese Comic Company). A wittily imagined reverse of the famous sleeve. Unless you know the original In Rock front cover, this would mean nothing to you at all. **King Curlee**, a Japanese guitarist with a passion for both Deep Purple and parody. He covered Highway Star and more on this 2005 album on Fun House Records (artwork and photos by Akihiko Musha). Austrian rock band **Krautschädl**'s album Im Kraut was issued in 2007 on Sony (artwork by Ronald Putzker and Gina Steffen). Even **Ian Gillan** joined in the fun, commissioning this none too subtle dig at his former band-mates on a solo single No Good Luck issued in 1990 just after he'd been fired from the band. Teldec quickly reissued it in a new sleeve making this quite rare. Artwork by Repo Zest (pun intended I assume).

A Various Artists tribute by or for German rockers **Prollhead**, I can't quite work out which. Fordert Tribute came out in 1995 on Virgin (artwork Jörn Zimmermann, photo Bela Hoche). Belgian boy / girl pop duo (augmented here on a concert recording) **Vive La Fête** recorded this ten minute version of Child In Time at a live show in Mexico. It's surprisingly faithful too, authentic organ sound, long guitar solos, screams and all, albeit with a modern edge, especially the drums (Ian Paice, never a big fan of drum machines, would hate it.) Issued by Surprise Records, 2006, cover designer not known.

The **Japanese DVD** cover remains a mystery, and lastly comes another **Various Artists** effort Strassenkreuzer In Rock from 2003. We can't discover anything about the bands, but strassenkreuzer is the German word for American muscle cars. Artwork by Arthur Engler and Wolfgang Gillitzer, photo Michael Matejka.

Many of these images come from Covered! Classic Sleeves And Their Imitators, compiled by Jan Bellekens for Easy On The Eye books, which contains many more examples of how famous sleeves have been reappropriated. See details on the left.

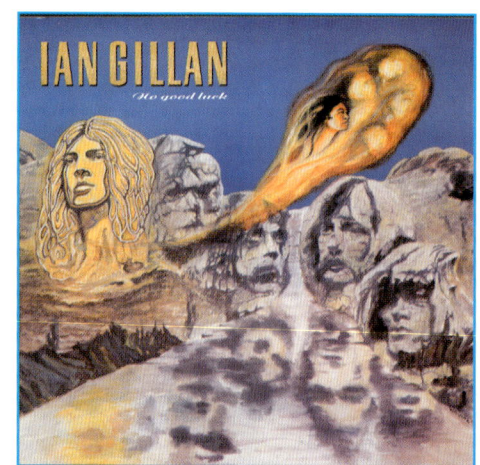
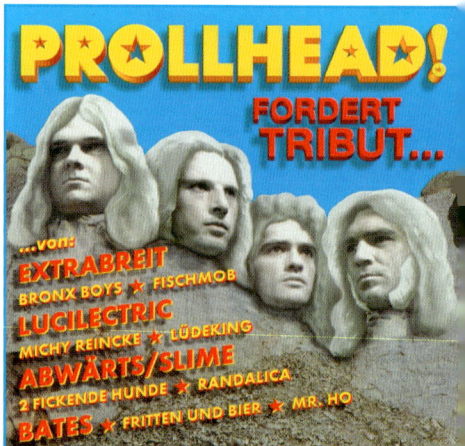